Mountain

of the

Holy Cross

by Mary S. Child

To Re-Order Please Visit:
www.thegentlewomanfoundation.com
The Gentle Woman Foundation
P.O. Box 154
Hanson, MA 02341
Or Call: 339-613-7592

To my husband, with love

Printed by Ingram Books

Published by The Gentle Woman Foundation

www.thegentlewomanfoundation.com

Copyright, 2011, written by Mary S. Child

*All rights reserved. No part of his book may be
Reproduced or transmitted in any form or technology –
Electronically or mechanically, including photocopying,
recording or by any information storage
and retrieval system,
without permission in writing from the publisher.*

Library of Congress Control Number: Pending

ISBN: 978-0-9835592-1-4

Printed in the United States of America, First Edition

THE CROSS OF SNOW

In the long, sleepless watches of the night,
A gentle face – the face of one long dead –
Looks at me from the wall, where round its head
The night-lamp casts a halo of pale light.
Here in this room she died; and soul more white
Never through martyrdom of fire was led
To its repose; nor can in books be read
The legend of a life more benedight.
There is a mountain in the distant West
That, sun-defying, in its deep ravines
Displays a cross of snow upon its side.
Such is the cross I wear upon my breast
These eighteen years, through all the changing scenes
And seasons, changeless since the day she died.

Henry Wadsworth Longfellow, 1879

CHAPTER ONE

Sunday, August 23rd

More than thirty-years before Ashley Moran was born, Starlight Cottage on Olive Branch Ranch was sealed and so it remains.

On days when Ashley found the summer heat oppressive, she often sought the tranquility of Starlight Cottage on the southwest border of the ranch where she lived with her parents Sean and Corrine and her grandmother Kit Moran. Sunday, August 23rd was such a day.

Around three-thirty in the afternoon, Ashley saddled her brown stallion Cocoa and headed out to the cool knoll surrounding the little cottage. She loved Starlight's aging gingerbread exterior. Throughout her entire childhood on Olive Branch Ranch, however, she had never seen the interior of Starlight Cottage. Kit Moran possessed the only-known key.

When she reached her teens and was able to venture out on the ranch alone Ashley's curiosity regarding the cottage grew but her father Sean, Kit's only son, insisted his daughter give up her quest to discover the reason the cottage was sealed.

"The reason is private," was Sean's standard pronouncement on the matter. "Your grandmother will tell us all one day – when she's ready."

When Ashley was a child Kit often took her for long walks along the river. Inevitably, these walks included a routine check on Starlight Cottage. In this check Kit's activities were always the same: she turned the old key in the lock, had a peek inside, relocked the door, then slipped her golden-key back into its silver sequin case and dropped the case back into her pocket.

Thick black blankets hung over the windows from the day Kit decided to lock the cottage. Quite incredibly, these blankets never lost their shape, nor did moths bore any holes. There was something mysterious about Starlight Cottage and at the same time, everyone in Cody knew Kit Moran's integrity was beyond reproach.

Several hundred feet along the tree-covered cart-path running between Northridge, Kit Moran's home and Starlight Cottage, Ashley dismounted Cocoa and led him the remainder of the way. As they neared Starlight, the trees gave way to lush green grasses where Ashley tethered her horse in the shade of several cottonwood trees running along the far side of the property. Then climbing onto her favorite terracotta stone at the river's edge, she took off her shoes and splashed in the clear running water. For over a million years, the melting snows from the Grand Teton Mountains just across the river smoothed the colorful rocks beneath her feet.

After wading in the river a while, Ashley freed Cocoa from his saddle and spread his blanket out on the spongy green grass so she could rest in the glorious sun. Overhead the cumulus clouds were moving slowly and creating "heavenly works of art," which captivated Ashley's imaginative spirit.

Quiet moments alone at Starlight always fueled her girlish fantasy of making improvements to the property. She would love to give the exterior a whole new look sometime in the future, to say nothing of what she dreamed of doing to the inside.

Unknown to Ashley the fate of Starlight Cottage was on Kit's mind as well that afternoon. Giving no previous indication of her financial concerns to her family, at that very hour Kit Moran was meeting with her attorney Thompson Smith at Northridge, the main home on the ranch. Kit asked Thompson for a special meeting to discuss with him the permanent distribution of Olive Branch Ranch and her entire estate.

Now 83, Kit Moran was all too aware of her age and she was very grateful to Thompson Smith for helping her in her time of need. When Thompson arrived, Kit readily offered him a thick file containing a detailed account of her estate. Thompson accepted her computations at face value, and never considered that his client and friend was holding back on her assets. He knew Kit always to be a shrewd and straightforward executive. Although Thompson was a close friend of Sean Moran and sole legal counsel for Kit's operations at Olive Branch Ranch, he always noticed that Starlight Cottage was the one entity Kit never discussed.

At the end of that first meeting, which centered specifically on updating Kit's will, Thompson assured his client he would trace the Moran files back to the early 1960's. At that time, her late husband John Charles Moran inherited the Olive Branch Ranch when his mother Jane passed away. Thompson wanted to ensure that he had not missed any important information or addendum before presenting his recommendations to Kit. Kit adored her late husband and more than four-decades after his passing, intended to consider John Moran's wishes in her estate planning.

"I've stalled long enough," she told Thompson over the phone several days prior to that first meeting. "Finally, I'm ready to make Sean my sole heir and put an end to my appalling procrastination. It must be now. We all know my days are numbered," Kit said sadly.

"I'll make it happen," Thompson responded with resignation.

Back at Starlight Cottage, when Ashley felt the afternoon sun fading, she began her return trip home to Amour where she had lived with her parents her entire life. Her great-grandmother Jane, who studied French abroad before she fell in love with George Moran and joined him in his venture west, named their home Amour, which means "love" in French.

Amour was set atop a rolling meadow and just across from the ranch's guesthouse. Known as the "Hub" of the ranch, this small area was the actual hub for the first fifteen years of the ranch's existence after which a new and larger hub known as the "Centre" was on forged one-hundred acres running along the river some twenty-five feet below Amour.

Kit's home was locked and her driveway empty, when Ashley walked Cocoa past Northridge then on toward Amour. She remembered her grandmother mentioned having a dinner engagement at Logan Mountain that evening so Ashley had no reason to be concerned. Her next thought as she walked along was that she would be home alone that evening as her parents, were attending a kick-off barbeque for the teaching staff at Cody High School where Sean taught science, and Corrine, mathematics.

"We're on our way over to the school for the barbeque, Ashley," Sean said, as she walked through the door.

"Hey Dad, before you go, I've been meaning to tell you Professor Rogers sent me a text this morning and he offered me the two additional classes I need before I begin the Master in Education program in January."

"That's fantastic, Ashley," Sean said.

"Corrine, did you hear that?"

"I did. That's great, Ashley. I can't wait to hear all the details. Good night, Sweetie," Corrine said as she kissed her only child. Sean, already at the door blew Ashley a kiss adding, "Let's all have an early breakfast tomorrow and take a good look at how our schedules are shaping up for the fall." Corrine and Ashley agreed.

After Sean and Corrine left Amour, Ashley felt the day begin to cool, and stepped out to the Hub to return a few text messages from friends. From her favorite place on the fence outside her home, she could see Jake Lewiston, veterinary-pharmacist and family friend, leaving pharmaceutical supplies for the veterinary clinic at the Centre. His visit was a preliminary check of medical supplies as Kit began preparations to present this year's stallions at Cody's Annual Show of Excellence on September 7th.

This was a banner year at Olive Branch Ranch. Kit Moran's team of seasoned ranch-hands broke 43 stallions, an unusually high number for presentation and sale at Cody's Annual Show of Excellence in a single year. The Annual Show of Excellence, which attracted the best owners and breeders in Wyoming, was the highlight of the entire ranching community, and produced the majority of Olive Branch Ranch's annual revenue.

Ashley liked Jake Lewiston. She felt he was a kind and gentle man but as he headed his pick-up truck up from the Centre, she hoped he would not stop to talk. She had been avoiding all conversation with Jake for some time because a friend informed her that his oldest son Patrick expressed an interest in her at a party in his honor just prior to his leaving for an assignment with the American Red Cross.

Two years ahead of Ashley at Cody High, she and Patrick travelled in completely different social circles. She knew Jake and Rita Lewiston's younger son Michael through the Lewiston's business but she never developed a relationship with Patrick Lewiston. A tender soul, Ashley was most comfortable with her peers, and at times, she was uncharacteristically shy with certain people. She had always considered Patrick Lewiston in this category and with heightened sensitivity after she learned of his interest in her.

As Jake's truck pulled up from the Centre, he spotted Ashley on the fence and stopped to say hello.

"Hi, Ashley! How's your summer been?"

"It's been nice, thank you. How about yours?"

"Great." Jake smiled then continued. "Have your folks gone to the barbeque at Cody High tonight?"

"Yes, they just left," she answered warmly. Then as if she could no longer control her friendly nature, Ashley walked a bit closer to Jake's pickup and continued the conversation.

"Has Michael started to look at colleges for next year?" she asked.

"That's next on our agenda. But for now we've all been pre-occupied with Patrick's homecoming from The Republic of the Sudan."

Believing Ashley would be interested in Patrick's heroic service with the American Red Cross, and specifically to the Sudanese people, Jake listed a number of his son's recent accomplishments.

"We're planning a big bash for him mid-September before he leaves on his next assignment.

"Oh, that's great news, Jake," Ashley said, hoping her disinterest in Patrick did not show. "I'm sure you will all enjoy having him around for a while."

"I know we will. Take care, Ashley. Have a great year at the University, if I don't see you before you leave."

She thanked Jake and waved good-bye. Then she headed into the house.

Crossing the threshold of her home, Ashley felt a sudden and extraordinarily deep chill penetrate her spine. Immediately, she felt there was something wrong with her. Leaning against the door, she took a deep breath then turned back to lock the door. Holding the wall for stability, she walked the length of her home's center hallway ever so slowly. Physically and mentally, she felt disoriented – and her spirit filled with a feeling of agitation. In a state of complete confusion, she thought maybe she was suffering a medical condition perhaps an aneurism or then again, maybe it was just nerves. Was the conversation with Jake too much for her? She knew that seemed a ridiculous consideration. Her emotional constitution was strong, although at that moment she was no longer sure of anything.

In a shear panic, Ashley hurried to her bedroom closet and grabbed her warmest robe. She did not want to call Corrine and worry her, so she convinced herself if she could just settle down, the state would pass. Five minutes of disorientation and indescribable anxiety pressed in on poor Ashley before she entered the family's large central foyer, lit the gas stove, and curled up in the rose colored wing chair Kit passed on to her family some time ago.

As time went on, her anxiety grew and she began to wonder if she was experiencing some kind of a panic attack. She let another long five-minutes pass but when she found no relief, she reached for the phone to call Corrine.

Across town, Police Chief Peter Travers rushed toward the scene of an accident with bodily injury and as he approached the crash site, he immediately recognized Sean Moran's mangled gray crossover. The scene was ghastly. The crown of Sean's head pressed against the broken windshield. Beside him, Corrine Moran was completely still – her face and forehead resting down on the dashboard.

Travers checked Sean's pulse, though he was certain his lifelong friend was dead. Hearing a slight murmur from the passenger side, he reached over Sean and took hold of Corrine's slight wrist to get a pulse. Seconds later, her heart stopped and her hand went limp in his.

After meeting the medical examiner at the scene, the chief raced to Olive Branch Ranch. He thought it best to stop first at Northridge but as Ashley noticed a short while earlier, Kit's old Towne car was gone. Leaving Northridge, he drove just a few hundred yards to Amour where he hoped to find Kit with Ashley. The chief knew that time was of the essence, as shocking news always travelled like wildfire in Cody.

Just as Ashley dialed Corrine's number, a weak-kneed Chief Travers rang her front doorbell.

Through the sash, she noticed the chief's look of anguish.

"Ashley, Chief Travers here, may I come in for a moment?"

At once Ashley recognized a note of urgency in the chief's calm familiar voice, and a rush of adrenalin surged through her own veins. With a shaky hand and shallow breath, she opened the door.

"Is there something wrong, Chief?" Ashley asked. She drank in Peter's death-pale complexion and searched the lines of his face for something – anything – that would stop her growing dread. She saw nothing reassuring. The man Ashley had always known to be unshakable in every circumstance seemed extremely nervous and disheveled.

"Chief, has something happened?" Ashley asked again. "Is everything okay? If you need my dad for something," she said as she noticed Peter closing the door behind him, "he and my mom are at the teachers' barbeque at the high school. You know he wouldn't mind if you stopped in on him there. Call him. I'll write down his cell phone number. No, I'd better give you my mom's number. I think Dad left his phone here."

The fact that she was the only one speaking did not

escape Ashley. She slowed for just a moment, but before Peter Travers could speak, Ashley started in all over again, "May I get you something to drink, Chief?"

"No thank you, Ashley," finally, the chief's tone was absolute and commanding. "I would like you to come over here and sit down. Please sit down," he said as he directed her to the wing chair.

After Ashley sat down, Peter moved toward the chair, put his hand on the wing, then knelt by her side and asked, "Do you know where Kit is?"

"She's gone to visit the Crawfords over on Logan Mountain this evening."

"Well, I'm going to ask you to take me to her but in the meantime I must tell you, there has been a dreadful accident this evening."

"Oh, no," Ashley said, already sensing what was coming next.

"Ashley, I am so very, very, sorry to tell you, both of your parents are dead."

"Dead?...Dead?... But this can't be, Chief! I just saw them! There must be some mistake. How can this be? They can't be dead. I just saw them! I just saw them!"

"I'm so sorry Ashley, but it's true. The medical examiner is already at the crash site. It was not your parent's fault. Another car crossed into their lane. Your father died upon impact, and your mother died just after I arrived."

"I want to see them," Ashley pleaded.

"That wouldn't be wise, my dear." Peter struggled. "In the long-run you will see that it's best not to view the crash scene. Would you like me to have my dispatcher call Christina and Drew Patterson to take care of the necessary details for you while we go to find Kit?"

"Yes, please," Ashley, said. "Then we must go quickly to tell my grandmother, before she hears the news in another way."

As Peter called the Pattersons, dear friends of Sean and Corrine, Ashley took two white fleece blankets from the hall linen closet. She wrapped herself in the first as defense against her feelings of physical shock, and carried the second blanket for Kit.

"Chief Travers, do you know where the Crawford family lives?" Ashley asked as they approached Logan Mountain. Peter nodded in the affirmative.

The Crawford family home, a spectacular marble mansion at the summit of Logan Mountain, is a local landmark. Peter remembered attending a charity ball at the mansion nearly a decade ago, which for him ended the dream of many in Cody, to see the interior of the Crawford Mansion. How the good chief now wished as he entered the pristine drive, he was doing so for any reason than the one at hand.

When Ashley mentioned the number of guests, she believed to be in attendance as ten Peter decided to park the car at the kitchen entrance. He would ask Jean-Pierre, the Crawford's butler of thirty-years, to assist him with their entry into the party.

Once inside, Ashley spoke firmly to Peter and Jean-Pierre, informing them she intended to tell her grandmother of Sean and Corrine's deaths. Jean-Pierre, stunned by her maturity and insistence that she be the one to inform Kit of their loss, still thought of Ashley as the mere child he knew from birth. Her remarkable courage amazed him.

The friendship between the Crawford and the Moran families now span more than sixty-years. Fran Crawford's husband Theodore, Sr., a land developer in Cody at mid-century, passed away a few years before Kit's husband John. When it became clear the family mansion was too much for Fran to care for alone, her loving son Ted reorganized the Crawford assets and returned to Wyoming from a high-profile banking career in New York to attend to his family's affairs.

Jean-Pierre motioned to Ted Crawford through the swinging door that separated the dining room and kitchen. Ted responded at once. He was surprised to see Peter and Ashley waiting out of sight. Peter delivered the tragic news to Ted and informed him Ashley would be telling Kit of their mutual tragedy.

"I'll bring you into the dining room," an ashen Ted Crawford said gently. "Your unexpected presence here alone, will be enough to startle poor Kit."

In the next room, Fran Crawford sat at the head of the table with Kit at her right hand. A white damask tablecloth, fine crystal goblets, gold flatware and gold-rimmed place settings sealed with the Crawford family crest, covered the dining room table. With Beethoven's *Ninth Symphony* playing in the background, elegance filled the room.

Slowly Ashley entered the dining room. From her perspective, the scene was surreal. One at a time Fran's guests noticed Ashley and their conversations ceased. To all Ashley's appearance was one of grief and was certainly in contrast to the young beauty they had all known for years. With her back to the kitchen door, Kit who was engaged in a conversation with Fran about Fran's gat-about grandson Tate was the last to see Ashley.

At first, the fact her granddaughter was out of place did not register with Kit. Filled with apprehension, just seconds later however, the elderly Moran asked, "Ashley, what are *you doing here?*"

The trembling young woman approached her grandmother and knelt by her chair. Then taking Kit's hand Ashley spoke. "Nan, I'm afraid there has been a terrible accident."

Drawing deeply, a final breath, Ashley finished what she had come to say. "My mother and father are dead." With unwavering strength, Ashley looked into Kit's dazed eyes and made the dreadful pronouncement again.

"Nan, my parents were in a head-on collision on Highway 20 about an hour ago, and neither one made it."

"Sean is *dead?* That's impossible," Kit pronounced with a strong surge of denial. Looking from one friend to the other, she longed for the return of the chatter and clanging of dishes that filled the room just moments before.

"Sean *and* Corrine?" Kit questioned. A weeping Ashley nodded. "No…no…no…no…no…!" Kit cried out at increasing decibels as she pushed her chair away from the table. Then in anguish, she threw her hands over her face and bent forward as if unable to hear any more news.

"It's true, Kit," Peter Travers said with authority.

Kit Moran had led a life of authority but now she was weak. In this moment, when she realized death had stolen away her dear son, she knew it was best to submit to Peter's word. As she stood to reach for Ashley, who was still trying to digest the news, Kit's entire body succumb to shock and she passed out cold. Luckily, Peter Travers was near enough to prevent a serious fall.

Ted cleared the dining room. He then suggested that his guests have tea in an adjacent room. When Kit regained consciousness, Peter guided her into the living room where a warm fire burned brightly.

"Kit, I'm so sorry. I want you to know I will do anything you ask of me to help you and Ashley get through this tragedy," he said.

"Oh, Peter, I know you will, and I thank you," Kit said, shaking her head. "If you could, I'd like to know the condition of the other driver?" It was so like Kit Moran to think of others, even in her hour of need.

"The other driver is of course shaken, but sustained no bodily injury."

"Oh thank goodness," Kit said.

Ashley sat taking everything in. Certainly, she knew whoever took her parents' lives had enough to bear already, and any injury sustained by the other driver was outside the realm of immediate justice. Nevertheless, she wanted to know who caused the accident before she could be as generous as Kit.

"Chief Travers, do you know who the other driver was, and what happened?"

"We do know who the other driver was and that he caused the accident not your dad. We are still investigating the exact cause. The young man's name is Dylan Bates and he is about to enter his senior year at Cody High. He was unaware who the victims were but I'm sure he knew both your mom and dad.

"I've heard his parents moved into Cody his freshman year in high school," Peter continued. "Outside Cody High, the Bates family does not appear to be particularly well-known. Do either of you know the family?"

The Moran women agreed they were unacquainted with the Bates family.

"Such a terrible burden they have in front of them now," Kit said. "I'll pray for Dylan and his family."

Ashley knew Kit always spoke this way, and at times, she found her grandmother's spiritual platitudes just too much to take. Her own life thus far was void of religious sentiments, as Sean and Corrine abandoned the practice of their shared Catholicism before Ashley was born. Early on, Kit lost the battled she waged for Ashley's baptism and sadly, watched her granddaughter grow without the opportunity to receive a Faith formed in Jesus. Silently, she wondered now just how her dear granddaughter would cope in life with less than a marginal belief in God at best.

When the Morans were able to consider returning to Olive Branch Ranch, Ted escorted them through the mansion's tall white pillars at the front entrance. He held their arms tightly and took them down the pink marble walkway one at a time. Wrapped from head-to-toe in the white blankets that Ashley carried from home, the two women rested in each other's arms during their return to Amour.

They found Amour, a welcome sight at that hour and Christina, and Drew Patterson, who were waiting at the door to receive them home, a true comfort. Christina, Corrine Moran's best friend since childhood, was as familiar with Corrine's home as her own. Christina and Drew were unable to have children and were always happy to be part of Ashley's many childhood milestones. Waiting for the women to return, Christina brewed a strong pot of coffee and set a few fresh muffins on the table.

"Even if no one is able to eat," Christina thought through her own state of shock, "the least I can do is set a warm table. That's what Corrine would do."

Leaving the Morans off at Olive Branch Ranch, Chief Travers continued on to the home of Thompson and Sarah Smith to inform them of the death of their dear friends, but he was too late. Just moments earlier Sarah, a general practitioner at West Park Hospital, received a call from a colleague informing her of Sean and Corrine's passing. With Peter's visit, however, the three decided Thompson should represent the family as spokesperson, if Kit did not object. Sarah especially, agreed this action was entirely appropriate, as Thompson was Kit's legal counsel but even more so because Thompson Smith was Sean Moran's best friend.

After Thompson's call suggesting this offer to Kit, she and Ashley rambled throughout Amour. They found the

Patterson's companionship reassuring that night though they too had difficulty settling in. Some one or another paced the floor the entire night. Exhausted when daylight finally came a slight sense of relief entered the home as well.

CHAPTER TWO

Monday, August 24th

Just hours after the loss of Sean and Corrine, Kit was already settling into the idea that it would not be long until she would see them again. These thoughts were only natural for someone of deep and abiding faith in her eighty-fourth year. Kit Moran's religious ancestry was Catholic and from her earliest age, Catholicism was a lively force in her life. As is true of most persons of faith, Kit's faith was tried and tested, and never more than during her beloved husband John Moran's battle with cancer and his pre-mature death in 1968.

Catholicism for Kit was her solid hope and her brothers and sisters in Christ, her lasting support. Even before the reality of Sean and Corrine's deaths settled in her soul, Kit was on her knees. She begged God not for consolation for herself, but for Ashley who had little knowledge of the Ways of Jesus and the comfort He brings to those in sorrow.

"O Good Jesus," Kit prayed in Sean and Corrine's empty room, "please provide. Please make Ashley completely whole again and give me the strength to guide her and comfort her as long as *You* allow. May she pass through the depths of this heart wrenching tragedy and live her life abundantly. Amen."

"Drew has gone into town," Christina told Kit, when Kit joined entered the kitchen. "But just before he left," she added, "Thompson called and left word that he has arranged a meeting for you at eleven with A.J. Lawser, the new owner of Blackstone Funeral Home. Thompson hoped that by meeting A.J. at his office rather than the funeral home he would be able to give you the support you might need for the details ahead of you."

"Of course we'll be there," Kit, answered. "It's so good to have dear friends to count on in our darkest hours."

Then turning to Ashley she asked, "Are you okay with this, too, dear?"

At the thought of whatever details lay ahead, Ashley became overwhelmed with grief and she had difficulty speaking. She answered Kit as well as she was able.

"To be honest, Nan," she said through her tears, "I've never been to a memorial service of any kind, let alone a funeral. Will we have a Catholic funeral for Mom and Dad? I know they were raised Catholic."

"We'll do everything together, Ashley. It will all work out. You'll see." Kit hesitated addressing the fact that there would be no Catholic funeral rite for her son and daughter-in-law but Ashley's further inquiries forced the issue.

"Would you call Fr. Evers to see about a funeral at St. Anthony's, Nan? I've always heard his is wonderful."

"Oh, Ashley, I'm certain Fr. Joe would be more than happy to help us, but sadly I must tell you that your mother and father cannot have a funeral at St. Anthony's."

"But *why?*" Ashley asked, disheartened by Kit's solemn pronouncement.

"Well, they haven't belonged to the Catholic Church in years. And while it's true reconciliation was open to them, they purposely never took this step. I know this must sound almost cruel to you and the fact that we are already discussing the arrangements so very difficult – but I'm certain your mom and dad won't be able to have their funeral at St. Anthony. Just to be sure I can ask Fr. Joe for you, but I'm quite sure he will be unable to grant your wish."

"Isn't your Church supposed to be about compassion? At least that's what you've told me in the past."

"In many instances of extenuating circumstances in Catholicism today, the Church is able provide for the bodies of the deceased. In our case however, I believe It will be unable to do so."

"What do you mean in *our case*? Do you mean specifically in the case of my mom and dad?"

"I do."

"I don't understand," Ashley went on, "especially when they didn't have time to say they were sorry if they made a mistake in leaving the Church."

"Ashley, the Church has certain criteria even in times of exception. Do you remember when your parents endorsed the abortion clinic in Cheyenne by adding their names to its public notice, just last month?"

"I do. But they always told me they were pro-life privately, and pro-choice in their professional lives."

It was clear to Kit at this point that generations of progressive attitudes were afflicting their conversation. She knew Fr. Joe Evers was out of town, but promised to ask him to clarify their situation as soon as he returned.

As an alternative, Christina suggested they consider using the high school gymnasium for a memorial service, which lightened Ashley's spirits considerably. Kit decided they would approach their preparations with this possibility in mind.

Just before eleven, the Morans left Amour and drove to Thompson Smith's office in downtown Cody.

"Ashley, Kit, come in," Thompson said, when he met them at the door. "I am so sorry for your losses."

"We know you are," Kit said, "as we are for you. After all, you lost two very dear friends."

"Thank you, Kit. This is true, but my work for now is to take care of you," he said choking back his tears.

"I do have an urgent request," Kit said.

"What is it, Kit?"

"I'd like to have you become executor of my estate, immediately."

Thompson looked at Kit in awe and knew that the greatest act of compassion he could render was to accept her request. Taking a page from his conference table drawer Thompson scrawled his name on the Executor Change Form and Kit signed on the appropriate line as well. Neither mentioned the painful fact that Thompson had just taken Sean's place.

"Done," he said.

A productive first meeting, the group decided burial of Sean and Corrine in the Moran family plot at Riverside Cemetery on Saturday, directly following the memorial service at Cody High School. A.J. Lawser suggested a second meeting at the ranch the next morning to discuss specifics for the memorial service. All agreed.

As that first afternoon passed without Sean and Corrine, Kit's long-time homemaker Elaine Cain answered a steady stream of deliveries and condolences offered by the good people and businesses of Cody. In spite of the increasing activity as word of her loses spread, Kit tried to relax in her natural environment. "Whenever I am most in need, Northridge gives me such peace," she said to herself.

"Ashley, why don't you ask Elaine to go Amour with you to pack a bag and come to stay here for a few days?" Kit asked her granddaughter. "You can stay in your old room upstairs. That way we can be together."

"You know Nan, I'd love to do that. Thanks for offering. I'm not sure which way to turn right now."

"I know. Of course you don't. If you stay, perhaps we can think about the music and Scripture Readings before we meet with Mr. Lawser tomorrow morning. Now you go along, dear. There must be some things you need from home."

Ashley admired her grandmother's strength and her way of taking charge of things, even in the worst of times. She learned early on that Kit was an incredibly strong woman, especially in tragedy; and now, really for the first time, she could see these personal qualities in full-measure and admired her grandmother in an entirely new way.

When alone, Kit began moving through Northridge, checking supplies to ensure they would have everything needed for the next few days. Fran Crawford called to check in, and then Thompson called with some unexpected news.

"Kit, how are you holding up this afternoon?" he inquired.

"As well as possible," she answered.

Then as always, her thoughts turned to others. "How are you and Sarah doing with the shock of all this?"

"We're okay. We both know the loss of Sean and Corrine will affect us forever. On a much deeper level Kit, I'll miss Sean more than I'll ever be able to tell you. Your son was such a terrific guy, and both were incredible teachers." Thompson would love to have said more, especially about Sean, but realized it was just too soon for both of them.

"I wanted to let you know my office has fielded several offers of assistance from the community. In fact, my assistant and I have answered more than a dozen calls between us."

"That's amazing."

Clearing his throat, Thompson went on. "Kit, I do have a specific reason for calling. There's a situation I must tell you about, and at the same time, I want to offer to handle this matter for you."

"What is it, Thompson?"

"Well, it concerns a personal request Sean made of me."

"Go on," Kit said.

"One day about a year ago, Sean stopped by my office and left an envelope, which he asked me to hold apart from the Moran file. He told me that I should open the envelope if anything ever happened to him."

"Have you opened the envelope?" Kit asked.

"Yes, early this morning. But I decided not to discuss it with you in front of Ashley."

"What did Sean say?"

"He asked that Lucy be notified of his passing and invited to his funeral."

"I see," said Kit as she paused thoughtfully. "You must call her for Sean, Thompson. Would you please? Whether or not she comes back to Cody is up to Lucy, but his sister must be informed of his passing and of the arrangements, just as Sean requested."

"Of course I will. I have told you already I want to help you. But, Kit? Are you sure you are up for this?"

When Kit heard the inflection in Thompson's voice, she recognized his deep concern over the fact that she and her only daughter were estranged. Kit learned long ago to suppress the unpleasant memories of Lucy's last year in Cody. The painful truth was her eldest child had not been part of her life for the last forty-years.

"How many years has it been since you've heard from her?" Thompson inquired gently.

"Many," Kit answered sorrowfully. "In the beginning there were a few phone calls." Kit hoped Thompson would not press her statement, as it was just too difficult to speak of Lucy's last call. It was a call of desperation.

The cold fact was that Kit had not seen Lucy Moran since she married Gary Gallow in 1970 on an old platform on the grounds of the Woodstock Festival, in upstate New York.

"Lucy will always be my daughter and Sean's older

sister, Thompson," Kit said softly. "She must be told. I do extend my deepest gratitude to you though, for your added concern for me."

"I'll make the call today," Thompson assured Kit.

"Please do let me know if you reach her. I'm assuming Sean left some kind of an address or phone number with you."

"He did. I'll speak with you soon, Kit."

"Indeed. Oh, and Thompson, Sean decided early on not to tell Ashley about Lucy. The fact that she has an aunt will come as a great shock, I'm sure."

"Good luck, Kit," Thompson said. Everything Kit had yet to deal with truly unnerved Thompson and his compassion for her rose beyond what he thought it capable.

As Kit turned off her phone, Ashley came through the front door. The two women decided to have tea together out on the grand porch with its beautifully manicured lawns atop a rock barrier leading down to the Shoshone River some twenty-five feet below.

"Nan, last night at Crawford's, I heard you say you would pray for Dylan Bates," Ashley said as they settled in their wicker chairs.

"I did, and I have prayed for Dylan and his family today," Kit said in response.

"Is that difficult for you?"

"Although it might seem so, it really isn't. Does this surprise you?" Kit asked, unsure of how Ashley was feeling about Dylan Bates.

"Because I know you so well, it doesn't surprise me that you are willing to pray for him and his family, but what I can't figure out is how you are able to do this without first feeling anger like I do."

"What do you mean, Ashley? How can I not be angry about what Dylan did?" Kit said gently.

"Exactly."

"Oh, the anger is there, and I'm sure it will be for some time but it's an emotion within me, and I do have some control over it. As far as praying for Dylan, without years of practice no human can arrive at this mindset quickly. Forgiveness is a chosen activity and the base of many good deeds."

"Forgiveness, yes, but it seems to me you've jumped over the part about justice," Ashley said.

"I suppose it does seem that way, but justice will prevail. Over the course of my lifetime, wisdom has taught me to forgive sooner rather than later. It's far less painful to forgive than to hold on tight for a while maybe even years. Who sustains the most pain when we hold on? The one who needs forgiveness certainly carries pain, but experience has shown me that the one who needs to forgive often carries so much more.

"What happened to your mom and dad was an accident. In other words, it was unintentional. The consequences for vehicular homicide are extreme and should be. Nonetheless, in almost every accident, the fact that the event was unintentional usually prevails.

"Accidents are part of the human condition and because we are all susceptible to them we must forgive as soon as we are able. At least that's how I feel about it, dear."

"I suppose you're right," Ashley agreed with hesitation. "You've forgiven, Dylan?" Ashley asked.

"I have," Kit replied, and then added encouragement for Ashley.

"Ashley, you will have to follow your own heart and arrive at forgiveness for Dylan Bates in your own time. My respect for your feelings is an important part of *your processing your grief* successfully. My only hope for you is that your day for forgiveness will come sooner, rather than later."

"I hope so too," she said but clearly, she just was not sure.

An hour after sunset Ashley went up to her room, the room where she had stayed as a child as often as her parents allowed. In those early years of her life Kit kept Ashley's room filled with stuffed animals, and covered her granddaughter's bed with a white fun-fur coverlet. Whenever she ordered new books from *The Book of the Month Club,* Kit purchased a new book for Ashley too. Eventually, the tall white bookcase filled with books of every kind including some religious books as well. This was Kit's silent contribution toward Ashley's spiritual growth in her early years.

Ashley loved Northridge. The Shoshone River was much closer there than to Amour. Whenever she stayed with Kit, she felt the river moving deep in her soul. Often she sat on a window-seat upstairs and counted the stars in the sky and the moonbeams dancing on the river while Kit, Sean and Corrine chatted in front of the fireplace in the dining room below. Whenever her parents agreed, Ashley stayed and had the most wonderful overnights with her grandmother.

When Ashley climbed the stairs and entered her room that night the entire house was deadly silent. There were no lively conversations. The only light remaining after she turned off the lamp on her nightstand was Kit's light shining through the crack of the master bedroom, which was three steps up at the end of the hall.

Ashley always took great comfort in her grandmother's protection. Tonight however, she recognized a profound new sense of protectiveness toward Kit within. Although just over twenty-four hours had passed since the accident, in Ashley's mind Kit had turned from pillar of strength into a fragile bird that might fly off and leave her too. At this thought Ashley trembled.

The sole member of the fourth-generation of the Olive Branch Ranch Morans, Ashley Moran was beginning to realize that life, as she had always known it had just come to a complete end. With this heavy realization, all she could do was close her eyes and cry herself to sleep.

CHAPTER THREE

Tuesday, August 25th

A cool dry air mass enveloped Northridge on Tuesday morning. From her bedroom, Ashley heard Kit and Elaine speaking for a few moments, then heard Kit's car leave the yard.

"Nan?" Ashley called, to see if Kit was still home.

"I'm here, dear. I have some warm muffins and fruit for you and the coffee is on. I've just sent Elaine out for supplies."

"I'll be right down," Ashley answered with a sigh of relief.

Kit felt a degree of tension over the list of pending details for Saturday's memorial, as well as the possibility Lucy might decide to return to Cody. Whether or not Lucy would return, Kit knew today was the day she had to inform Ashley her father had a sister. As she waited for Ashley to join her at the table, she thought back to the day Corrine and Sean asked her not to discuss Lucy with their daughter.

At first, Kit thought this request was preposterous. As time went on however she agreed that any mention of Lucy would stir up unpleasantness in the presence of a child who filled all of them with such joy. Long before Ashley was born, those close to the Moran family insisted that locals refrain from discussing Lucy amongst themselves. All of Cody loved Kit and no one wanted to add to the grief of her early widowhood so, the entire community took an unspoken oath never to mention Lucy. Unfortunately, with Sean's unexpected death, Kit knew she must be the one to inform Ashley about Lucy – and that this must be done right away.

"Good morning," Kit said, as Ashley poured her

coffee. "My dear, there is a family matter of which you are unaware, that I must discuss with you this morning."

"What is it, Nan?" Ashley asked while stirring her coffee.

"It's something you may have many questions about, but before I tell you I want you to understand that your parents wanted to protect you and eventually I agreed with their decision."

"Is this some sort of a family secret?" Ashley asked. She was now feeling some apprehensive.

"Ashley, do you know I have an older daughter?"

"You do?" Clearly, this was the first time she had heard this news. "Who is she? Was Grandpa John her father, Nan, or were you married before?"

"No dear. John Charles Moran was my only husband, and Lucy is most definitely our daughter born in 1950 – almost a year to the day after our May wedding reception in 1949. Lucy grew up here at Northridge but left home permanently after your Grandpa John passed away four-decades ago."

"Why haven't I been told anything about Lucy, Nan?"

"Well that's a long story. You see, Lucy's reputation was in shambles when she left our ranch with a young couple of questionable character. Her departure was a powerful rebellion against my values and was, frankly, a great embarrassment for your dad and me. Certainly, we would have considered her amends at any time, had Lucy decided to confront her wrongdoings. She never did. Later, and because of Lucy's questionable character, your mom and dad decided it would be better not to tell you about an aunt you might never meet."

"How dreadful that must have been for you, Nan, to lose contact with your only daughter." Kit felt Ashley's compassion and appreciated her acceptance of the "forced" decision made on her behalf so long ago.

"It was really difficult, Ashley. But rather than fall into a world of regret in seeking a relationship my daughter clearly did not want, I focused on my own life, your family, the ranch, and on touching the lives of those who accepted my love."

"Does Lucy know about my dad and mom yet?"

"Your dad left his number with Thompson a while ago, in the off-chance something ever happened to him. I'll know more when Thompson gets back to me. He's trying to reach Lucy today."

"Does that mean she might come here, Nan?"

"There is that possibility. But let's not think about this detail until we have to."

Ashley sensed that without question Kit would prefer that Lucy not come. "I'm glad you finally told me, I have an aunt. That took courage, Nan, especially now."

Ashley gave Kit a warm hug and both headed upstairs to prepare for their meeting with A.J. Lawser. As each was dressing, Kit's phone rang.

"I've been out of town for a few days," Fr. Joe Evers announced, "and just heard the news. How dreadful for you, Kit, and of course for your son's daughter as well."

"Yes, it is. And of course this is just dreadful for Ashley, Father."

"Tell me what I can do to help you? I'll do anything Kit."

"Thank you so much, but I'm afraid there's not much you can do. Do you recall my telling you how my son and daughter-in-law were absolutely firm in their stand against the Church?"

"Yes I do. Regardless Kit, I might be able to help you and your granddaughter in some way. And, of course you'll have my prayers, as will Sean and Corrine. You must not forget their time came early and that God will consider all the good they have done, and how they felt about Him at the moment of their deaths. God *is* mercy. We're not judge or jury, my dear."

"Thank you for reminding me of God's beautiful mercy," Kit responded. "Of course this knowledge is a great comfort to me."

"What else? What else can I do for you, Kit? You've done so much for us, at St. Anthony's."

"Well Father, are you busy right now?"

"Not if I can be of service to you."

"A.J. Lawser will be arriving from Blackstone Funeral Home any moment. Would you come out to Northridge too, and sit with us? We're planning a memorial service and I know we would appreciate your guidance.

"Our family ancestry is Catholic on all-sides, but Sean and Corrine's decisions against the Church left their daughter without a religious upbringing. Her parents decided to allow Ashley to choose her Faith, if any, when she was grown. I'm afraid the consequence of this decision has left my poor granddaughter wanting in her hour of need."

"I understand completely, Kit. This is happening to our children more now than we can comprehend. Entire families come to the doors of St. Anthony's to bury their dead without any understanding of the religious significance of our funeral rite, or of the necessary reverence or etiquette. Please don't misunderstand me. I'm happy to see they desire a Catholic burial for their loved ones but I often wonder if I ache more over their losses or from their spiritual depravation."

"You'll love Ashley Therese, Father. Her innocence is refreshing. And, I'll pray God will give you the insight to help her in some way."

"I'm leaving now," Fr. Joe told Kit. "I'll be along in a few minutes."

Fr. Joe Evers knew all too well that Sean and Corrine

Moran made a firm commitment against the Catholic Church. In fact, he had recent contact with the couple but knew this was not the right time to disclose the gist of these communications with their survivors unless necessary.

As far as Father could see now, Kit's initial judgment regarding her son and daughter-in-law's denial of a Catholic burial was correct. Kit's knowledge of this fact was astute, but if Father revealed a conversation he had with the couple just weeks ago, Kit and her granddaughter would see it was Sean and Corrine who made it impossible for the Church to overturn Its position. Father's greatest hope as he headed off to Northridge was that his need to disclose his recent meeting with Corrine and Sean Moran would not arise.

When Fr. Joe and A.J. Lawser joined the Moran women in the dining room at Northridge, Kit opened their four-way discussion by addressing Ashley first.

"Ashley, why don't you share some of your ideas about the service?"

"I will," she answered vaguely. Then surprisingly, she changed the subject. "But first, I have a question for Fr. Joe." Ashley's tone was firm and commanding.

"What is it, Ashley?" he asked.

"Well Father, you probably know my mom and dad were both baptized Catholics at birth, and I'm having a very difficult time accepting my grandmother's explanation for the Church denying them a Catholic funeral."

Frankly, Ashley's candor surprised Kit. She had no idea her granddaughter was still struggling with the location for the funeral, and was sorry she had not recognized her distress. She was not however uncomfortable with Ashley's persistence on the matter.

Nothing would have pleased Kit more, than to find out her initial statement of what she believed was the Church's stance in their case was incorrect. As far as she was concerned, this would be the best possible outcome.

"I understand your particular situation completely, Ashley. I'm sorry to say that St. Anthony's Parish, or any other Catholic parish for that matter, would be unable to have a funeral service for your mom and dad."

He hated to move on with his next explanation but now there was no avoiding the facts if he was to support the women honestly.

"Unfortunately, it came to my attention several weeks ago, that your mother and father endorsed a pro-choice rally in Cheyenne. I noticed their names appeared in the *Wyoming Tribune-Eagle* in an advertisement indicating their financial support for NARAL – Pro-Choice America."

"Oh, I know all about that, Father," Ashley said in quiet defense. "That's what they felt they *had to do* to remain in good-standing with the *Advance Teaching Movement*, but they told me that personally they were pro-life."

"Ashley, as painful as the Church's stand might be for you to accept in your present situation, I truly want to help you to celebrate your parents' lives and to be a Catholic presence to you, Kit, and the entire Cody Community."

"I'm trying to understand, Father, but I need some help because as my grandmother has probably told you I'm not Catholic. I'm not even baptized."

All at the table felt an unmistakable edge toward Sean and Corrine in Ashley's last comments, and they shared in the young woman's plight. Silently each reflected on her profound love for her parents – and how distressing it was for her now to live out the consequences of the greatest mistake parents can make – failure to prepare their children for life's inevitable losses, in which only God will suffice.

"Ashley, please don't take the Church's decision as an affront on your parents," Fr. Joe continued.

"It is a privilege to belong to the Catholic Faith, but that privilege carries certain obligations to which the faithful must adhere, if they are to receive the Church's outward blessing in death."

Father stopped and said a little prayer before he revealed Sean and Corrine's last dealings with the Church.

"Kit, Ashley, I really hate to tell you this, but I met with Sean and Corrine when I saw their endorsement of NARAL."

"When was this?" Ashley asked.

"Last month." Fr. Joe's response was firm yet filled with compassion. "When I saw their names in the advertisement, I decided to contact them hoping to open some sort of dialogue. To be courteous they accepted my invitation to meet with them but at that time they made it very clear they were unwilling to review the latest materials I prepared for them on the sanctity for life." Fr. Joe remembered how irate Sean was in particular, but decided it was not necessary to give Ashley these details.

"A few days after we met I received this letter with both of their signatures," Fr. Joe said as he pulled the Morans' letter from his pocket. Your parents' letter make it irreversibly clear, Ashley, that we will not be able to bury them from St. Anthony Parish. To confirm this statement Fr. Joe read an excerpt from the text:

> *"...While we thank you for your spiritual concern, as we explained at our brief meeting, we no longer consider ourselves Catholic and plan never to return to "the fold." Please keep this letter as a permanent record of our decision..."*

The room went silent. Ashley's sorrow tore through Fr. Joe. He could see she suffered more at the conclusion of his explanation than she was suffering when she first posed her question. This pained him.

"Ashley, let's work together to develop a beautiful memorial for your parents," he suggested. I'll give you my total blessing for this purpose, and I promise to be there for you in the days ahead."

Exhausted by the intensity of the meeting, and with nowhere to go with her disappointment, Ashley finally conceded to Fr. Joe's kind offer.

Fr. Joe Evers was a man of great faith. He was a contemporary sort, of average height, physically fit and a man who enjoyed Wyoming's great outdoors. His personality was warm and hospitable – and without exception, parishioners and visitors always felt welcome at St. Anthony Parish.

As a parish priest, he was not subject to a vow of poverty, therefore he was free to keep up with technology, a means he frequently employed to capture the energetic minds of his young parishioners. Now approaching forty, Fr. Joe could be a comfort to his peers in their struggles, and an understanding ear for the elderly and their caretakers. Whenever possible, he extended the same care to his aging parents as well. All around, Fr. Joe was a wonderful priest, however at meetings such as this, the poor man felt sorely inadequate.

"Ashley, if I may have your permission, I'd like to share an idea I had with all of you," Kit said. Ashley nodded her approval and things seemed to move on from there.

"Because your mother and father chose not to participate in any religion in town but did give their lives as teachers to the entire community, perhaps we could ask a representative from Temple Shalom, the United Church of Christ and you Fr. Joe, to offer an ecumenical service."

"I'd like to suggest the memorial be held at two on Saturday," said Mr. Lawser who was relieved the conversation had finally turned to his area of expertise. "Ted Crawford called me and offered to be the master of ceremonies," he added.

"That's wonderful, A.J.," Kit replied.

"There were several other offers I'd like to present, if I may," Lawser continued. Nick Davis has indicated the Cody High Band and the Grand Teton Orchestra would like to prepare music of your choosing. As principal at the high school, Nick also offered to coordinate the town's academic community."

"Does your ecumenical program include readings from the New and Old Testament?" Fr. Joe asked A.J.

"Yes, definitely."

"May I ask a few friends to do the readings, Father?" Ashley asked.

"Certainly. However, I'd like you to select only those friends familiar with the written Word of God, if you will. There is an absolute difference between those who present God's Word with love, and those who simply read it."

"I'll do that," Ashley assured Fr. Joe.

The successful meeting adjourned at noon and Fr. Joe and A.J. Laser departed thereafter. Elaine prepared an early lunch and a pitcher of iced tea for the women, which they decided to have on the front porch overlooking Kit's rose garden and the river below.

Thinking Ashley would grill her about Lucy or discuss her disappointment over the funeral as they ate alone; Kit was pleasantly surprised to find her granddaughter much more interested in her early days at Northridge.

"Nan, would you give me a little lesson on Northridge? I mean its history – how it came to be. I've heard it told before, but the ranch and especially this home seem much more important to me now that I'm in the middle of a crisis." Kit agreed on both accounts.

Relaxed and relieved, Kit asked Ashley, "Where shall I begin?"

"Begin when you first came to Wyoming," Ashley commanded.

Happy to concede to Ashley's wishes, Kit said, "Of course, dear. A beautiful place to start." Then she opened her life's story to Ashley.

"I came alone to Powell, Wyoming in 1948 from my home in Salvador, California – the Napa Valley Region. I took a job with the California Department of Food and Agriculture (CDFA) after receiving my degree in agriculture at San Francisco University and accepted a summer assignment, examining a new dry-farming method Wyoming farmers were perfecting.

"When I completed the project, I decided to spend a few days exploring the beautiful Grand Teton Mountains before returning to California. I then came to stay at Olive Branch Ranch on the recommendation of a farmer I worked with.

"I was an experienced rider and was longing to explore the Grand Tetons on horseback. When I saw Wyoming's endless ribbons of wildflowers, the rainbow fields of Indian Paintbrush, yellow Primrose, and blue Mountain-Bell hugging the base of the mountain range from Highway 20, I was absolutely driven, to see it all first-hand. I wanted to experience the incredible aroma, to see the mixed-bouquets that grow quite naturally here, and Wyoming's glistening lakes and rivers, too. I remember being determined to follow the trails of at least one Grand Teton to its summit.

With her introduction complete, Kit sat pensively for a moment, trying to decide which of her early days with the

Morans Ashley would find most interesting. Before she could begin again however, Thompson Smith called.

Kit rose to her feet and took her phone to the white picket fence at the edge of the lawn. Hearty red roses, danced about her knees in the breeze, as she stood with her back to Ashley. Watching Kit, Ashley could see Kit's anguish and assumed the call was about Lucy.

"Did Thompson reach Lucy, Nan?" she asked as Kit headed back to the porch.

"Actually, she just returned his phone call. She'll be coming to Cody for the memorial on Saturday and will be arriving in town tomorrow afternoon."

"Are you okay with this? It seems so much for you to go through. We could send word it's best if she didn't come," Ashley said as she watched the color drain from Kit's fragile face.

"No, no," dear. We're going to go on living in the present moment. Lucy is coming, this is true, but I don't have to think about her arrival until tomorrow. That's soon enough.

"May I please continue on with my stories of Northridge?"

"Oh, please, Nan. But before you start I want to mention I've noticed your statue of Our Lady has disappeared again," she said. "But I'm sure I'm not telling you anything new."

While her family inquired occasionally about the statue's coming and going from its pedestal on the lower lawn, Kit never felt the need to give an answer. Today was no exception. She made this known with a wide but silent smile.

"Now, where was I? Oh, yes, now I remember. My first day on the ranch was so long ago now," she said with a sigh. "I've never left the ranch for more than a few nights from the time I was about your age and I've never regretted that decision – not even for a moment." Kit went on with her memories.

"As I pulled up to the guest house that first day, I saw your great-grandma Jane in her flower garden at Amour. She was lovely in both mind and spirit and her first impression was indelible. She was an aging beauty amongst the mature roses with long wisps of graying hair over-shadowing her golden complexion. I had called ahead for a room the night before, so she was expecting me.

"When I arrived Jane led me into the guest house where John, who was painting the front porch, held the door for me. It was love at first sight for both of us."

"Really?"

"Absolutely, and I would have to say that it was really from that moment on that my home became Olive Branch Ranch."

"It must have been awesome to be so sure of your major life decisions," Ashley said.

"It's easy to make such a decision no matter the timing when it's true love. John and I had wonderful time while I was a guest at the ranch. He took me to the summit of Mt. Owen and we rode all over the region on horseback covering a different area each day. It was glorious.

"When I was about to leave your grandfather decided he could not live without me. He proposed to me and I was thrilled. Within a week, we were married in what was once a little Catholic chapel in Yellowstone National Park.

Kit's memories of falling in love with John captivated Ashley who, as most young women her age, lived in quiet anticipation, hoping she too would fall in love.

"Oh, I wish I had known him, Nan. He always seems so wonderful to me whenever someone speaks of him."

"John was strikingly handsome, but it was his good spirit that simply knocked me off my feet. He was tall with dark brown curly hair. His build was medium, and strong. He had the hands of a worker and large blue almond-shaped eyes. John's personality was gregarious and dazzled those in his presence." Kit paused a moment, wrapped tightly in her intimate memory of her sweet husband. With the heavy cross of Sean's death to carry, Kit missed John Charles Moran more than ever.

"Did you tell me once that you and Grandpa John built Starlight Cottage together?" Ashley knew her question was manipulative but hoped Kit would forgive her. Her curiosity about the family cottage rarely ceased and she was never completely free of her desire to learn of its contents.

"John and I built Northridge by building Starlight Cottage first. Starlight, during our first year of marriage was mill-by-day and home-by-night. While the amenities were sparse, a small kitchen on the ground floor and a loft for sleeping above, it was a wonderful place for newlyweds.

"Each evening we mulled over blueprints for Northridge and then retired to the sweeping sounds of the Shoshone River just outside our door, as the moonbeams filled our little loft with soft sweet light.

"Besides being an expert rancher your grandfather was an extremely talented carpenter so Northridge came together quickly."

"Did Grandpa John do all the finished carpentry in this house?"

"Every bit. He wouldn't have it any other way.

"The beautiful split-wood stairs, the foyer, and all the shelves for the library?"

"Yes," Kit said.

"And that gorgeous mantel?"

"Yes, again."

"I know I've never heard this version of your life

before, Nan."

"When quite young, Sean and Lucy heard stories of the various items John tailored for our home, but children seldom value the work of their father or mother when they are young, and I never really expected them to. When John passed away, I considered this house the "remnants" of *my life*, not my children's future."

Suddenly Kit felt exhausted. "Ashley, I'm afraid I need some rest. I know from my experience with grief that the body needs more sleep while the mind wants less." Ashley agreed with Kit's assessment. "I'd like to lie down, so why don't we get together again at dinner. I will pull something light together later. I'm expecting Thompson and Sarah to come by around six."

"That will be fine, Nan. I think I'll lie down upstairs for a while as well."

Somewhat rested, Kit rose before Ashley and warmed a waiting casserole. Recalling an early seed of wisdom her own mother shared, she always did in sorrow the things she would be doing otherwise. Therefore, she set a simple, yet lovely dinner table for the two of them. Just as she called up to Ashley for dinner, Fr. Joe stopped by.

"Please come in, Father. You must have dinner with us," Kit insisted all in a single breath.

"Are you just sitting down, Kit?"

"I'm waiting for Ashley. She should be down shortly. I think you'll be a comfort to her, if you are able to stay."

"Well, I was out this way again today, visiting a sick parishioner. I really just wanted to see how you were both doing this afternoon, and to see if I can be of further service to you in any way. I've finished my part of the memorial service, but I'm somewhat cautious about

Ashley's feelings toward me and more specifically toward Catholicism. I'm afraid that she might feel that as a representative of the Church, I've let her down."

Before Kit could assure Fr. Joe, this was not so, Ashley glanced over the upstairs balcony. She hoped Father would stay for dinner. Having had time to digest their morning meeting she welcomed an opportunity to explain more clearly where she's coming from religiously speaking.

"Please stay, Fr. Joe," Ashley said, as she descended the stairs. "It would be good for Nan and for me to have your company. Maybe you'll have answers to a few more of my difficult questions," she said with a smile.

Before Father had an opportunity to accept their invitation, Kit whisked a third place setting on the table and pulled out another seat. Seated at the dining room table, Fr. Joe admired the beautiful oil depiction of a single snowcapped mountain hanging over the dining room mantel for the second time that day. While he chose not to comment on the painting when at Northridge that morning, his interest piqued as he viewed it for a second time.

"An original?" he asked of Kit.

"Yes, by Thomas J. Moran. You may know of him as one of the greatest early painters of America's western landscapes."

"Yes, I know of him. Any relation to your husband, Kit?" Fr. Joe asked without hesitation.

"Distant. This painting is called *Mountain of the Holy Cross,* and is a painting of Mountain of the Holy Cross in the Colorado Rockies." Fr. Joe was interested in Kit's answer but could not help but notice a formal – almost edgy tone in her voice. Between the lines, he heard, "Please, no more questions."

Over his fifteen-years of ministry, Fr. Joe learned when

to probe and when to be silent. Feeling he caused the tension in Kit's voice, he decided to tell the women his favorite icebreaker regarding his call to the priesthood; how while hiking with friends in the Rocky Mountains a black bear scared him right into the Arms of God. Both women enjoyed the humor in his tale. Fr. Joe was relieved.

When dinner was over, Kit decided to wait for Sarah and Thompson Smith's arrival out on the porch, which gave Ashley an opportunity to speak privately with Fr. Joe. In her present situation, he was not surprised that she still had questions.

"Fr. Joe, I have some new concerns," Ashley said.

"What kind of concerns?" he asked.

"Well, I've never given this much thought before, because my parents always told me that if we were good people we would all go to Heaven, even if we didn't worship God on Sundays." Ashley choked back her tears as she blurted out her greatest fear. "Do you think my parents are in Heaven?"

Fr. Joe felt the deep spiritual concern Ashley had for Sean and Corrine. Her eyes begged his answer. In his heart, he bore great concern for the salvation of all souls today, more than ever before, because so many of God's people stand firmly against Him and His teachings.

Father answered Ashley with great tenderness.

"The death of a loved one, or in your case Ashley, the tremendous burden of losing two loved ones, is frequently a moment of spiritual crisis, especially for the young.

After pausing briefly to acknowledge Sarah and Thompson had joined Kit on the porch, Fr. Joe attempted to respond to Ashley's pressing question.

"I think it's likely your parents first exited the Church when they picked up a very popular trend that was emerging around the Country when they married. Then as did many new parents at that time, they decided to allow you to choose your religion in adulthood. Unfortunately, young people seldom have the foresight to see the consequences in this error. I am sure your parents would have reconsidered their decision on your behalf had they known what you would be facing.

"I hope you will find a degree of comfort in knowing however this trend was considered mainstream in America at that time. Perhaps this is something even you and your friends might have considered if you were the young adults of that day.

"As young college students in their day, your parents probably considered themselves mainstream America and actually progressives in their native western culture. A common decision made by many young adults of that particular era was to postpone the religious upbringing of their children.

"As a result, many of our County's young today believe religion is unnecessary, or they postpone a commitment simply because they are so unsure which religion to join. This is true especially for people with parents of two different faiths, such as Judaism and Catholicism. If parents encourage their children to postpone making a decision as to which Faith they will join, when the child is grown, he or she may feel that choosing one religion over the other is like choosing one parent over the other -- an impossible consequence for most in this situation. I have witnessed this several times over the years and it's very painful for all involved.

"Although you have never had religious training per se Ashley, someday you will reflect on these days of trail and realize God is working in you, even as we speak.

"As far as your mother and father are concerned," Ashley, "while they chose not to grow to full-maturity in their Catholic Faith, they were faithful to each other and this is admirable. If they had a bit more insight when they were first married, perhaps your mom and dad would have decided differently. They were however married at a time of great change in society, and the Catholic Church often failed in Its mission to provide continuing education for Its young adults facing changes of historical proportion."

"You explanation is helpful to me," Ashley said thoughtfully.

"But do you think they will get to Heaven?" Ashley repeated.

"Only God knows for sure," Father told her, "but let me try to shed some light on this subject as well."

"Ashley, there are two more things I'd like to explain to you this evening, if you don't think it would be too much for you."

"Oh, I'm fine, but before you do, Father, would you like a little more coffee and some shortbread cookies?"

"You know, that would be great. Thanks so much."

While Ashley stepped into the kitchen and he was unobserved, Fr. Joe again had an opportunity to take in the beauty of the Thomas Moran painting over the fireplace.

"There must be more to tell," he thought to himself. Recognizing Kit was under no obligation to speak about the painting, and certainly not in these hours of trial, he decided not to pursue further questioning. Thinking back to Kit's response at dinner however Fr. Joe could not help but notice that her avoidance seemed rehearsed, as though it was her standard response to unsolicited interest. "I know Thomas J. Moran, Jr. as one of the greatest painters in American history," Fr. Joe's thoughts continued. "This work must be absolutely priceless."

Seated directly across from the painting, Father admired Moran's artistic ability. He soaked in thousands of strokes of natural oil pigment laid by the artist's hand a hundred-years ago. Exploring the painting, he examined one small area and then the next as he followed Moran's expressive brush patterns flowing from one pool of color to another. Fr. Joe's eyes moved from pine trees and river rocks at the base of the painting to the green forests lining the mountain top, on then to the beautiful white cross of snow that forms naturally in the deep ravines on the face of Mountain of the Holy Cross in Colorado each spring.

When Ashley returned to the table, she found Fr. Joe completely mesmerized by the landscape, but out of respect for Kit, she decided not to mention the painting.

"Here, I hope you like these strawberry-shortcake cookies, Father. They come from a little shop near Logan Mountain.

"I love them. Thank you."

"Ashley I'd like to explain the culture of young Americans that began taking shape in the 1960s to you, just as I do for others who have either directly or indirectly lost their Catholic Faith as a result of that turbulent decade. I think this will help you to understand some of the social pressures your parents were probably facing as young adults at that time. I'll just give it to you straight."

"Please," Ashley pleaded wholeheartedly.

"I think Kit told me once that your folks were married about 1979."

"1979, exactly," said Ashley.

"Well, the first of the two points I want to make is to describe the particular culture of your parents' time. For more than a decade preceding Sean and Corrine's marriage, America went through the Cultural Revolution, which initially came into being by mass objection to U.S. involvement in the war in Vietnam. This period in our Country's history, shook every aspect of America's social, cultural, sexual and religious foundations.

"For over four-decades now, we have been living in the

consequences of the Cultural Revolution – the deep scares really – of those remarkably turbulent times. Family life was shaken to its core during this period. The stigma of divorce was defeated by a new social acceptance and many marriages failed when one spouse or both demanded their freedom – often just for the want of a new sexual partner.

"At this time women began to fight, and rightly so, for equality in the workplace, then as couples decided to refuse the Sacrament of Matrimony and cohabitate, some Catholic priests bent to "the will of the people," giving in to the desires of those who wanted less stringent rules and obligations.

"In the end, every aspect of American life was affected by this revolution – this pandemonium really. Soon thereafter, as is so often noted following a period of social disturbance, every kind of rebel or existentialist and every radical social agenda imaginable was in tow.

"Ready or not, approving or not, America acquired a new scale for measuring moral, ethical and social norms."

"So this could explain the social diversity I see within my various groups of friends and their families even out here in conservative America," Ashley told Fr. Joe.

"Actually, there's even more to it."

"Tell me," Ashley said.

"The major effects of all this turbulence "trickled up" and rocked every older age group in society in the early 1970s and at the same time it "trickled down" to the next generation of students.

"My mom and dad were in that second wave of young Americans, correct?" Ashley asked. Fr. Joe nodded. "Do you think many young people lost their faith during this turbulent time, Father?"

"Oh, I know so, and because many beliefs were reformulated, it was easier for people to justify their actions."

"Do you think my mother and father justified their decision not to worship God?"

"Actually, I think that was likely the case."

"Do you think their decision against Catholicism, translated into a decision against Jesus? Do you think they made it to Heaven?" Ashley asked again.

"Well, as I mentioned before Ashley, no one really knows the condition of another's soul or how God interprets the soul's affection towards Him, and we certainly don't understand the Mind of God. Through the teachings of Jesus Christ, we know what God expects of us, but we have no idea the leniency He allows in judging us, or how He interprets our failures. He may see some persons seemingly hardened by sin, as not at all responsible because of circumstances out of their control. In these matters, we can have no understanding. By contrast, there may be individuals who appear to be living according to the proclamations of Jesus Christ, and profess all day long this is so, who may actually be steeped in grave sin. So in the matter of another's salvation, especially when there is a question, it's always best to depend upon the Divine Mercy of God."

"What is Divine Mercy, Father?"

"Ah, this is the second point I wanted to make before we conclude our chat for this evening. Divine Mercy is the "unfathomable" mercy Jesus Christ offers to all sinners if they seek Him. In other words, by His Death and Resurrection on the Cross, Jesus has died for every sin ever committed by humanity. And if we ask for forgiveness for whatever we have done wrong, particularly if we do this acknowledging the true mercy God has prepared for us, Jesus assures us of His immediate forgiveness and aids us in bringing our souls into His presence now – or at the hour of our deaths.

"How beautiful," was all Ashley could say.

"Ashley, as far as your parents are concerned, I want you to believe whole-heartedly that the mercy of Jesus was still available to your mother and father at the moment of their deaths. So many believing in the great gift of Divine Mercy, believe there may be a last opportunity for the willing soul to be immerse in the mercy of God.

"Have you seen ever seen this Image – the Image of the Divine Mercy?" Fr. Joe asked as he pulled a prayer card containing an Image of Jesus with rays of Blood and Water coming from His Sacred Heart.

"Yes, I've seen it. Nan has that very same card."

"Through St. Faustina, who received the directive to make this devotion known, Jesus has told us, that the pale rays represent the Water that makes souls righteous, and the red stands for His Blood, which is the life of souls.

"Ashley, you must learn to trust in the graces God has given to you by your innocence, and believe your mother and father have a share in these graces too. I want you to believe in this as a witness to your grandmother's lifetime of Masses and prayers for all of you."

"I will learn," said Ashley with true conviction. "Thank you, Fr. Joe. You have really helped me. Is it possible I could actually be feeling the effects of grace over me now? I feel so peaceful."

"Absolutely. I would interpret that warm sense of peace as God's immediate way of telling you, with regard to your parents, there is nothing to worry about."

As Kit and Thompson concluded the legal portion of their meeting, Sarah in particular listened well to Kit's apprehension over Lucy's arrival in Cody the following afternoon, and offered several practical tips for relieving her additional stress. Then Fr. Joe, Sarah and Thompson wished Kit and Ashley a good night and headed home.

CHAPTER FOUR

Wednesday, August 26th

Kit tossed and turned all night long. Lucy's arrival Wednesday was no small part of the distress that prevented sleep. Seeing Lucy again would be painful. In fact, Kit felt nearly as pained by her estranged daughter's arrival in Cody as by Sean's death. The pain was different in each case and how odd she thought it was to compare one to the other. "Any loving mother would understand that in both cases there is grief and there is pain," she thought as she sought to console herself at sunrise.

"How long has it been since you've seen Lucy?" Ashley asked at breakfast.

"It's been over forty-years, my dear. I have not seen Lucy since Sean and I made a trip to up-state New York to attend her marriage to Gary Gallow." As Kit began to discuss her daughter's past, Ashley's eyes widened.

"The day of her wedding, I was so happy to see Lucy again after an entire year apart however it was difficult too, to attend the small wedding she planned on her limited budget. John and I had always dreamed of her wedding here on this beautiful ranch. And, while Lucy had no remorse then for what she had done to disrupt our lives in the wake of John's death, I remained hopeful she would one day regret her exit from our lives. For my own peace of mind as the years went on with no change in Lucy, eventually I had to accept she was gone," Kit concluded with a palpable trail of remaining sadness.

"Until we know if Lucy's motives are pure, Nan, I have this vague sense of your needing my protection from her. For me, meeting Lucy is like meeting a total stranger, but for you it is an emotional burden beyond description. I don't want anything to happen to you with all this stress.

You are the only family I have now. I've just got to have more information about Lucy in order to protect you."

"That's sweet, dear. I know your desire to protect me is earnest. Sadly, you are no longer a child," Kit said with regret, adding, "and in anticipation of Lucy's arrival, I want to give you a few details about her life and departure from the ranch. That will help you to grasp a better understanding of our situation. With this information however you must remember, in so many cases, a person's character remains unchanged throughout life and we must go on the assumption this is true of Lucy as well, unless she proves to us otherwise."

Kit drew back for a moment, then said, "Let's not get ahead of ourselves by thinking all sorts of crazy things though; let me tell you more about your aunt and perhaps we'll discover something that will help us to deal with her while she's in town."

"Yes, please do," Ashley, said with conviction in Kit's wisdom on the matter. Then Kit began.

"Well, Lucy was nineteen when she left home permanently. In 1961, when Sean was two and Lucy was eleven, your Grandpa John received a cancer diagnosis. John and I lived through the ups-and-downs of his treatments alone for several years and we tried to protect the children, especially Lucy who was older and showing some signs of emotional distress. Our little family had already experienced tragedy when John and I lost a son, Stephen, in childbirth in 1955 and a daughter, Mary, with Sudden Infant Death Syndrome in 1957. As would be expected, because of her age, these losses affected little Lucy greatly.

"The loss of both children was extremely difficult on all of us, then when Grandpa John passed away in 1968, Lucy's spirit was profoundly affected by incredible grief for the third time in her young life, and of course her father's death hit her the hardest."

"But she left home, Nan? That doesn't make sense to me, *to leave* the comforts and surroundings that are dear to you, when you need them the most?"

"Well, as crazy as the world might seem to you today, the period Lucy grew-up in, left its own mark of instability on America's youth as well.

"Oh, Fr. Joe explained this period in our American history to me last night as the Cultural Revolution. This was all at about the same time, wasn't it?"

"That's exactly right." Kit stirred her coffee nervously.

"Near the end of that first year without John, I tried desperately to change the focus in our home from one of sadness to one of anticipation, as we prepared for Lucy's high school graduation and her future at college. Your dad was eleven at that time."

"He must have been so cute," Ashley said, with a crack in her voice.

"He was adorable. In many ways during that first year without John, it was young Sean who offered me such kindness and distraction, too, by insisting at least once a week that we take a ride on the ranch or go fishing.

"Well, anyway, as the academic year progressed through the fall and into the holiday season, I noticed profound changes in Lucy's attitude toward me, toward Sean, and frankly, everyone she knew.

"Then one day in late January, 1969, I was contacted by the principal of Cody High, Mr. Resmond, who told me he had serious concerns over Lucy's behavior as well. He related that Lucy had become isolated and a loner at school, and that earlier that day he saw her leaving an empty English classroom, which was off-limits at lunchtime.

"Mr. Resmond asked Lucy to empty her purse on the spot. She in turn, handed over its contents one piece at a time – a lip-gloss, a few personal items, and $3.00 plus some change – until the bag was empty. Without proof of any wrongdoing, Mr. Resmond let her continue on her way.

"But that same afternoon Lucy's math teacher saw her pull a $20.00 bill from a false lining in her purse, just after an English teacher reported $20.00 missing from her briefcase. To carry a $20.00 bill to school then would be equivalent to a high school student today brining a crisp $100.00 bill to math class. Something that is not encouraged, I'm sure. When Mr. Resmond realized what had happened, he called me immediately.

"After that, rumors at the school began to fly and they continued without end. Lucy's stellar reputation after nearly twelve-years in the Cody school system was in absolute ruins."

"Wow, Nan! That must have been so tough on you especially because integrity is your personal hallmark."

"Oh, believe me Ashley, Lucy almost broke our family's reputation. The whole experience was emotionally harrowing for me on so many levels," Kit said as she shuttered at the memory. "In the end however, the entire ranch stood in God's grace.

"As the weeks went on, the rumors about Lucy got worse and spread throughout Cody and beyond, and as her conduct worsened, Sean and I, and our business suffered the consequences.

"In June, as Lucy climbed the platform on the football field at Cody High School to receive her diploma, I fought back a flood of tears as I sat alone. It was hard enough to arrive at this most important milestone in our daughter's life without John, but to have the entire community think so little of Lucy was devastating.

"I remember the graduates discussing their futures that day, but not Lucy. A week before graduation, I made the

56

decision to withdraw her acceptance from the University of Wyoming because her reputation was so severely damaged and her overall stability was in question.

"I told her if she restored her recommendations I would help her apply again the following year and that was the best I could offer her."

"Did you present a way for her to do this?"

"Yes. Definitely. Several wonderful people in the community including: Mr. Resmond, Police Chief Jack Blake and Fr. Francis Doyle, the pastor at St. Anthony's at that time, came forward with a way to help Lucy recover her reputation and gain their recommendations for college the following year.

"Their comprehensive plan was to include, a paying job as room attendant at Eagles Inn and a volunteer position with the Guardians of the Range protecting Cody's wildlife. We all met right here in the dining room a week or so after graduation to discuss the plan."

"What was Lucy's reaction to the proposal?"

"As quickly as the last car left Northridge that evening, Lucy ran up to her room at the head of the stairs and slammed the door behind her. She dismissed every suggestion the men made on her behalf. Rather than seeing any potential growth in the generous offerings, she rejected the opportunities angrily and without deliberation.

"Lucy spent the next few weeks sulking and Sean and I did all that we could to avoid her. Then suddenly she became incredibly belligerent toward both of us, but most powerfully toward me.

"Slowly, I began to put two-and-two together and realized she was reading all about the new American Cultural Revolution and idealizing the moral freedoms of the youth she was reading about in California. Soon I found out Lucy didn't have a fleeting interest in the revolution, she wanted to join it."

"She did? Really? Is that the reason she gave you for leaving home?"

"Oh, she never gave me a reason. Instead, she just slipped away from home one just before dawn one morning without my knowledge and never returned.

"When almost a year had passed and I realized she would not be returning home, I let go of my anger for my own health and for your dad's future. I simply had to let go of my daughter, in order to save my son's childhood.

"But fear of my being angry was not the reason Lucy stayed away. By the time she married Gary Gallow the following summer, she seemed completely lost to me.

"What was Gary like?" Lucy asked.

"Gary Gallow was a rebel Lucy met in her travels, and she absolutely idolized him. Not long after they were married, he formed a small real estate company and began bilking average investors by convincing them to buy unusable house lots for vacation homes in northern Vermont.

"Eventually, the government prosecuted Gary. While he awaited trial in jail he died unexpectedly from a cerebral hemorrhage," Kit shook her head. "Lucy held me responsible for Gary's death.

"When Gary was first arrested, she contacted me hoping I would make his bail. But when I refused and Gary died, she called and blamed me for his death. Since that call, some thirty-something-years ago, I've heard nothing about Lucy, and without her apology, I never felt any inclination to initiate reconciliation."

"I just can't believe all that you have been through during your life, Nan," Ashley said with deep compassion.

"That's true Ashley. At times, it's all been quite unbearable, really. Certainly Lucy never made things any easier."

"When Thompson delivered word she is flying into

Cody this evening, he mentioned she will be traveling from Vermont. So I'm assuming she never left the Lake Champlain region. But beyond this, I know nothing more about the present life of my only daughter."

"Would you tell me more about Lucy and the Cultural Revolution?" Ashley asked adding, "If it's not too difficult."

"Oh, no," Kit said, "it's no longer difficult and could be quite educational for you to hear my take on the whole thing." Therefore, Kit added her perspective to what Ashley had already learned from Fr. Joe.

"The weeks following Lucy's graduation," Kit went on, "when Lucy's behavior was so vile at home, she began making daily trips to the library in town. She was disgruntled and miserable to say the least, and began to escape the painful realities of her life by devouring every article she could find on the Cultural Revolution.

"When I sought answers to the mystery of her disappearance after I realized she was gone, the head librarian Felicia Fillmore told me Lucy spent hours each day mulling over *Rolling Stone* magazine. Later I would learn the editors of *Rolling Stone* featured one article after another on the Cultural Revolution, which began in the Haight-Ashbury district of San Francisco in the west, then spread east to the Greenwich Village section of New York City.

"While Lucy was immersing herself in these materials, the Cultural Revolution made its way onto the national nightly news and I became greatly concerned that my daughter would somehow grab onto the revolution's ideologies.

"The first confirmation of Lucy's concrete interest in the revolution came when she insisted I let her go to the Woodstock Music and Arts Festival, first advertised in

Rolling Stone magazine as the "Aquarian Festival," a three-day music festival in upstate New York. Of course, I refused.

"To make matters worse for me and for other concerned parents all over the Country, as the advertisement for the Aquarian Festival ran dramatic clips of one Dr. Timothy Leary's drug induced behavior ran simultaneously on television every night. Timothy Leary led the Cultural Revolution and promoted mind-altering drugs, LSD and the like, and introduced these drugs to disenchanted American youth all over the Country via staged video recordings.

"Before I understood the grave consequences of the Cultural Revolution on our children everywhere, it had Lucy in its grip."

"Way out here in Cody?" Ashley asked.

"Oh, yes. The circumstances were somewhat remote, but Lucy managed to join the Cultural Revolution right here in Cody."

"Go on, Nan," Ashley said. She was now enthralled with all the details.

"When I discovered Lucy was missing, I met with Felicia Fillmore, who recalled a young married couple, Roy and Samantha Winters sitting down in the main library with Lucy one day.

"Who were the Winters? Did they know Lucy before this meeting?"

"They were a young couple who considered themselves elite members of the Cultural Revolution en route to the Aquarian Festival. A far more accurate description of the Winters was scam-artists who looked for the vulnerable and rebellious in every community they passed through.

"Lucy was the couple's Cody scam."

"Really?" Ashley questioned in disbelief.

"As Felicia later reported, one day Lucy was returning

to her usual seat with the newest issue of *Rolling Stone* magazine in hand, when she was approached by Samantha Winters who seemed to be about twenty-three years of age. Samantha's heart-shaped face projected initial warmth, but her ice-blue eyes revealed her cunning personality.

"As the woman approached Lucy, Felicia heard her say, 'My husband and I are new in town. I'm Samantha Winters, and this is my husband Roy.'

"Then signaling behind her Roy Winters moved forward. 'Roy is an artist,' she told Lucy, 'and I am a fashion designer.'

"Taking in Samantha's clear but cold beauty, Lucy became enthralled and couldn't help but notice her clothing bore a striking resemblance to the same clothes photographed in *Rolling Stone* magazine. Giving Samantha a quick reply, Lucy gasped, 'You are a *real* fashion designer?'

"Samantha smiled, as she easily recognized Lucy's gullibility and moved from Lucy's left to the other side of the table. A cool pink peasant blouse and bell-bottom jeans covered her tall, lean, body. Felicia related that she noticed Roy was dressed in a similar manner wearing jeans identical to Samantha's and a green tie-dyed T-shirt. His black shoulder-length locks were pulled back in a ponytail and his wide hazel eyes did nothing at all to warn Lucy of his criminal record.

"For her part Lucy, who spent much of her life in riding clothes, was entranced by the Winters appearance. With numerous cons under their belts, once they realized she was captivated by their lifestyle, they raised the curtain on their real-life drama."

"Drama?" asked Ashley.

"Yes, drama. The Winters had been dodging hotel bills and restaurant tabs for days as they travelled toward the

Aquarian Festival and Lucy became a temporary means to an end for their financial woes. She promised to give them the necessities they needed for that night, and a few dollars cash in exchange for a ride to New York."

"Later as I looked back I remembered, everything between us that particular evening was raw, and the animosity Lucy harbored toward me, especially was just so deep. When she was up in her room that night and your dad was settled in bed, I remember sitting alone out here and crying my eyes out.

"That hour was my lowest moment of grief in those early years without John. I had absolutely no idea what to do with Lucy. Her behavior was just so painful, that when I learned she was gone, I actually felt a tiny twinge of relief."

"How do you do it, Nan? With all you've been through how do you hold everything together so well even now with the deaths of my dad and mom?"

"I trust in God, Ashley. And I always allow Him to unfold His plans around me."

"Was it somewhat easier to see Lucy leave because you trusted in God to take care of her?" Ashley asked.

"I wouldn't say easier, because in Lucy's departure I felt a great deal of sadness and shame. But there were times when Lucy's well-being would haunt me, and it was during those times especially, I put my trust in God.

"Realistically, I knew there was nothing more I could do for my adult-child at that point in her life except trust in God to take care of her. I recognized that she would need to live the life she chose by exercising the freewill God gave to *her* as a gift. My acceptance of this fact is what finally made it easier."

"I can understand that," said Ashley, taking a deep breath as she exhaled some of the pain she felt for her grandmother.

Ashley's beautiful green eyes twinkled a bit as the sparkling waters of the Shoshone hit her face. She reflected for a moment, staring down at the river, and then noticed the air was warming as the sun rose higher in the Wyoming sky. Standing, Ashley stretched for a moment, swinging her long arms over her head; touching the white planked-ceiling of the porch with her fingertips, then leaning all the way forward to grab the tips of her toes.

"Have you had enough for now, Ashley? You must have some messages and things you need to care for back at home."

"Christina offered to go over to Starlight with me this afternoon to soften the blow of my going home to an empty house. But I still have a little time. Please tell me what happened next."

"Let's see," Kit said, as she recalled her place in Lucy's story. "Oh yes, now I remember. To make good on the promise Lucy made for a night's shelter, she told the Winters how to find Starlight Cottage."

"She sent them to Starlight? To your little cottage?" At this news, Ashley was both shocked by Lucy's nerve in allowing strangers to sleep in Kit's cottage and a little envious too, that Lucy and a couple of hippies had seen its interior. Just as quickly as this thought entered Ashley's head however, it left leaving her once again on Kit's side against Lucy.

"It was wrong of Lucy to hide strangers anywhere on the ranch and especially at Starlight, but she was only nineteen at the time. She was so rebellious as many are at that age and terribly affected by the loss of her father."

"Do you still have compassion for Lucy, Nan?"

"I suppose a mother always has at least a shred of compassion for even her most unruly child. This is probably so for me as well, but to be honest, I won't know for certain until I see her tonight."

"Thanks for sharing all of this with me, Nan. I don't really know what to make of things but at least now, I have some idea of whom Lucy Moran might be.

"On another note, I'm wondering if Thompson was helpful to you last night? He seemed to have stacks of files with him when he left."

To avoid any conversation regarding the details of her discussion with Thompson and Sarah the previous evening, Kit answered Ashley in a controlled and authoritative voice. "Everything is under control, my dear."

"Good," was Ashley's only response, and Kit was relieved she seemed satisfied.

"Will Lucy be here when I get back?"

"I'm planning to meet her in town. Thompson indicated earlier that she has decided to stay at Eagles Inn and he promised to make a dinner reservation for us after speaking with Lucy this afternoon."

"Great. If you're not here when I get back, I'll be waiting for you this evening. Please be careful, Nan."

"Life is so strange," Kit, said to herself. "To think I must be cautious when meeting my own daughter. Realistically speaking however until I know more about Lucy, Ashley is absolutely right."

Ten minutes later, Ashley left Northridge for Amour with Christina as Kit watched from the front door. The sun was pouring down upon her lovely island garden at the front of the house and everything seemed so peaceful. Kit was happy to be alone. Though she much preferred having Ashley with her than not in their present circumstances, she had lived alone now for many years and solitude was a natural part of her life. Solitude was just what she needed before seeing her only daughter for the first time in forty-years.

As she wondered what she would say to Lucy, her mind filled with waves of new suspicions. Kit sincerely regretted the depth of her negative thoughts. She found it unlikely however that Lucy was coming to Cody just to pay her respects to her brother Sean.

Thinking ahead to that evening, Kit searched a drawer in her bedroom for her red and white silkscreen scarf. She laid the scarf out on her vanity table along with the silver butterfly brooch John gave her on their fifteenth-wedding anniversary. Next, she carefully descended the main staircase, passed over the foyer and through the French doors, across the porch, then down a half-dozen grey steps that lead to the lower lawn. There she hoped to enjoy some time alone in the sun.

She loved the furniture on the lower terrace. Between a yellow Adirondacks lounger with a bird painted here and a bee there, were matching chairs of lime green and tangerine. Fresh lavender spilled about the lower lawn. As Kit stretched out on the lounger, she was fully aware Jesus was revealing His refreshing beauty all around her.

Kit always found comfort in Jesus Christ and today was no exception. She opened her heart to her Savior as she sat in the sun and released her troubles to Him. She prayed that He would take them to the river and simply wash them away.

Finally, she realized a state of peace and a deep sense of gratitude to Thompson and Sarah Smith for their efforts in her affairs. As she relaxed, Kit now had a few minutes to reflect on their discussion the previous evening.

"Thank you both for coming all the way out here again," Kit said as the Smiths arrived on her porch Tuesday evening.

"You seemed concerned," said Thompson.

"I am. I have something of great importance to reveal to you regarding my estate. I have a secret I've been holding now for more than sixty-years. And as usual Thompson, I'll need your legal aid."

Kit's voice sounded ominous and Thompson was concerned, first for the additional stress she seemed to be carrying, and then for the scope of his own legal capabilities.

"What's this all about, Kit?"

"Well, I don't really know quite where to begin."

"Just begin," he urged her with confidence, yet adding softly, "and we'll just listen."

"Yes," Sarah said, "that's exactly why we came – to listen."

The couple could see clearly that whatever Kit Moran was about to tell them, was taking an emotional toll on the poor woman. They waited patiently, as their dear friend gained control over her anxiety.

"It has to do with Starlight Cottage. It must be included in my assets in a most definitive way. There is so much to tell you about its contents, but I think you will grasp a better understanding of what I'm talking about if I begin with the day of John and my wedding reception in 1949." With this first statement, Kit began to unload years of personal torment.

"On May 1, 1949 to be exact, John and I hosted our wedding reception right here on this beautiful porch. We didn't have a reception when we were married the previous fall, because we were in the middle of constructing this home. So, we decided to have an all-day event the following spring to celebrate our marriage and to dedicate Northridge.

"It was a splendid event," she went on. "I was just twenty-two at the time and remember exactly what I wore – a double-layered stiff pink organza with a beautiful sweetheart neckline. And John wore a classic black tuxedo."

"How elegant," said Sarah, who was already drawn into the depths of Kit's memories.

Speaking with an unpredictable feeling of satisfaction Kit continued. The quality of her voice, suddenly quite steady, carried a hint of joy as she described the day of her wedding reception to her younger friends.

"The dedication of Northridge was at noon and our wedding reception at one. John's mother Jane was with us but his father was no longer living. And while my family was unable to make the trip from California, we had many friends as a new couple, and John had many lifetime friends in Cody as well. Overall, I would say, we had at least fifty people with us at any given time throughout the day.

"I remember that we placed a small advertisement in the *Cody Enterprise* to announce the event, inviting everyone with an interest just to stop by in the afternoon. I must admit, entertaining was so different then."

"You're right," Sarah said. "There was no need to worry about security then as we do today." Kit agreed.

"Our special day was absolutely beautiful. Everyone, including all of the children in attendance, danced the entire afternoon to the string quartet we hired from the old Blue Moon Tavern.

"I remember standing in this very doorway in the late afternoon with John," Kit told the Smiths as she pointed to the beautiful French doors, "and as we took in the wonderful day, a cool breeze rose from the river and blew through the entire first floor. The sun was beginning to lower in the sky and the sunbeams glistening on the river became all the more prominent. As we were taking in this marvelous scene, John looked up from our conversation and saw a tiny, elderly woman standing just inside the front door.

"Our late-day guest had striking white hair pulled high

on her head and wore a navy blue velvet dress with a white lace collar and small rhinestone belt about her waist. I have never forgotten the impression this woman made, so long ago. She was very elegant, almost angelic, and she came to us as we thought later in a rather mysterious – yet prophetic way.

"Upon seeing the delicate figure in the doorway, John sprang across the room to welcome the woman into our home. I followed. The woman seemed to know John before they met and extended her hand to him as he approached.

"'Hello, John,' I remember her saying, 'My name is Sophia Moran.' With his typical charm, John took Sophia's hand and bent toward her.

"'How do you do, Miss Moran.' John said. 'It is so nice of you to come. May I ask, are we related somehow?'

"'We are, though we've never met,' was Sophia's reply. She went on, 'I read the announcement regarding your open house and my long-time friend and chauffer, Andrew Reed drove me here from Riverton. In essence, I've come regarding some of my late father, Dr. Marcus Moran's unfinished business.'

"John guided Sophia, who we would later learn was ninety-two, to the new rose-colored wing chair his mother gave us as a wedding gift, and assured Sophia he had all the time she needed to explain the reason for her trip.

"'You see, John,' Sophia began in earnest, 'your great-great-grandfather Michael Moran and my great-grandfather Matthew Moran were brothers. We have a common ancestor in their father Franklin Moran, five-generations back on your side of the family and four back on mine.'

"'Franklin Moran's two sons – Michael and Matthew were born in Bolton, England. Michael had two sons,

Philip and Nicholas. Philip Moran was father to Thomas Moran, Sr., who was father to Edward, Leon, Thomas, Jr. and Peter, an entire family of incredibly talented English artists from the turn of the twentieth-century, whom you may know are now world-renowned for their influential talent.

"'Among the Moran artisans, Thomas J. Moran, Jr. is of greatest acclaim for his many oil and watercolor interpretations of the Grand Teton and Rocky Mountain ranges, the Grand Canyon, and a vast number of other locations extending from his native England, as far east as Venice, Italy.'"

"Yes, of course," Thompson said, interrupting Kit's account of Sophia's revelation, "you have Moran's *Mountain of the Holy Cross* in over your fireplace, that is, if it's the original."

"Oh, that's absolutely the original," Sarah piped-in before Kit could confirm this fact. "With all of Thompson's scholastics, Kit, art-history was not one of his strong points. Even though he has seen your painting more times than he could count, he has probably never given its origin much thought."

"Sadly, Sarah's right, Kit," Thompson confessed.

"Well, Thompson," Kit said, as she offered a curious smirk, "all that's about to change."

Shifting his slouched position of listener, to a forward position of active participant, Thompson was ready for Kit to continue.

"Sophia went on. 'Nicholas Moran, Michael's second son, was my grandfather,' Sophia announced to John, 'and his son Marcus was my father. Nicholas and Marcus were both physicians and came to southern Wyoming, as well as I can ascertain now, about a decade before your parents settled here in Cody, to the north.'

"'I'm sure this fits in with my parents' arrival in Wyoming,' John answered. 'I will ask my mother tomorrow. I am sorry I cannot introduce you to her now, she retired to her home a short time ago.'

"'I understand, please give her my regards,' Sophia said, then she continued. 'My mother, Belle Palmer Moran, passed away from tuberculosis just two-years after I was born. I was an only child,' Sophia said.

"'Belle was the absolute love of my father's life. He decided never to marry again. After my mother died, Dr. Marcus, as his patients called him, fussed over me so I never did feel completely free to leave him. I pushed marriage off until it was really too late. But just the same, I've been happy throughout my entire life.'

"As she went on with her tale, Sophia became more and more animated. Although we had no idea what was coming, the real reason for her visit seemed to delight our guest.

"'On your branch of our family tree, John, Franklin Moran's second son, Matthew, had a son named Carroll, who was father to your great-grandfather Terrance. Terrance then had Joseph, whom you must know, was your father George's father.'

"John nodded in response to these facts, his own father having confirmed these relations with him when he was a young boy.

"'I have a wedding gift for you, which my chauffer Andrew Reed will bring in, as soon as I ask. I want to give you both a Thomas J. Moran, Jr. original, *Mountain of the Holy Cross,* which belonged to my father, Marcus Moran.'

"'You see,' Sophia went on, 'I am the last of my father's branch of the Moran family with no descendants at all so I want you to have this great painting. Your youth predicts that you'll have many, many years to enjoy your cousin's work.'

"Sophia told John she had no idea of the painting's value, but had been told by an appraiser some years earlier that it was considered one of Thomas Moran's most valuable works."

"So that's how you became owner of this marvelous painting," Thompson said, as he leaned back in his chair and glanced through the French doors to the painting's resting place above Kit's fireplace.

"Yes, this is how the paintings began arriving at Olive Branch Ranch. And this one has been on display over the fireplace for the better part of sixty-years."

"Paintings? There are others?" Sarah asked with wonder and awe. Sarah had listened intently during Kit's revelation, but also found the fact that there were other paintings absolutely fascinating, as she and a colleague were in the process of establishing a small art gallery near the entrance to Yellowstone National Park. Presently, Sarah was attending an art-history refresher course, covering the great *Hudson River School* artists, the foundation of American Landscapes artists including founder Thomas Cole, Samuel Colman, Frederic Edwin Church, Thomas J. Moran, Jr., and his mentor, Albert Bierstadt.

"Yes," Kit answered with a smile, "there are more. But if you please, I'd like to continue with me explanation.

"John and I met Andrew Reed when we walked Sophia out to her car that day. After a brief introduction, Andrew opened the rear door of the black Model A, lifted the unwrapped painting off the backseat, and handed it to us ever so gently. Andrew conversed with John briefly, as I thanked Sophia for her generosity, and then bid her farewell."

"What did Andrew say to John?" Thompson asked.

"He told John that Sophia had Thomas J. Moran Jr.'s

entire collection and that she asked him to begin delivering the collection to us. Further, Andrew told John, Sophia Moran was an extremely private woman and had never attempted to bring the paintings out for a public viewing.

"According to Andrew, Sophia, who was twenty-years his senior, was the sweetest woman he had ever known and was extremely generous as well. But apparently, the distribution of such fine works of art grew more and more problematic for Sophia, as she aged. When she reached her nineties, she became overwhelmed with disposing of her assets but was relieved when she learned John and I had married. She found us a likely solution to her problem.

"Then sadly, a few months after all the paintings were delivered, Andrew called to say Sophia had passed away.

"And my news, in case you have not surmised my friends, is that the entire collection of Thomas Moran, Jr.'s paintings, over five-hundred of his original works still belongs to me."

"This is extraordinary, Kit!" Thompson exclaimed. "Absolutely extraordinary! I would never have guessed."

"Nor would I," Sarah followed.

"Well, perhaps this won't be such an extraordinary revelation after all," Kit said in a deep concerning tone, "when you hear that I have done absolutely nothing to protect the paintings legally by including them in the Olive Branch Ranch inventory of assets, or by having them underwritten. In other words, I have never insured a single painting or worse, provided any environmental protection for these incredible masterpieces.

"And as if things were not bad enough, after John died I apparently fell victim to the same sort of profound anxiety over the paintings that Sophia suffered after Marcus Moran passed away – over my neglect of the paintings and have never assessed the condition or the value of the collection.

"For years now I have been caught up in a vicious cycle of denial over the necessity to do something about Moran's fantastic work. Now, I'm so fearful my neglect has damaged the paintings, I am absolutely paralyzed."

Sarah, especially, was very compassionate toward Kit. She had seen elderly patients, one after the other, facing this same type of predicament. And although she had to admit never seeing anyone quite as anxious over their affairs as Kit was at the moment, neither had she seen anyone facing so much new wealth at her age either, let alone the tragedy with which she was also living.

"I had intended to tell Sean and Corrine all about the collection." Kit went on. "Andrew Reed gave us a copy of Marcus Moran's handwritten inventory, which I've had locked in my desk for years.

"Sean didn't know?" Thompson asked.

"I don't think so. All of the paintings were already in storage by the time Sean was old enough to have noticed them. *Mountain of the Holy Cross* is the only one I hung in the house." As Kit's attorney, Thompson felt bound to pry with one final question.

"Kit, where are the paintings now?"

"They're all in a closet out at Starlight Cottage," she said as she exhaled an intense sigh of relief.

"It is done," she thought as she recalled the previous night's meeting with Sarah and Thompson, and she thanked God for the friends He sent to share in this life-long burden.

As Kit rested under the warm August sun, her confidence in Thompson's ability to advise her in the distribution of her assets grew stronger. The huge weight she had suffered under for years was finally off her shoulders.

By allowing Kit to bear her soul, the Smiths helped to alleviate her guilt over neglecting the Moran collection all those years. Sarah urged her patient to release the stress she was holding, telling her it was not good for her heart. Next Thompson assured her that because she is sole owner of the paintings and had never used the collection as collateral, whatever solutions they employed to help her get control of the situation would be far easier than had various other scenarios been in play. If Moran's works were somewhat damaged, Thompson reminded Kit, there remained the possibility that some or all of the paintings could be restored.

The guilt Kit carried all those years for neglecting the collection lessened tremendously when the Smiths shared their wisdom, and she put her implicit trust in the matter in these professionals, who were also dear friends. Moreover, she was pleased beyond measure when Sarah offered to use her new ties to the art world to find a reputable fine arts appraiser. Finally, Kit felt a host of solutions was possible and her anxiety over the paintings all but faded away.

"Kit?" Elaine called down from the porch. Her reprieve out on the lower terrace was about to an end.

"Thompson just called to tell you Lucy contacted him on her way to Eagles Inn. He suggested you meet her at the inn for dinner at six. No need to call him back unless this doesn't work for you. I left Lucy's cell phone number on the dining room table."

"Thank you, Elaine," Kit said as she came into the house.

"Kit? I hope you don't feel I'm overstepping but please be careful with Lucy. I mean no disrespect, but you've been through enough, and still have so much more to go through. Cody still remembers Lucy's final year in town. People here care deeply for you personally, Kit. What they can't say to your face, they say to each other with genuine concern. Please be careful."

Kit looked at Elaine with deep appreciation for these beautiful words, which overpowered the shame she continued to carry over Lucy's life. Elaine's true concern for Kit was palpable and she filled with gratitude. Yes, time had passed, but Cody retained both its public and private histories in which memories of Lucy Moran's last year in town were permanently forged.

"Thank you for your concern, Elaine, and for your compassion as well. These days are truly among the most difficult days of my life."

"Kit, would you let me call Peter Travers and ask him to drive you home from your visit with Lucy this evening?" He asked me to let him know if there was anything he could do for you.

"Yes, certainly. Everything is so emotional for me right now. I think it would be best if I didn't drive tonight."

"I'll give him a call," Elaine said.

"Then, please don't worry about me this evening, dear. I'm sure by the time I get home from dinner, Ashley will be here."

"I'll call Peter for you. And, I promise I'll try not to worry. See you in the morning, Kit."

At Amour, Christina proved a warm and loving spirit for Ashley in her time of need. Christina, Corrine's dearest childhood friend, and Drew were included in many Moran family festivities over the years. Now that her parents were gone, Ashley was not surprised that her natural inclination was to draw even closer to both of them. She actually felt a need to share some of her present feelings with Christina and as she did, Christina listened with great compassion.

"Christina, do you believe there are times when some people are forced to grow-up in an instant?" Before Christina could answer, Ashley added, "The moment my parents died, I know my childhood fled and my adulthood arrived."

Clearly, Christina felt her young friend's pain. "You are so young to be left without your father and mother, Ashley. Forgive me, if what I am about to say seems premature, but you will survive this trial and you will be happy again someday, no matter how impossible this seems right now." As she drew a deep breath, Christina decided to make a striking revelation.

"I went through this, too," she began.

"You did?" Ashley asked with great surprise.

"Yes, but I was much younger than you. I was an only child and my mother and father planned a wonderful weekend away to celebrate my seventh birthday in Colorado.

"We owned a private plane and my father was an experienced pilot, but the engines died just after take-off on our trip home. My father had strapped me into the backseat before takeoff and of course, he and my mother were up front. When the plane came down it split in two pieces and my parents died instantly.

"Patricia Nelson is my real mother Marilyn's sister. Patricia and her husband Bernie drove to Colorado immediately and nursed me through a compound fracture to my right leg. When I was well enough we returned to Cheyenne, but the Nelsons felt I would be better off with a fresh-start in life so we moved to Cody. As soon as they thought it was emotionally prudent to do so, they asked me to call them Mom and Dad."

"I never knew," Ashley said with true sorrow for

Christina.

"I never told anyone but Drew, not even your mother because it was just too painful and because the Nelsons, who were my real aunt and uncle, asked me not to."

Ashley was stunned by Christina's story.

"Back in those days," Christina continued, "adoption papers were sealed in the courts and it was necessary for many people to submit their adopted children to a life of endless questions. I think I was luckier than most in this regard, because I knew I was adopted. But my new mom and dad asked me not to tell, in order to protect me from the pity and the painful inquiries I would face if people knew what had happened to me. They really wanted me to learn to cope with the loss and not to become accustom to pity. Now, so many years later, I'm incredibly grateful for the wisdom they exercised in that decision. Today, I feel I'm the best person I could be having survived such a terrible tragedy.

Christina's story slowed but Ashley's eyes begged her to go on.

"I met your mom on my very first day of school in Cody, and the rest is history," she said with a teary smile.

"Corrine and I related well to each other, as we were both only children which is a much different way of life than having siblings. At least that's what I've been told.

"I hope I did the right thing by sharing my early life with you now," she said to Ashley.

"Oh yes, you did. It must have been painful for you to share this with me today, but knowing you survived a similar experience has given me so much hope."

"Although I'm not walking in your shoes, in many ways I do understand exactly what you are going through, and I loved Corrine as the sister I never had."

Suddenly Christina's revelation drained her emotionally, and she found a need to seek the comfort of her own home. "Ashley, will you be all right if I go along now?" she asked as she watered the last plant in the foyer. An avid baker she had promised several trays of teacakes and pastries for the mourners on Saturday.

"Try to get some rest," she added as she reminded Ashley to take good care of her own physical needs.

"I'll take your advice. I have a couple of friends stopping by for a little while, while Nan is at dinner with Lucy. Then I'll head back to Northridge to be there when she gets home."

Christina's startled silence at the mere mention of Lucy's name spoke volumes. She could offer Ashley nothing in return.

"I'll be home baking tomorrow, too," her voice now softened to near silence. "Call me if you need anything."

"I will. I love you, Christina."

"I love you too, Sweetie."

Ashley walked Christina to her car in front of the house and watched her drive away. She found hope in Christina's story of survival and renewed courage in the challenges she would face without her own parents.

Returning to the house, she sat to read some of the cards she received. There were several from her parents' colleagues at Cody High School and notes from various friends and civic organizations throughout the region as well. As she came to the end of the pile, she found a small envelope containing the return address: P. Lewiston, Cody, Wyoming.

Ashley was surprised by her feelings of gratitude toward Patrick Lewiston for offering his condolences. After her conversation with Jake, she was beginning to realize her avoidance of Patrick was child's play.

With gratitude, she opened his note and read nine simple words, "Dear Ashley, I am so sorry. Sincerely, Patrick Lewiston."

So humble she thought. Through this simple note, Ashley learned that Patrick, like Michael and their father Jake had inherited the Lewiston family traits of kindness and humility.

Across the field at Northridge, Kit sat at the vanity table in her bedroom as she prepared to meet Lucy in town. Brushing out her hair, she spoke to her late husband John, just as she did so often. "Oh John," Kit said aloud, "please be with me. I need you now as much as ever." She pulled her coarse salt and auburn hair back into a knot at the nape of her neck then fastened it with a tortoise-shell clip.

Then Kit, who was an ardent student of the Holy Spirit, turned the outcome of that evening over to God. She was no longer worried that any new suffering she endured that evening would overwhelm her. "Somehow," she thought, "God will prevail."

When the late afternoon sun hit her reflection in the mirror Kit noticed how pale she was, especially against the black knit dress she had chosen for dinner. She gave her cheeks a little pinch to simulate color then fastened on her silver earrings and the scarf and broche she set out earlier. Just as she stepped into her black-beaded shoes, the phone rang.

"Hello, Kit. How are you doing?"

"Oh, Thompson, I'm okay. Have the plans changed?" she asked nervously.

"No, not at all. Actually, I'm calling for a different reason. Kit, do you know if you still have a copy of *The Old Man of the Mountains* by Norman Nicholson?"

"Oh, that was one of John's favorite books. I have an idea where it might be, if I still have it."

"How are you getting into town this evening?"

"That's a great question. I know Elaine called Peter

Travers to bring me home after dinner. I guess I was still thinking I'd drive myself in, but of course, that won't work. Goodness, what am I thinking? Oh, Thompson, you have no idea how confused I've been feeling."

"We all go through that even when we are under half the pressure you are. I think you're doing well, just as you are," he assured her.

"Kit, I'm going to send my new assistant Brendan Snyder out there right away to help you find the book we need, and to drive you into town."

"That would be helpful," she answered. "But you haven't told me yet why you need *The Old Man of the Mountains*."

"There's a clue in John's file. If my hunch is correct, the book may contain an important piece of information regarding your estate."

"Please don't let Lucy rile you. And just a note of caution, be sure you don't give her too much personal information, or information about the ranch just yet. I'll come by in the morning to discuss everything."

Kit Moran was made with a pure heart, filled with generosity, and the ability to excel in her efforts to tolerate the intolerable, by loving the world as the Lord did. A spiritual director once told her that her heart resembled that of Nathaniel, the man Jesus saw at a distance beyond a human's ability to see.

Jesus told his disciples that Nathanael was without hatred or deceit.* Jesus' miraculous vision and His knowledge of Nathanael's interior life amazed Nathanael and he followed Jesus permanently.

---

* John 1:47   Jesus saw Nathanael coming to Him, and said of him, "Behold, an Israelite indeed, in whom there is no deceit!"
New American Standard Bible, 1995.

From her earliest years, Kit had a long history of heroic love just as Nathanael did. She loved all peoples and things of creation. Her love began with her first breath of life and continued without interruption. Even her earliest years were filled with gentle expressions of God's love. In particular, an early fight for justice against a budding cruelty at Redwood School, the small primary school she attended in California, was to serve as hallmark for her entire life of generosity.

Early on little Kit became aware that some of her classmates were ridiculing another child simply because she was impoverished. A popular leader among her peers, when Kit offered her friendship to Polly Mason, all scorn from the other children ceased.

Polly was poor beyond the other children's wildest imaginations. Small and frail, she and her mother lived alone and without heat in a rundown cabin near the edge of town. Through her efforts to ease Polly's trials and pain, heroic love took shape deep in Kit's heart. Later, Kit would come to realize she was able to exercise heroic love through the Power of the Holy Spirit repeatedly, because He empowered her to do so. Moreover, it was the Holy Spirit Who strengthened her to keep the door of her heart-room slightly ajar when she heard Lucy would be returning to Cody.

While waiting in her living room for Brendan Snyder to arrive, Kit created a plan she hoped would help her to keep a clear head when in Lucy's presence that evening. She devised a way to judge the condition of her daughter's heart that would help her to determine if reconciliation with Lucy would be possible.

Twenty-minutes after Thompson's call, his young assistant arrived at Kit's front door.

"Mrs. Moran, I'm Brendan Snyder. Attorney Smith sent me to help you look for *The Old Man of the*

Mountains among your things and then escort you into town. But first the tall, thin, young man with black hair and dark-rimmed glasses reached for Kit's hand and said, "Please accept my condolences on the loss of your son and daughter-in-law."

"Thank you so much, Brendan," Kit said gratefully. She then changed the subject quickly, hoping to avoid a fresh wave of grief. It's nice to finally meet you."

Brendan offered Kit his left arm for support as she led him to the library-foyer where she hit the recessed lighting to illuminate the titles.

"Would you please go to the right of the doors there Brendan, and look up on the top-shelf? If I remember correctly, *The Old Man of the Mountains* is a slim book. It may be a sea-green color with red ink accents. if I remember correctly."

"Here it is Mrs. Moran," Brendan said, pulling the book down off the top shelf, "just as you said. I'll slip it into my briefcase for safekeeping." Kit thought this hasty move on Brendan's part was delivered at Thompson's urging, so she would not have any additional stress factors that evening. She complied.

"I know Thompson needs this book to help decode the details of your estate, this much I can tell you," Brendan offered apologetically. "Are you ready to go into town?"

"Yes," Kit said as she drew in a deep breath. "I'm as ready as I'll ever be."

As Brendan made the final turn onto Inn Road Kit's nervousness consumed her inner thoughts, "How will I greet Lucy? Will she be waiting for me? Will I even recognize her?" she asked herself.

Just as her anxiety grew beyond measure, Brendan pulled his car up in front of Cody's famous 1880 yellow antique Colonial inn, known for miles around as Eagles Inn.

It was quite some time since Kit had been to the inn and she found its curb-appeal striking. The wild-flower gardens behind the white picket fences on either side of its front entrance were gorgeous and a true representation of Wyoming's natural bouquets. A wavy brick walkway flowed between the two gardens and a black period lantern hung over the inn's main entrance. Once inside, the interior foyer boasted a second-story antique chandelier, which when lighted, added to the inn's lovely ambiance.

As Brendan helped Kit out of the car and on to the walkway he thought, "At this moment, Mrs. Moran looks like one of these fragile flowers to me. But at the same time I can feel her amazing strength."

Although a newcomer to Cody, Brendan too found himself slipping into the community's present sorrow over the loss of its two esteemed citizens.

"Oh, Kit," hostess and long-time acquaintance of the Moran family Margie Cooper said, as Kit entered the dining room, "I am so sorry."

"Thank you so much, Margie," Kit replied stoically.

"May I seat you?" Margie asked, assuming Kit and her young escort would be dining together.

"A table for two please," Kit answered as Brendan leaned forward to say good-bye.

"It was a pleasure driving you into town, Mrs. Moran. Here's my cell phone number in case there is anything you need," Brendan said as he handed Kit his business card.

"How thoughtful, Brendan. Thank you for everything."

"Oh, are you expecting someone, Kit?" Margie asked as she led her guest through the dining room.

"I am. Actually, my daughter Lucy is joining me in a few minutes."

A former childhood acquaintance of Lucy Moran,

Margie Cooper knew well of the women's decades-long estrangement and assumed Kit's loss of Sean was helping to bridge their relationship. She was happy to seat Kit at the finest table, but she never mentioned Lucy. While Kit waited for Lucy to arrive, she gladly took in the recent changes made to the dining room's interior.

In recent years, the inn's owners had done much to retain the Early American feel of the main dining room. All four interior walls, which included an original exterior brick wall, were painted in federal white. Two large, lit, colonial-style sconces framed the fireplace on the far wall and a royal blue period rug tied the colonial décor together. Kit always loved Eagles Inn and its fine furnishings. The table Margie chose for her that evening was covered with burgundy linen, set with Colonial white china, and overlooked Cody's Historic Hayden Village.

When she was seated, Margie handed her a menu that Kit fingered nervously until Lucy arrived.

"Hello, Mother," Lucy said as she approached the table from behind Kit's shoulder. Her voice, now a deep and formal tone, had aged over time.

As Lucy carelessly brushed her mother's side, she sat down across the table and offered Kit an executive's handshake but nothing more. Kit's first impulse was to excuse Lucy's chilly persona but then she remembered her plan to read her daughter's heart. In light of that first impression, she felt it necessary to implement a new set of guidelines. "She must utter slander against other persons three times this evening, a habit Lucy enjoyed during her rebellious years. If she is kind and loving, then I will know she has corrected this fault. If cold and sarcastic as she was that last year under my roof, I will have my answer."

"Good evening, ladies," their server said as she filled the water glasses. "May I bring you something to drink?"

"I'll have Chablis," Lucy answered, clearly leaving Kit to fend for herself.

"Nothing for me. But thank you, dear," Kit said to the server. She tried to overlook Lucy's rush to order before giving her the courtesy of going first but it hurt just the same.

During their first few moments together, Kit searched Lucy's face for signs of the life she had been leading since they last spoke over Gary Gallow's death. While she thought her daughter's appearance was meticulous and her attire, a navy blue suit, entirely appropriate, there was still an edge to Lucy, an obvious sign she had not mellowed over the years. Clearly, this saddened Kit.

As Lucy sipped her Chablis, the women began to settle into an evening of uncomfortable conversation. Lucy made a feeble attempt to offer her condolences to her mother, but Kit found her words contrived and distant, as though Lucy was speaking to someone, she had just met.

Kit groped for a change of subject. "How was your trip to Wyoming?" she asked, hoping to gain some fresh traction.

"To be honest with you, Mother," Lucy blurted, "the trip was absolutely dreadful. I flew standby from Burlington and took the only available seat between two elderly peasants from who knows where. They absolutely reeked of poverty."

Kit's natural love for humanity was so profound that Lucy's very first comments about the less fortunate were an emotional blow to her entire system.

Putting herself above others was one of the blatant defects Kit last remembered about Lucy. At this moment, she found her daughter's lack of compassion for others, especially if they were less fortunate than she, beyond words. She despised Lucy's characterization of the less fortunate. This alone was enough for Kit to leave the table, but in an honest attempt to remain in control of her emotions, she remained seated. In her mind however, she issued, "Strike one!" against Lucy.

The server approached their table again and the women placed an order for the evening's special, roasted chicken over rice. Kit ordered hot tea and Lucy a second glass of Chablis.

"I'm sure Thompson must have mentioned to you that Sean asked him to notify you if anything ever happened to him," Kit said. She watched to see if Lucy showed any kind of tenderness toward her brother but nothing of that sort came. Instead, what she heard pass over Lucy's lips next was nothing less than astounding.

"Tell me, Mother, just what did Sean and Corrine do to deserve all the attention they're receiving? They seem to be the talk of the town."

"Strike two!" flashed in Kit's angry mind.

When Lucy saw appall written on her mother's face, she tried to soften her comments but only made matters worse.

"Oh, I'm sorry Mother. It's just that there's so much more out there in the world beside Cody, Wyoming. It's too bad really, that Seanny didn't see things differently, especially in those early years of his career.

"In Vermont I've been able to mix with real New York socialites and yet retain a sense of country class. I give credit to my New York contacts for helping me shake my Wyoming accent and folksy attitudes. If only Sean had been able to let go of your apron-strings Mother, he might have made a *real* mark on the world. I thought he had the right-stuff."

Kit fought hard to keep control of her anger over these insulting remarks. Clearly, she did not need this stress. While Lucy was teetering on the very edge of Kit's receding tolerance, she managed to keep her cool so she could speak justly in Sean's defense.

"Lucy, Sean had a perfectly brilliant career, which was *not* of my making. You probably know that he taught science at Cody High. And, I'm certain you'll find the tribute to his life on Saturday very moving. He and Corrine touched many lives here in Cody. Lives that went on to touch others, everywhere."

"Did you like Corrine, Mother?"

"What kind of a question is this?" Kit asked herself. "I won't dignify this question with an answer! What would be the point of sharing the intimate side of my wonderful twenty-five year relationship with Corrine who was more a daughter to me than Lucy has ever been?" How Kit despised admitting it, but she had to be honest. For questioning sweet Corrine, Kit had to level Lucy with, "Strike three!"

"Have you done much with the ranch, Mother?" Lucy asked next in an effort to change the subject on one hand, and exploit the circumstances surrounding her real reason for returning to Cody on the other.

"How ironic she would ask about the ranch now," Kit thought as she felt a wave of repulse rise within.

"I'm just wondering if you have kept up the property with your age and all," Lucy repeated with a slightly different twist.

All the years and hours of labor Kit had given to maintaining and improving the ranch, in good times and in duress, filled her weary head. Knowing that Olive Branch Ranch boasted the finest ranching complex for miles around, Kit became filled with indignation over Lucy's implications, but managed to lift her head just slightly and answered softly, "I have."

"Really? Northridge, too? Did you bring it out of the Stone Age?"

Inwardly enraged, but outwardly as peaceable as humanly possible, Kit indicated the interior footprint of the house was exactly as it was when Lucy had last seen it. Then she remembered Thompson's warning not to give her daughter too much information, and hoped she had not crossed that line.

"And do you still have that wretch Elaine Cain working for you?" Lucy dared to ask.

"Strike four!" Kit thought. She was actually happy to level one more than necessary, thereby eliminating any doubt in her decision against her only daughter. "I could sit here all evening and Lucy's derogatory remarks would never cease. She is absolutely despicable!"

Again, Kit chose silence, as she came to the difficult realization that Lucy was still filled with hatred. In fact, if Kit did not curtail their visit by paying the dinner bill, Lucy's rants may have gone on longer.

"What do people wear to this sort of thing?" Lucy asked. Clearly, she was referring to her brother's memorial service. "I haven't been anywhere with ranchers in so long, and I haven't stepped into a church in years."

"Call the funeral home if you have any concerns," was the only answer Kit felt Lucy deserved.

"I will. Thank you for dinner, Mother," Lucy said, choosing to stay seated as Kit departed in search of Peter Travers.

"Good night, Lucy," was all Kit could say, as she turned her face away from her child to hide her pain. "At least," Kit thought, "I still have my dignity."

Peter was waiting in the reception area to escort Kit to his cruiser. Well aware she was under an incredible strain, he treated her with the utmost compassion and considered it an honor to transport Sean's mother to the comfort of her home. Ashley was waiting at front door at Northridge when Peter pulled his cruiser into the yard.

It was obvious to the chief that though separated by two whole generations there was something special between these two Moran women. It was not hard for him to see the difference between Ashley's gentle love for her grandmother and the cold, hard, face of Lucy Moran, who remained seated when Kit departed the inn. Human nature never failed to surprise the chief.

While the Moran women met at Eagles Inn that evening, Thompson Smith evaluated a brand new piece of information regarding the Moran estate. He could only hope John Moran's handwritten "criteria for distribution" of the Olive Branch Ranch assets, which Thompson found in *The Old Man of the Mountain*, would provide Kit with a true sense of relief.

Thompson now knew something Kit did not. Her loving husband had provided for this very moment in her life, at the very hour of his own death. With John's criteria in hand, Thompson was certain Kit would never feel obligated to consider Lucy in her new will, unless she choose to do so. Leaning back in his red leather chair, Thompson read John Moran's notes once again and was amazed at the timing of his findings.

CHAPTER FIVE

Thursday, August 27th

Before retiring the previous evening, Sarah and Thompson worked from their respective home offices at Waterbury Ranch and cleared their schedules for a leisurely ride out to Olive Branch Ranch Thursday morning. They were hoping to get a first-look at the contents of Starlight Cottage then go on to Northridge to meet with Kit.

Things were fairly well under control at Thompson's office when he called Brendan around seven-thirty and instructed him to see Judge Aire at Cody District Court on behalf of the Moran Estate first thing that morning. When Brendan followed-up with Thompson around nine, he estimated it would be at least eleven before he could bring the documents Thompson requested for Kit out to Olive Branch Ranch. "Actually, that would be perfect timing," Thompson reassured Brendan.

Remembering they could reach Starlight Cottage if they followed the Shoshone River from Cody proper, Thompson suggested to Sarah that they take a look at Thomas Moran's works as they travelled the back way to Kit's home.

"I really do want to get a good look at Starlight, Sarah."

"I do too," Sarah said. "It's likely I'll have a fine arts appraiser booked to evaluate the paintings by the end of the day. I'd love to see just what the appraisal I'm seeking will entail."

Around ten, the Smiths saddled their horses, Hunter and Sweet Lady, and left Waterbury Ranch. Although they were just beyond mid-point in their lives and in their careers as well, both were the picture of health. Sarah's sandy-blond hair was long and she pulled it back in a ponytail when she rode. She looked lovely that morning in spite of everything they were going through.

Thompson's deep brown-hair now had distinguishing gray at the temples. In spite of all the long hours spent behind the desk, he was strong physically. Beyond his physical strength and his outgoing personality, Thompson's strongest personal attribute was his self-assuredness. His colleagues rated his most difficult cases by this strength, the more difficult the case – the greater his confidence.

Over the years, Thompson and Sarah learned to depend on each other's opinions in some of their most difficult professional cases. Today was no exception. Each had a professional case to discuss with the other as they rode out to the Moran's ranch.

Sarah opened their discussion. She was working on a medical case that was very near and dear to her heart. In her role as family practitioner, she was the only obstetrician in Cody. Her laboratory paged her at home early that morning, and the clinician in charge confirmed the pregnancy of a young woman named Rosie Hart whose live-in boyfriend had a temper and worse, wanted Rosie to have an abortion.

As a new patient, the young woman sought Dr. Smith out specifically because she knew Sarah to be a true advocate for the Unborn and their mothers. Unwed mother cases were usually difficult cases and by taking them on, husbands and boyfriends had threatened Sarah's life several times over the years. Often these cases had domestic violence at their core, and Thompson always worried about his wife's physical welfare as she worked with such patients.

"This time I think you need Peter involved, Sarah,"

Thompson answered when she asked him what he thought she should do. "I know he is affiliated with some great Wyoming negotiators who might just be able to bring some sense and direction to the young man involved. How old is he?" Thompson asked.

"He just turned nineteen. His father put him out of his house, as did Rosie's parents when they realized she was pregnant. They are both living with his grandmother right now. I checked with Nick Davis at the school and they are seniors. It's a challenging case, because it's so early in Rosie's pregnancy, Thompson, but I think you've given me a great idea with a police negotiator."

"Maybe it will work, Sarah. It may just be that the kid feels his life is so out of control."

"I hope it's that, and not a personality disorder," Sarah replied. "I'll give Peter a call this afternoon. Thank you."

The Smiths always worked well in this manner, sharing confidences and giving each other added resources and resilience for whatever new situation was at hand. With one problem solved, they continued on their way, taking in the exceptional beauty of the Wyoming wildflowers along the base of the Grand Teton Mountains.

At the base of these mountains, nature arranged wild-bouquets of flowers as if the reflection of a double rainbow in the sky. The beauty before them offered a stark contrast to the violent deaths of their dear friends. Rich scenes of color stretched as far as the Smiths could see and coaxed their minds from their present-day burdens by offering them a brief sense of reprieve.

This morning in particular, there were carpets of Wyoming Blue Flag Irises and Wild Sunflowers in bloom everywhere. Thompson led them toward the shallow riverbed ahead, and then turned to Sarah for her approval before taking the horses across at Hayden's Arch. Sarah waved Thompson on, and once they cleared the river and loosened the reigns of their horses, Lucy Moran became their topic of conversation.

"How do you think Kit is doing today, after seeing Lucy for the first time in years?" Sarah asked Thompson. "I hope she was not spooked by Lucy's presence the way I was," she offered before Thompson answered.

When Sarah arrived home late Wednesday evening, she informed Thompson that as she was preparing to leave her office a short while earlier, when she found Lucy Moran in her darkened waiting room. Not wanting to relive the experience when she got home that evening, she promised Thompson she would fill him in on the details of her encounter with Lucy on their way to Northridge Thursday morning.

"Did you recognize her right away?" asked Thompson.

"Not exactly. It took a moment to realize who she was. I had just dimmed the lights in the waiting room by remote control and was preparing to leave through the back entrance. With keys in hand, I decided to see if my staff had secured the front door properly.

"When I entered the darkened waiting area Lucy was standing at the end of the counter, where she had a straight view back to my desk. I wonder now just how long she watched me before I noticed.

"That's unbelievable Sarah. You'll learn soon enough however, that with Lucy Moran no one ever knows what to expect." With this statement, Thompson began to recall Lucy's younger years in town.

Sarah went on. "I really did the best I could to greet her as I would another patient, but I was definitely operating in my threatened mode. I went around her and straight to the light switches by the door. Once all the lights were on and the waiting area was bright, I invited her to sit down on the sofa, but I sat next to the door just in case."

"As soon as Lucy told me who she was, I took immediate control over the conversation by offering my condolences regarding Sean and Corrine. It was obvious she had no idea I'm grieving them as well. Her interest in Sean and Corrine seemed remote. If I hadn't known otherwise, I would think she had come to Cody for a vacation rather than her brother's funeral."

"That's exactly the impression I had of Lucy as well," Thompson responded, "and exactly the way I remember her so many years ago."

"The whole situation is just so odd. That was my first experience with Lucy Moran and I certainly hope it's my last," Sarah said, who moved to Cody several years after Lucy had departed.

As the couple approached the property line at Olive Branch Ranch, they agreed they would be silent in case their voices carried along the river. They thought silence would be best under the present circumstances even though they knew the area surrounding Starlight Cottage attracted few visitors.

"Before we get to the ranch Sarah, would you sit here a minute?" Thompson asked as he pointed to a downed tree.

"Lucy was trying to confirm that you are Kit's doctor, is that right?"

"I think she is assuming I'm Kit's doctor, because you are her lawyer. It was obvious to me that she's aware of patient confidentiality, but I do think she would have discussed Kit if she thought I was open to it. I have a feeling she intended to press me, but suddenly realized her inquiries might prompt me to ask more serious questions of her as well.

"I think you're right about that," Thompson agreed. "Let's try to use your unsettling experience with Lucy, in light of my own and we may be able to help Ashley and Kit survive Lucy's stay in Cody."

"How did she get in to see *you,* Thompson?" Thompson finally had time to fill Sarah in on the details of Lucy's impromptu visit to *his* office before Lucy met Kit for dinner.

"Brendan was not expecting to meet Lucy at the office or anywhere else this week. He was totally engaged in the Moran estate, and taken aback when she came through the front door. He seated a rather impatient Lucy Moran in the conference room with the door closed and then came to my office to inform me of her arrival.

"One of the details Brendan was looking for in the Moran file at the moment Lucy arrived was any mention of Lucy Jane Moran, Lucy Gallow or anything to that effect. Therefore, Brendan found Lucy's arrival at that precise moment unbelievably eerie.

"Did he find a mention of Lucy in the file?"

"No. But while looking, he discovered a scribbled reference John Moran made to a favorite book, a play actually, about the Prophet Elijah called *The Old Man of the Mountains.*"

"Now I'm lost, Thompson. You really need to explain how all of this fits together."

"I will soon, but I'm still putting all the pieces together myself. I scheduled another appointment with Lucy at four this afternoon. Hopefully, I'll have all the information I need to ward off any financial motives she may have for returning to Cody."

"You're going to see Lucy *again*?" Sarah asked with a tone of disbelief. "Don't you think it's a bit risky to get so involved with her right now?"

"I have to see her, Sarah. I need to surmise exactly what she's up to, every angle if I can, so I can advise Kit. Let me update you on what I know so far, I really need your opinion, too.

"Go on," Sarah said gently.

"I received a call this morning from Luke Webster, the handwriting analyst I've engaged to confirm John Charles Moran's handwriting on a note I found in Harold Loft's old files in my office last week. I believe I mentioned to you that Kit asked me to begin her final will a few weeks ago."

"Yes, you did mention that."

"I found another note dated March 26, 1967, which was about a year before John died, on my second pass through the file yesterday. This note supersedes John's signature on his original will, dated December 21, 1960. In this note, John Moran referenced the possibility he might place an additional update to his last wishes inside his copy of *The Old Man of the Mountains,* should he feel his death drawing near.

"It is quite possible of course, that John took Harold Loft into his greater confidence as his battle with cancer raged on. At any rate, once we found the note in the old file, we needed to check *The Old Man of the Mountains* – and right away.

"When Brendan went out to pick-up Kit yesterday, she gave him the book from her library and there was, in fact, a signed and sealed envelope tucked in its center. On my orders, Brendan slipped the book into his briefcase and whisked Kit out the door to dinner.

"I just figured she had enough going on last evening, so I asked Brendan to handle things this way. Anyway, Brendan is now having John's writing in this note authenticated by Luke Webster as well. Judge Aire will forego the usual waiting period for John and Kit's estate and promised me he would take care of signing-off on everything he has on the case this morning."

"Okay," Sarah said. "I understand the process, but can you tell me what's in John's final note?"

"No, I can't do that just yet as Judge Aire stipulated the

envelope and its contents must remain sealed until I give it to Kit. He plans to send John's note back to me in a district court envelope. Brendan told me earlier he thinks he'll be able to bring the envelope along to Northridge late this morning."

"You've accomplished all this already this morning? That's amazing," Sarah said to her husband.

The Smiths were just a minute's ride from the cove to the oblique granite marker indicating the southernmost boundary on Olive Branch Ranch. When they arrived on the property, they dismounted Sweet Lady and Hunter and tethered their horses to two cottonwood trees. The Shoshone River was running to their left and Starlight Cottage was just a few feet ahead on the right.

As they moved, closer to the cottage Thompson showed Sarah a narrow footpath that ran from the right side of Starlight Cottage out to Highway 20 where a small overgrown double-parking space served as another entrance to Starlight. Sarah would need to use that path to bring the appraiser to Starlight on Saturday.

Sarah smiled nervously as they neared the front door. Drawing a deep breath, Thompson took Kit's antique key out of his pocket. When he inserted it into the keyhole, they heard the old lock tumble. Then the door hinges creaked as Thompson pushed the door wide open and the couple entered the little cottage. Their first impression was a positive one; the dry air was an excellent indicator that Starlight's climate was actually conducive to the preservation of material goods.

To let some light in, they took down the blanket next to the front door.

"No moth-holes, Thompson," Sarah reported.

"That's another good sign," he added.

"I'll take all the blankets down. We need more light," Sarah said as she climbed the ladder to the loft on the left side of the main room. There she took down a blanket on the window facing the river and folded it. Next, she removed the blanket on the window facing Northridge. Returning to the first floor, she uncovered the window on the Northridge side and then the riverside as well. Finally, Sarah removed the cover on the window where the horses stood. She then folded all the blankets and placed them on a side table under the front window.

"Can you see anything in there?" Sarah asked Thompson who was already hunting through some of the paintings in the large closet Kit had described.

"It's tough but I can see there are paintings everywhere. It's absolutely packed. I'll pick three at random so we can have a look. Help me, Sarah, if you can. Take the paintings as I hand them out to you. There are several oversized works in here but they are too much for me to handle alone. Here's one of the medium-sized paintings. I can feel a tag on the back. Be careful Sarah."

"Oh, you know I will. Have you forgotten I'm now a student of fine arts?"

"Actually, I had. It's hard for me to imagine you with any interest other than medicine."

"I know," Sarah responded with a smile. She was happy to have other interests at this point in her life and something new to share with her patients as well.

Thompson handed out three of Thomas J. Moran, Jr.'s paintings: *The Much Resounding Sea, An Indian Paradise* and *Summit of the Sierras,* all done in oil. They would soon learn these paintings carried estimated values of $10,000, $8,000 and $7,500 respectively in the early 21st century market.

"These are in wonderful condition," Sarah said to Thompson excitedly as she placed the first, *The Much Resounding Sea*, on an old rustic table in the center of the room. "Of course I'm an amateur at evaluating art but besides being incredibly dirty, there seems to be no corrosion by the elements." Taking a closer look Sarah added, "This painting appears to be untouched by any infestation of mold, insects or rodents. After all these years, this is a remarkable find, Thompson. What wonderful, wonderful news for Kit and Ashley."

"When all the dust clears, and I mean both literally and figuratively, my dear, we shall see," Thompson said as he rubbed his itchy nose.

Once seen in daylight, the lettering on the tags on the back of each painting was as clear as on the day Dr. Moran dated them in 1928.

"Perhaps the Stock Market crash in 1929 is the real reason these paintings never made it to exhibit while they were in Dr. Marcus' possession," Sarah said. "Certainly he must have known they would never retain their true value, until the economy stabilized once again."

"As so many other doctors did in that period, he was probably able to support his household with his medical practice, by accepting livestock or fresh produce in exchange for care," Thompson suggested. "With a flattened investment market, Marcus Moran may have decided to hold onto the paintings to secure Sophia's future.

"The paintings have survived being "underground," here on Kit's ranch for six-decades, which is a very long time," Thompson said. "If the first three works indicate the condition of the rest, I think Kit will be absolutely astounded." Then Sarah spoke.

"When the paintings entered Marcus Moran's care, a complete inventory of Thomas Moran's paintings was most likely already published, as Moran passed away in 1926. I would guess that by the time Sophia had the paintings delivered to John and Kit, the public had lost interest in Moran's work, and the inner circles of the art world simply found the trail too cold to pursue. However, Moran's work is just too valuable for its absence from the market to go unnoticed forever. There may be some museums and art dealers still speculating about the collection location even now."

With *The Much Resounding Sea* still on the table, and the other two painting resting at his knee, Thompson heard the horses stir outside. He froze solid.

"Quick Sarah, look outside," he said firmly.

Sarah looked out toward the tethered animals.

"The horses are sensing someone's coming, Thompson."

"Step back Sarah and push the door closed without shutting it completely. S-l-o-w-l-y. That will buy us sometime. Hurry!"

Sarah did as Thompson asked without question, while he slid *The Much Resounding Sea* off the table and put all three paintings just inside the closet door.

"Quick," you head up to the loft and look busy, or at least make it as far as you can. I'll check the window again," Thompson whispered. He moved to the window and looked to his left toward the path out to Highway 20.

"Sarah," Thompson screamed in a whisper. "It's Lucy! It's too late to escape her inquiries. She knows someone is here."

"H-e-l-l-o?" the Smiths heard Lucy call from outside. It was a relief to both that Lucy was unable to identify their horses.

Now each wondered how they would escape her inquiries. Then suddenly Sarah heard Thompson whisper the word, "play." Immediately Sarah began to laugh aloud as though Thomson was initiating a romantic interlude. "Oh, Honey, stop it," she said as she increased the strength of voice.

"H-e-l-l-o?" the Smiths heard Lucy call again. This

100

time with a guarded edge in her voice.

"It's working," Thompson whispered, as Sarah descended the ladder.

"Keep it up and follow me."

The couple slid behind the closed portion of the front door. This time Sarah took the lead.

"Don't you dare tickle me, you big moose," she pleaded in a ragged tone.

Thompson leaned toward his wife and gave her a thumbs-up as he mussed her hair. Then in baited breath, he furthered their cause, "Cool it! Q-U-I-E-T! I think I hear someone out there!" Quickly he moved from behind the door and opened it just the width of his body and then Sarah popped out from behind him, in a burst of youthful energy.

There was no getting out of meeting Lucy face-to-face but with a little ingenuity on their part; they were able to prevent her access to Mill House.

"Oh, my goodness," a startled Lucy exclaimed, "I *never* expected to see *you two* here." With greater apprehension over her relationship with Thompson than his wife, Lucy felt more comfortable turning her attention to Sarah.

"Dr. Smith, how are you?'

"I'm quite well, Lucy. Thank you for asking," Sarah answered as she pulled her hair back in a fresh ponytail and straightened her shirt, hoping she had been successful in creating an embarrassing scene. In the tension of the next moment, Lucy made her true motive for being in Cody known.

"What are *you two* doing here on *our* property?" she snarled at the Smiths. In an instant, her sweetened tone had disappeared. Though she tried to look calm, Lucy was overtly hostile toward her mother's friends.

Sarah tempered Lucy's hostility by asking her if the place had changed much since she had last been there.

While Lucy looked about for a moment, Thompson turned the antique key in the lock, and then slid the key back into his pocket.

"It has changed," she said, as she peered into the uncovered windows. "It looks as if it's gone through some renovations since the last time I was here, but then let go again."

"Perhaps you are right," said Thompson.

"Beautiful little spot, isn't it?" Sarah said as she hastened the conversation to focus anywhere but on them. Sarah talked on about the Kintzley's Ghost Honeysuckle growing over the roof and then how green the grass remained in the little knoll in spite of the dry summer. As she talked, Thompson untied Sweet Lady and Hunter from the shade trees and handed Sarah her horse's reins. Thompson, who was already mounted on Hunter, encouraged Sarah to mount Sweet Lady while she chatted on with Lucy.

All but aloof, Thompson reminded Lucy of their appointment that afternoon. Then the couple wished Kit's daughter well. Turning their horses toward Northridge, the Smiths then headed into the woods and travelled the same path Ashley used to come and go on Sunday afternoon. Lucy left Starlight by the path to Highway 20, just as she had come. She simply did not have the nerve she needed to stop the couple from heading to Northridge and of course, she was unaware of their scheduled meeting with Kit.

The sun cast a warm, magnificent glow over Northridge that morning and the moss baskets of white and purple mums, which Kit hung along the ceiling beams over the porch rail, swayed gently in the breeze and added to the home's beauty. No aesthetic beauty however, could account for the sheer tranquility the Smiths felt as the wooded trail opened onto Kit's lower lawn. There Sarah and Thompson both entered what appeared to be an evolving scene of utter magnificence encompassing all of Northridge.

Before their eyes, an incredible golden light rose up over Kit's home, a light that penetrated right through the windows in her small first floor office. This golden light cast a stream of majestic gold rays through the French doors, over the porch railing, down the stairs and across the lawn, where these rays came to rest at Sarah and Thompson's feet. In addition, as if this astonishing light was not enough, in the next moment the sun itself appeared to dance along Kit's rooftop.

"I've never seen anything like this, have you, Sarah?" Thompson remarked.

"N-e-v-e-r!"

Clearly, the couple had no idea what to make of this fantastic display of light.

"Are we seeing the same thing, Thompson?"

"You know we are. And the peace this light carries is utterly amazing."

Dazzled by the light's final display and then its retreat, the Smiths were soon left with only a memory of what had just occurred. Frankly, they were stunned and unable to speak of the beautiful yet truly odd phenomenon. Sarah could count the number of times Thompson was speechless over the thirty-years she had known him on one hand. This day was one of them. In total silence, he took the reins of their horses and tethered them to two trees. Then placing his hand under Sarah's elbow, Thompson moved her along toward Kit's front yard while *he* continued to look back over his shoulder to where the streams of golden light had been.

When they arrived at the front of Northridge, Elaine Cain answered the door. Elaine had known Thompson

Smith all of his life. In fact, when she was in high school Thompson's mother routinely hired Elaine to be his babysitter. Then when he brought his new young bride to Cody, Thompson made a special point of counting Elaine among the first to meet Sarah.

"How are you two?" Elaine asked in a whisper.

Taking Elaine's cue, Sarah and Thompson returned the whisper as well, without knowing exactly why.

"Is Kit still asleep?" whispered Sarah, taking a stab at Elaine's motive.

"Oh, no. Not at all. She's in her office with Fr. Joe Evers."

"Oh, I see," whispered Thompson. Sarah realized they were both so preoccupied with the spectacular scene in Kit's backyard, neither one of them took note of Fr. Joe's car in the yard.

It was common knowledge throughout Cody that Sarah and Thompson Smith had not attended church regularly for years, having taken their lead from the Cultural Revolution as Sean and Corrine had done. Knowing this, Elaine took the moment-at-hand to remind them why Fr. Evers came to visit.

"Fr. Joe brought Jesus Christ in the Eucharist to Kit this morning."

"Do you mean she is receiving Holy Communion?" Sarah asked.

"Yes," Elaine answered without hesitation.

Suddenly Thompson understood that Elaine's whispering was her way of demonstrating respect while being in the Presence of Jesus. "Oh, now I see. Forgive me Elaine," Thompson whispered. "It's been such a long time since I've given proper reverence to Our Lord, that I missed your cue completely."

"Thompson, there's no need to ask for *my* forgiveness. We are friends, and in Christ, we are brothers and sisters.

None of us gets through this life without failing Jesus in some way. That's why He needed to save us."

"I've been away from my Catholicism much too long," Thompson admitted to Elaine, recognizing he was speaking to a woman of great wisdom and even greater love for Jesus.

Without Thompson realizing it, Elaine was able to see what was going on inside him. She had grown familiar with many of the reasons or justifications men and women make for why they moved away from the Lord. As she looked at Thompson, she had compassion for the mental gymnastics she knew he was playing.

"Really, it's okay," she said softly to Thompson.

He went on however with his feelings of regret. "I have solved so many problems for people over the years," Thompson said as he looked at Elaine. "In recent years I'm afraid I've grown to feel *I have* all of the answers. After this week, I wonder if I really know *anything* at all. At least that's how I feel right now."

Elaine had nothing to add to Thompson's profound self-analysis. She had done her part. It was now time to let Jesus do the rest.

"Hey, you two," she said gently, to break the solemn moment. "I'll get you both a glass of ice water and you can relax here in the dining room for a few minutes. I'm sure Fr. Joe and Kit won't be too long."

"Thanks, Elaine," Sarah said, "that sounds great."

Elaine's absence gave each a few moments to reflect on their own lives. Their lack of reverence for the Lord was uncomfortable on one hand, but on the other, each was now convinced the Real Presence of the Lord was at Northridge, and that Jesus was actually drawing them to Himself at that very moment. They could feel His love.

"Here you go," Elaine said as she placed the water before them.

"Thank you," they both replied.

"I'll see you at the memorial service Saturday," Elaine said.

"If we don't get to speak with you, please keep us in your prayers," Thompson said with complete awareness that Elaine was in fact so much closer to God than he. With all sincerity, he was asking for the grace he knew she could obtain for him. After promising to pray for them, she left for town to do a few errands for Kit.

The Smiths sat at Kit's dining room table in silent reverence of the Lord's Presence. Sarah had her head down for a moment when suddenly Thompson took her hand.

"Sarah?"

"What is it?" she asked.

"I want you to look at that painting."

"Okay," she said as she raised her head. "It's *Mountain of the Holy Cross*, the first painting Sophia Moran left here at Olive Branch. We've seen this painting many times."

"Yes, but I want you to *really look at it*. The cross on the mountain is *gold*. I've seen this painting at least a hundred-times in my lifetime and the cross has always been as white as snow. Today it appears to be real gold."

"You're absolutely right!"

Thompson went on. "There seems to be something mystical going on here at Northridge today."

"Amazing," was all Sarah could say to express what she knew was beyond words to describe.

"I'm not sure what to make of all of this," he continued, "but I do think now is the time for us to return to the Church. I'm afraid we have both made a rather serious mistake by shrugging off our Christian duties."

"You're right," Sarah said, her voice weakened by her own sense of shame.

Fr. Joe concluded his prayers with Kit and left her in her office where she rested in silent meditation after Holy Communion. Stepping down quietly over the foyer stairs and onto the green Oriental rug in the living room, Father gestured for the couple to remain quiet.

"God bless both of you for all that you have done for this family and particularly for Kit," he whispered as he sat down with them at the table. "She's overwhelmingly grateful to you."

"She is something else," whispered Thompson.

"Yes, she is," Fr. Joe replied. Though he had not known Kit long, he recognized her virtues with ease and learned from other parishioners and members of the Cody community, that she was well loved and well respected by all.

"How is she today, Father?" asked Sarah.

"She's doing pretty well, I would say. I think she was greatly saddened by her visit with Lucy last night but she seems resigned. She also seems resigned to say good-bye to Sean and to Corrine on Saturday as well." Father added, "Her faith is very strong."

"Father?" Sarah said.

"What is it, Sarah?"

"We would like to show you something." Thompson objected.

"Oh, Sarah, let's not bother Fr. Joe with what could be a figment of our imaginations."

"Well, it's more than our imaginations, Thompson," Sarah shot back in self-defense. "After all, we *are* rational people. I know *I am*," she whispered to Father with gentle sarcasm.

Now Father's interest was piqued and his curiosity had the best of him. He simply had to know what was going on.

"Well, Father, I've been to Northridge at least a

hundred-times in my lifetime and I've seen this wonderful painting by Thomas J. Moran, Jr., a distant cousin of Kit's husband, just as many times. In fact, Kit would always ask those gathered at her table to gaze upon the white cross and remember God's physical and spiritual blessings to all of creation – as our grace before meals."

"You have a great memory," Fr. Joe replied.

"It's easy to remember Kit's blessing now, though I have not thought of it in years. The events of the last few days have led me back to my early days at Northridge with Sean. It's all so strange. Sean and Corrine's deaths have given us a different perspective on everything. Just now Sarah and I have admitted how terribly wrong we've been to exclude the Lord from our lives. Isn't this so, Sarah?"

"Yes. I must admit everything Thompson has said so far reflects my sentiments as well," she answered.

"Now I want to ask you something."

"Anything," Father said to Sarah.

"We want to ask you what color you see on the cross in the painting."

Fr. Joe turned, expecting to see the cross of snow he admired while dining with Kit and Ashley Tuesday evening. When he looked at the painting and the cross this time however he did not hesitate to exclaim, "It's gold! Oh, my gosh! It's solid gold!"

"Exactly!" said Sarah.

"What's all this chatter about?" Kit asked from the foyer. "Good morning, my dear friends," she said, greeting her guests as she came down the foyer steps.

"Good morning, Kit," Sarah replied.

Thompson rose from his chair to meet Kit. "Come over here," he said as he took her by the arm. "We'd like to show you something."

Pressed with a million worries at that moment Kit's

face registered her definite misgivings.

"What do you want to show me?" she asked in a voice that seemed unusually frail.

"It's the painting," Fr. Joe answered gently.

Before anyone could say another word, Kit looked up and was completely shocked. She reached for the high back of the empty dining room chair in front of her for stability. There she stood, completely dumbfounded. Her friends watched closely as she gazed upon the painting.

"Oh… my… goodness! Oh… my… goodness!" was all she could say. Kit was stunned by the change in the painting. She moved to get a closer look and then after a long minute she finally spoke.

"I sat on that sofa last night," she said as she pointed to the living room, "and followed the details of this marvelous work up the mountain as I so often do. The painting has always brought me such peace. But I can tell you friends that the cross was white last evening. In fact, I imagined that the snow was melting, and pouring down through the ravines washing away the pain I was feeling.

And, then, I allowed my imagination to take me back to the days I spent sledding down a giant hill behind my home in California when I was a small girl. For an instant before I retired for the evening, I sent myself up the snow covered cross in my mind's eye, and then flew down its center on my old Radio Flyer.

"So this is how she survives when she is confronted by terrific grief," Sarah thought.

"I can tell you without a doubt," Kit went on, "the cross was white last night. But now its gold – and not just some sort of gold-wash – it SPARKLES – like precious metal."

"Yes, it does," said Fr. Joe. "I believe it's safe to say this is truly a gift to all of us in our sorrow. In addition, in a special way, Kit, because this painting belongs is yours, you should consider this a very special gift to you from Almighty God.

"I saw something similar happen once before in my early years as a priest, when God sent an apparition to a mother who had lost her teenaged daughter to suicide. The woman placed her faith in her daughter's salvation in Our Lady's hands and several months later, she saw a picture of her daughter's face come through her favorite image of Mary. I saw the image appear with my own eyes and took the phenomenon to my bishop, who accepted the transformation as a miracle.

"I don't hesitate to encourage you to accept this physical grace as a special sign from God as well, Kit. May this gift bring you much peace in your grief."

"Oh it will, Father, especially because it seems to have appeared when Our Lord Jesus was present here."

"He's still here for all of us in you, Kit. Allow His Presence to strengthen all of you today."

"We will," Kit said, on Thompson and Sarah's behalf.

Though wonderful people it had been a long-time since the Smiths had thought about the condition of their own souls relative to their early formation, and the couple was spiritually shaken by all they had experienced that morning. They were not disturbed as much by any of the phenomenon they witnessed, as by the profound truth, that in spite of all their accomplishments and personal riches they were very poor Catholics.

When all had settled down, Fr. Joe took leave of Northridge, stepping out the front door as quietly as he came in. As he approached his car, he greeted Brendan Snyder whose disheveled appearance reminded him that everyone connected to the Morans was working their hardest to help them.

When the two men crossed paths, Fr. Joe mentioned to Brendan that he would find Thompson in Kit's dining room.

"Thanks, Father," Brendan said with an appreciative wave. When he reached the door he knocked, then entered Northridge to deliver the documents Thompson was waiting for. Thompson thanked Brendan then asked him return to the office right away.

As he headed toward his car, Brendan saw Ashley Moran for the first time. Although they had never met, Thompson mentioned each to the other, but when he saw her, he honestly felt Thompson had understated Ashley's beauty. When he finally had the opportunity to see her with his own eyes, he thought she was absolutely lovely, even her grief.

Not wanting to impose with a forced introduction, Brendan continued on to his car on the other side of the circular drive and offered Ashley a passing wave. Without voice, Ashley returned the courtesy.

"Hi Nan," she called into the dining room, as she entered the kitchen. "I'm just going to pick-up a few things from your cupboards to take over to Amour. I saw the floral arrangements for Mom and Dad when I was in town and they are lovely. Everything is all set for Saturday."

"Oh, hi," she said to the Smiths, "I had no idea you were here. I didn't see your car. How did you get here?"

"Our horses," Thompson said. "They're down back."

"How are you doing, Ashley?" Sarah asked.

"As well as I can be, although I'm a bit tired. I thought I'd go home to Amour and tuck myself into my own bed for the afternoon."

"I think that's a great idea," said Sarah.

"I do, too," Kit agreed. "I'll have dinner ready for us about six. Will you be back by then?"

"Definitely. I'll see you soon."

"Nan, I'll call you if my plans change," Ashley said as

she took a canvas bag of supplies from the kitchen counter and headed home to Amour.

As she waited for Thompson to finish organizing her estate file, Kit quietly stirred her tea.

Sarah, seated at Kit's left hand, was lost in the mystical experiences of the beautiful golden light and dancing sun over Northridge, the gold cross in the painting over the fireplace, and the presumed preservation of the Thomas Moran collection at Starlight. She wondered how, with all the grief that had come upon all of them, they seemed to be operating in the midst of an incredible spiritual mystery as well.

Breaking the silence between the three of them, Thompson brought their little meeting to discuss his recent findings to order.

"Before I fill you in on my latest discoveries, Kit, I must ask you about your encounter with Lucy last evening. I feel it will help me from a legal perspective."

With quiet determination, Kit tried to enlighten her friends on her odd encounter with Lucy.

"Thompson, you have described it precisely. I had an encounter with Lucy, and a challenging one at that, but nothing more." Without her need to say so directly Sarah recognized the fact that Kit had "closed the book" on any possible reconciliation.

"Actually, we've discovered a great deal since we met with you Tuesday evening," Thompson said, "and if you are at all worried that Lucy's aggression could undermine whatever final arrangements you make for your estate, I want to share this information with you now. Kit looked bewildered but Sarah offered reassurance by gently patting Kit's arm.

"Try not to worry," Thompson said offering his own reassurance.

"We can only imagine how difficult all this must be for

you," Sarah said, "but please, try to trust us. We love you Kit, and want the very best for you – especially your peace of mind."

"I know you do and I thank you," Kit said. "Now tell me what I need to know and please don't sugarcoat anything."

"Well, after her arrival in town yesterday, I was the first one to see Lucy," Thompson began. "She paid me a little visit at my office late yesterday afternoon shortly after she checked into Eagles Inn."

"She did? What did she want?" Kit asked.

She came by to confirm that I'm still your attorney, something she should already know. Do you agree?"

"Oh, yes, I agree completely with your assessment on this point." Kit paused then asked, "Was that all she wanted?"

"I'm fairly sure there is more but that was all I could make of things yesterday. I was telling Sarah on the way over, that I set up another appointment with Lucy for this afternoon. I'm hoping I'll be able to confirm my suspicions regarding her ulterior-motive for returning to Cody. I'm afraid I'm convinced it has nothing to do with Sean and Corrine's funeral, but rather, this is her excuse to make a trip she has wanted to make for a while."

"So is *that* everything?" Kit asked hoping Thompson could put an end to her immediate miseries regarding Lucy.

"No, Kit," Sarah said while treading gently, "Lucy actually came to see me, too."

"She did? At *your* office? What time was this?"

"I'm quite sure it was after you left Eagles Inn to go home last evening," Sarah replied.

"Peter drove me home about seven-fifteen," Kit added without hesitation.

"Yes, well as I told Thompson this morning, I was

getting ready to leave my office through the back exit about that same time but decided to recheck the front door. When I entered the reception area, there she was." To spare Kit, Sarah decided not to let on just how much Lucy's intrusion had frightened her.

"She introduced herself as your daughter and then she inquired about your health. She seemed embarrassed when I counseled her on doctor-patient confidentiality but bounced back immediately by showing an unexpected interest in my office décor. Then she went on to mentioned how lovely your home is and asked if I had seen Northridge lately. I think she was trying to establish the depth of our relationship."

"Lucy asked me about Northridge, at dinner last night as well," Kit confirmed. "She was interested in how much things had changed."

"But it was what she said just before she left that was the real clincher, Kit. She spoke fondly of Ashley and mentioned what a lovely young woman she is. Then she excused herself, and left quite abruptly."

Fully aware that Lucy had never met Ashley, Kit found her daughter's comments unnerving, and her thoughts turned now to protecting her granddaughter.

After a brief moment of contemplation, she responded angrily to what Lucy had done to Sarah. "I can see Lucy has been *very* busy!"

"But that's not all we have to tell you about her," said Thompson. "We saw her together, again this morning."

"You did? Where?"

"At Starlight Cottage," Sarah jumped in. "Thompson thought this morning would be a great time for us to have a look at your collection."

"You did? So soon?" Kit asked, with the same angst she carried through their conversation about the paintings out on the porch Tuesday evening. The poor woman's

114

emotions were in such turmoil she had no idea which issue needed her attention first, so the Smiths continued to lead.

"Yes and the news about the paintings is absolutely incredible," Thompson informed her. "The three paintings we were able to view before Lucy interrupted us are in near-mint condition, as far as Sarah can tell."

"*Really?* How could this be after all these years?"

"I can't answer that, Kit," Sarah said. "I'm still an amateur, and it does seem a bit of a mystery. I've hired a fine arts appraiser, Annabelle Marsh from Casper, to come out to Starlight Cottage on Saturday and I hope she will confirm my opinion.

"Annabelle and her father, Neil Marsh, have a wonderful reputation as fine arts appraisers. Neil, who is nearing eighty, is a local authority on the *Hudson River School* artists from the turn of the 20th century, and all the Moran family artists specifically. The Marshes will be working together on your collection. I've spoken to Annabelle alone on this matter and she has promised to deal with your appraisal with much discretion. In fact, she doesn't plan to reveal a single detail about the assignment, even to Neil, until I meet them on Saturday."

"What wonderful reassurance, my dear. Thank you, for going to all of this trouble."

"This is no trouble at all, Kit. Let me tell you a little bit about Annabelle's background, before we fill you in on Lucy's visit to Starlight this morning. A little good news before the bad," Sarah continued.

"Annabelle is licensed by the state of Wyoming, and has a PhD in art-history and restoration. Although you probably have all of Thomas Moran's works in your possession, she obtained a recent market-analysis which lists several of Moran's paintings and their extraordinary value, based on inflation and desirability, if offered on today's market. I'm sure you'll find this startling Kit, but

I must tell you that *Mountain of the Holy Cross* if found in mint or near-mint condition, which we believe it to be, is worth $4.9 million dollars on the current market.

Kit opened her mouth as if to speak but made no sound.

Sarah went on. "I've asked the Marshes to come early Saturday and they plan to work through the day. I'm hoping with most everyone in town at the memorial service, they'll be undisturbed as they view the collection."

"Now I'd like to fill you in on our encounter with Lucy this morning," Thompson said reluctantly. "Apparently, she drove to Starlight Cottage and parked in the overgrown lot out on Highway 20. I had just taken three paintings out of the closet when Sarah noticed our horses stirring. I was able to get the paintings out of sight and luckily, when Lucy heard us in the house, she walked to the river's edge instead of entering. She would never have known our horses so she was probably to trying to get a feel for who was inside."

"Did you get the impression Lucy was there for a specific reason?" Kit asked.

"Actually, that's what we hoped you might know. My first and I'm afraid my only inclination is to think she is up to something. We really must assume from this point on that she knows more about the paintings than less," said Thompson. "We can't take any chances and to be frank with you Kit, I don't have a concrete reason for Lucy's appearance at Starlight Cottage. But I plan to pursue this matter among others. I've scheduled an appointment with her for four this afternoon."

"I see," was all Kit could manage to say.

"Now I must introduce you to another matter regarding John Charles Moran's will, the authenticity of the note he added to his will a year before his death, and the contents of the envelope we found in *The Old Man of the Mountains*. It's all good news – at least I think it is."

"Yes, please. I simply can't believe I'm about to hear something from my Dear John, today."

Then with an obvious shift in his posture, Thompson began bringing all the facts of the Moran Estate to the table.

"Do you remember that when you asked me to review your whole estate a few weeks ago, I told you things were not all in one place and that I'd need to pull several old files from storage?"

"I do," Kit replied.

"Well, it was in one of the old files that I first came across a reference to *The Old Man of the Mountains*. To make a long story short I've uncovered John's last wishes, a set of criteria, which he apparently slipped into that book the day he died."

"He died Easter Sunday, late in the evening," Kit stated.

"Yes. Brendan checked back to 1968 for me and noted this fact. Just this morning, Kit, Judge Aire at the Cody District Court put his stamp of approval on my expert handwriting analyst's testimony that the note in the book is written in John's weak – but authentic hand."

"Go on," said Kit.

"Judge Aire's legal confirmation of John's final signature now clears the way for me to work-up your will, and include John's wishes as well."

"We must get my final will on paper right away," Kit said with definite urgency.

"Yes, that's why I'm here, but now we have a set of criteria in John's handwriting to consider as well. I don't think you've known a thing about these criteria."

"I'm actually shocked by this information, Thompson," Kit said.

"I wanted to see you today to go over John's notes. But before I tell you about it, I need a full-page of your handwriting. It can be anything that you have handwritten, just for me to have on file in case I ever need to verify *your* signature."

"I've kept a gardening journal for years," Kit said as she headed to her office. "I'll tear a page from that."

"That's perfect," Thomas said.

Instead of conversing over the details of the transaction before them while Kit was gone, Sarah and Thompson sat quietly and looked at *Mountain of the Holy Cross* over the fireplace once again. Their silence was reverent. They were in awe of what they continued to see – the solid gold cross on the mountain covered in snow.

Returning to the table, Kit tore a page from the back of the journal she had been keeping for a quarter-century. "I hope this will do, Thompson. My last entry was August 1st."

"That will be fine. Now, I'll read John's final letter Kit."

Kit, who could not imagine what she was about to hear from John, listened carefully to Thompson as he read the following:

> *<u>To Whom It May Concern</u>: Praise be Almighty God that this letter has found its way into your hands.*
>
> *I have had difficult time dealing with my cancer and with leaving the incredible responsibility of the distribution of my family's wealth, including the Thomas J. Moran, Jr. collection, to my beloved wife, Kit Moran.*
>
> *I have had many hours alone to contemplate how to treat my heirs fairly and as my death approaches, it is my heart-felt desire that these*

individuals, be it my children or my grandchildren, should share in the ownership of the Moran estate, provided they pass three important criteria which follow: 1) They must be individual(s) of integrity, law-abiding, and love America. 2) They must demonstrate they are proud of their family heritage, and try in a significant way to draw strength and ability from our family tree. 3) Last but not least, they must practice the Catholic Faith of their ancestry.

I, John Charles Moran, have written this final letter with the intention of sending it off to Attorney Harold Loft tomorrow, to be opened by my wife Kit, Attorney Loft, or their representatives when the appropriate time comes.

I close now with my heart full of love for Kit, Lucy and Sean Moran. May God be your guide in the future in determining how best to use Olive Branch Ranch and the historic paintings we, as a family, have been given to guard. John Charles Moran, April 17, 1968

"Kit, as present owner of Harold Loft's original practice, I qualify as Harold's representative, and while this criteria was not part of your file at my office, it appears to me this is simply because John was unable to request its delivery."

Then Sarah spoke. "I'm just in awe of your husband, Kit. What a wonderful man he must have been."

"Incredible," added Thompson. "In all my years of estate work, I've never met anyone as thorough, and as thoughtful. You must be so pleased."

"Oh my dears, I'm afraid you have both missed a very important point, if you think that John's instructions have consoled me!"

Kit's sharp statement surprised Thompson and Sarah.

"What have we missed?" Thompson asked, in near desperation.

"When preparing these criteria back in 1968, John could never have anticipated that our family, as in many other families in our world today, has not a single practicing Catholic in the next generation. I realize I'm assuming this is true of Lucy at the moment. It's an assumption I hate to make, but simply must by the way she behaved last night."

"No, my friends," Kit's voice was low and deliberate, "unfortunately I don't feel any better than I did when we first sat down together. I simply don't know what to do. I'd like to ask you both to reread John's criteria. Neither Lucy nor Ashley qualifies to inherit our estate as of today. Ashley already exhibits the character of a woman of integrity, and has a real love and appreciation for her family and Country, but Sean and Corrine baptized their only child.

"Lucy meets neither of these criteria and we know by her questionable land dealings in Vermont that she has failed the integrity criteria her dear father laid out. It's clear at this point Lucy has had no "about face" since her early years.

"While it's obvious that Ashley qualifies in love of family and Country, she does not qualify in John's stipulation of Catholicism, and I simply must adhere to my husband's criteria. There is absolutely no way I can do otherwise, if I want my last years on earth to be years of peace.

"How *can* this be?" Kit asked, through tears of frustration, not knowing whom to blame, Sean, Corrine, the world as it is today, or her own failing to convince her son and daughter-in-law that they were in grave error when it came to their religious decisions about Ashley.

"Is this true? "Ashley has never been baptized?" Thompson asked, trying to remember those early years of Ashley's life. Without waiting for an answer, he continued. "I just don't recall."

"I know that it's almost unthinkable, Thompson. But if Ashley were baptized, clearly you and Sarah would have been included in the celebration. I'm telling you that it never happened. I'm sure that's why you have no memory of such a day. Now, not only must Ashley go on without her parents, she has very little faith per se to lift her. I think when someone close is lost to death; it's all the more difficult for those whose early psychological development did not include a strong faith in God."

Kit had spoken. From what she said, Thompson found he now had a small taste from the "cup of anguish" she experienced over the spiritual condition of Sean's family. He now saw Kit as a woman of great personal sacrifice for the souls of her children, rather than some kind of religious zealot, a label she would surely receive if known to progressive America.

A defeated Thompson Smith was more than disappointed in his failure to bring resolve to Kit's situation that morning. Further, he realized that pressing her for an alternative resolution to her distribution of wealth, whatever that might be, would probably bring the poor woman more heartache. He accepted the results of their meeting without making further recommendations.

Then recognizing her husband's defeat, Sarah offered Kit a last word of comfort. "Try not to worry about any of this, Kit. You know God has a solution out there that will work for you. We'll help you find it.

"It's true that like Sean and Corrine, I haven't practiced my Catholicism in years, but I've seen plenty of miracles and difficult situations resolve among my prayerful patients. Please let Thompson and me carry the emotional burden of your estate for you now, so you can get through Saturday.

"What I can do for you right now is confirm that the paintings will be fully-appraised by Saturday evening. Hopefully then you'll feel that we're making a bit of progress, in spite all of the roadblocks."

"Oh, I think I really am in over my head with emotional fatigue at the moment, but I'm so grateful to you both. I know God has sent you to help me through these awful days."

"And you to help us, Kit, in *our loss* of Sean and Corrine. You get some rest, love," Sarah said, as she reached to touch Kit's hand.

"I will. Ashley's coming back a little later and we'll have dinner together. People have been so generous. Our refrigerator is still full and Elaine arranged everything today so we don't even have to decide what to eat."

"Wonderful," Sarah said in the tone of a concerned physician.

"We'll both work on your estate behind the scenes these next few days and hopefully we'll have an update for you on Sunday."

The Smiths then refreshed their horses at the river briefly, rode back to Waterbury Ranch and onto their respective offices for the afternoon.

Alone again, Kit took went to her room for a short-while where in secret she questioned John over his criteria and waited for a response for an idea, a feeling, or a sense of what she should do. But nothing came.

Then, faced with all the news of the day and the tragedy of the week thus far, she did what anyone would do. She put her head down on her pillow and cried.

Sarah had late-rounds to make at West Park Hospital Thursday afternoon, and Thompson still had Lucy to deal with.

"There's no escaping Lucy Moran. Not now," Thompson said to himself as he got into his car. He needed strength to deal with her guile, and recognized that his intense dislike for the woman was continuing to grow.

As he drove into town, he had full-recall of an incident with Lucy as he and Sean were playing in a field behind the Centre just after John Moran died. Thompson still remembered the ugly scene as if it were yesterday. Lucy, who appeared from nowhere, began to abuse Sean verbally.

"You filthy little pig, Sean!" she screamed in her young brother's face as she moved within two feet of the terrified boy. "You disgust me! And so does this wiry little runt of a friend of yours!"

Lucy's rant that day was the first time young Thompson Smith ever experienced the true sting of human venom, and his memory of the dreadful incident was never far from his conscious mind. Today, however this memory served to remind Thompson not to let his guard down, as far as Sean's sister was concerned. He knew Lucy's natural disposition all too well.

To his chagrin, Lucy was waiting for him when he pulled in. After a brief hello, the two entered Thompson's office. Thompson ushered Lucy directly to his conference room then joined her several minutes later. His main objective that afternoon was to find out if she knew about the Moran paintings at Starlight Cottage. He intended to initiate the conversation in earnest, but Lucy dominated their first moments together with a wave of endless prattle.

Thompson tried to interrupt Lucy but before he could move the conversation to solid ground, she made a brazen request of him, which revealed the real reason to return to

Cody. She was in fact in Cody seeking financial gain and saw Thompson as a means to this end. She agreed to meet with Thompson, not to suit his needs, but to solicit him into going after a painting she stashed in the attic at Northridge when she was ten-years-old.

With a cold and solid stare Lucy told Thompson exactly what was on her mind.

"There's something at Northridge I'd like to have and because I'm not planning to visit my mother's home, I'd like you to get it for me."

"Go on," Thompson was leery.

"I know how much Mother trusts you with access to all of her properties. This became quite clear to me when I saw you lock Starlight Cottage this morning."

Thompson's surprise flashed across his face.

"Oh, I did see you, my good man," Lucy said sarcastically. "I saw Mother's antique key flash in the sun as you pulled it from the lock then slipped it into your pocket.

"She's already one-up on me," Thompson thought, with a new dose of infuriation.

"I'll be happy to pay your regular hourly rate plus a handsome bonus if you are able to retrieve the item I need. How would $1000 be?" Lucy was not prepared to accept "no" for an answer and reached for her checkbook.

"So that's it," Thompson said to himself. "Lucy has factored my accessibility to Kit's properties as the main element in her plot against her mother." He was incensed that she was attempting to exploit his relationship with Kit, and further, astounded she would use her family's tragedy for financial gain." He was now certain that Lucy Moran would stop at nothing.

Immediately, Thompson began to consider how to turn Lucy's scheme to Kit's advantage. While his "wheels" turned, she continued.

"You see, Thompson, I've fallen on terrible times. Desperate times, really." She lied in order to manipulate Thompson.

For Kit's sake, he decided to meet her request but planned to do so in the offense. Now, *he* would take charge.

"What's Kit holding for you, Lucy?"

"Well, I wouldn't say Mother is actually holding it, I'm not even sure she knows it's there, and I certainly don't want to disturb her now when she is going through so much. I'd like you to retrieve a small painting by Thomas J. Moran, Jr., a famous artist and distant cousin of my father's. Recently I've read that if this particular painting is found, its worth $10,000."

Thinking back to Annabelle's market-analysis and the value of *Mountain of the Holy Cross*, no matter what painting Lucy had in mind, Thompson knew she was underestimating its true worth. What little Thompson knew of fine art, he thought it was odd that she had not used either of the two highest professional classifications for a painting. The classification "mint condition," reserved for flawless works, is seldom used. Lucy did not use this term. Neither did she use near-mint condition, which is used to rate works in excellent condition.

"Apparently she's unaware of this fact," Thompson thought to himself.

While disappointed that Lucy was aware of this one painting, Thompson now had to presume that she remembered *Mount of the Holy Cross* in the dining room as well. He was not convinced however that she knew Thomas Moran's entire collection was at Starlight Cottage. Whether or not Lucy knew about Starlight's contents, the fact that she knew about John Moran at all and assumed at least one of Kit's paintings belonged to her made Thompson nervous. Further, as he looked across the table at his opposition, he realized Lucy repulsed him – quite literally. He refused however, to let his contempt for her show. This much *he could do* for Kit and Ashley.

"Does the painting you are referring to have a name?" he asked.

"Really, I don't know. I think it was a scene at Yellowstone Park. I seem to recall it had some sort of mystical quality. And I do remember something else."

"What's that?"

"I remember that Mother has always kept another painting on display at the house, it's of a mountain with a cross of snow. I think this is Moran's *Mountain of the Holy Cross,* though my mother never said so. I believe she had this painting over the fireplace for years. But I have no idea if she still has it."

Lucy was hoping Thompson would confirm the "cross" painting was still at Northridge, but he never lifted his head from his notes. By his refusal to answer this question, however she assumed the mountain painting was still hanging over the mantel.

"You probably won't think very well of me when I tell you this Thompson, but I took the Yellowstone painting from our front hallway when I arrived home alone from school one day. I was in the fifth-grade.

"Mother had been rearranging things and was so preoccupied with Daddy and neglecting me, that I took the painting out of spite. Apparently, she never noticed it was gone. Thinking back now on that period, perhaps Daddy had already received his cancer diagnosis.

"I just remember feeling so angry as I carried the painting up to the attic and placed it between the studs and main chimney."

"Nothing was ever said to you about the painting?" Thompson asked.

"Nothing. I never mentioned it to anyone, but I did speak to Daddy about it the night before he died."

"You did?"

Taking a deep breath, Lucy continued.

"Yes. I went to him in his room late at night, while Mother waited downstairs for the hospice-nurse to arrive. He looked so peaceful and I said to him, 'Daddy, I've done something terrible and I want you to forgive me. I took a painting from the hallway one day a long time ago.'"

"Did your father acknowledge you?"

"Oh, not with words. He was lucid earlier that day, so I assumed he could still hear me. In fact, I found him writing some kind of a letter on Easter Sunday morning, so I wasn't aware that the end was so near when I asked him for the painting that evening.

"I made him promise me," Lucy said.

"You made him promise you what?"

"I made him promise me that I could have the painting," she blurted out like an evil child.

"No one else was there?"

"No."

"Lucy, maybe you would describe for me exactly what you said and what your father's response was to you. Can you remember?"

"Like it was yesterday," she said without hesitation.

"I pulled the stool from Mother's vanity over to the bed and sat right beside him, so he could hear me. After I confessed what I had done, I heard him moan. Then, I told him I was sorry and I asked him for the painting.

"'Daddy,' I said, 'I want to keep the picture forever. Can I have it? Please, Daddy, please?' Then he moaned again." Clearly, Lucy was heavily invested in the dramatics of her memory.

"And *this* is how you came to believe the hidden

painting belongs to you?" Thompson asked.

"Yes, exactly." Lucy's answer was firm.

As preposterous as this explanation was, Thompson knew Kit would absolve her immediately, especially in light of the fact that Lucy was just a child when she stashed the painting during her family's crisis. Moreover, knowing Kit as well as he did, Thompson knew that if there were not so many extenuating circumstances she would most likely give Lucy the painting she described outright. However, as Kit's attorney he would advise her not to do so, if she asked.

For now, Thompson agreed to go along with Lucy's scheme to retrieve the painting she insisted was in Kit's attic. He did not want her to come to any greater understanding of the true value of the Moran painting she described, which he was now certain was well beyond what Lucy believed.

Before accepting her proposal however Thompson excused himself, returned to his office, and sent Annabelle Marsh an instant message including the scant details of the painting Lucy provided. As he stood from his desk, Annabelle's response appeared on his screen.

> *Thompson: This could be Moran's Big Springs in the Yellowstone Park — which is a bold and beautiful interpretation of the Park resting in a mystical fog. I do know already that if the painting were in "mint condition" the current market value would be $662,500. A. Marsh*

Though floored by Annabelle's response, Thompson returned to Lucy to seal the deal. His demeanor was calm and his purpose, intentional.

"I wouldn't be asking you to help me, Thompson,

unless I really had to," Lucy insisted. Even without knowing the details of her business assets or about her lucrative marriage of ten-years to real estate tycoon Adam Whaler, Thompson knew her claim was a lie. Lucy was operating on greed, not in poverty.

"I hope you won't think too ill of me, Thompson, when I tell you I know Olive Branch Ranch is worth a fortune, and that only by the goodness of my mother's tender heart would she ever include me in her estate. I've done nothing to deserve her good favor, I tell you, absolutely nothing. So I'm hoping to have the painting I've described in my hands before I leave for home for good on Saturday."

Thompson all but froze in disbelief. He listened to Lucy's outrageous plan for his retrieving the painting however and agreed to it immediately. Now that he had her confidence, he turned the tables and began to dig further, hoping to discover if she knew of the other paintings at Starlight Cottage.

"Lucy? Did you find the old cottage as you remembered?"

"Not exactly. I last saw the place in the daylight, the day before I left Cody with a couple I let stay there. Today it actually looked better than it did when I was there last. As I mentioned this morning, Mother seems to have done some repairs. The drooping gingerbread trim on the roofline and the remnant of a garden lattice near the front door are new to me. The last time I saw the place it was very rough inside, with storage boxes up to the ceiling and no furniture at all.

"I took a quick look through the windows after you and Sarah left," Lucy continued, "and noticed that even though it was thick with dust, it still looked better than I remembered. It was apparent Mother brought a few of her old things from Northridge to the cottage. To the left of the woodstove I saw the cradle she used for Sean and me."

After hearing the details Lucy offered to him, Thompson asked, "Was Starlight Cottage the last place you and your friends were before you left the ranch?"

"Yes, of course. But why would you be interested in that?" she asked. Thompson's questioning, annoyed her but still she never stopped talking.

"Mother and Seanny knew nothing of my departure. I met the couple I left with at the library one day in late July and they offered to take me to New York State for the Woodstock Festival. For their trouble, I offered them a night at Starlight Cottage."

"Ah... yes... Woodstock," Thompson said with false admiration. Lucy's excessive pride in her attendance at Woodstock left the door open for Thompson's further questions.

"I can image it took great courage to leave home to go off to the unknown – communal-life."

"Do you think so, Thomp?" By Lucy's informal use of his name, Thompson concluded she was taking his bait.

"I do. It must have been so exciting to meet these new people. What did you say their names were?" Thompson asked.

"Roy and Samantha Winters. I snuck out of Northridge about four-thirty that morning and walked along the river to Starlight. I remember it was still dark, but instead of being terrified of the dark as I thought I would be, my first taste of freedom was exhilarating. We had planned to leave from the lot out on the highway at four-forty-five and Samantha was waiting for me outside Starlight Cottage when I arrived."

"Was everyone excited?" Thompson asked hoping to get more information.

"I was the most excited as the Winters had been on the road for days. When Samantha saw me we locked arms and danced almost all the way to the car," Lucy said with a reminiscent smile. We threw our things into the back and waited for Roy who was lagging behind."

"Why had Roy fallen behind? Did he have a heavy load to carry?"

"Because of a painting, of course."

"What painting?" Thompson asked.

"I think it may have been of Venice, Italy, now that I recall. Or it could have been some other dusty old landscape by who-knows-who. All I know is that by the time Roy finally got to the car, it was almost daybreak. I was so excited about getting out of Cody that when he opened the tailgate and announced he was taking the painting I just said, 'Who cares!' I remember the rush I felt at that moment as though it happened yesterday."

Now, Thompson was afraid to go further. He was almost certain that Lucy had come home to Cody for the Thomas Moran painting in her mother's attic and seemed unaware the painting the Winters fellow took that morning was one of hundreds at Starlight Cottage. Thompson surmised by Roy Winters' decision to take just one painting, he never saw the complete collection during his overnight stay.

"Very well, Lucy," Thompson said, "I'll find a way to get into your mother's attic and have the painting waiting at the end of the memorial service Saturday, but I'll need the check for $1000 now.

"Lucy, do you have a second set of car keys?" he asked. Lucy nodded. "Give them to me please and I'll ask Brendan to leave the painting in your rental car."

Thompson grabbed Lucy's personal check with staged satisfaction, hoping to convince her he could "bought" for a price. She seemed more than satisfied with his acceptance of the deal. It simply never occurred to Lucy, it could be otherwise.

With great relief, Thompson finally ushered a satisfied Lucy Moran out of the office. He debriefed Brendan immediately on all that had transpired, dismissed his young assistant for the evening, then settled into his old, worn red leather chair to review the Moran file one more time.

"Am I missing anything?" he asked himself repeatedly. "From Sophia, to John, to Kit, are there any other specific items of value Lucy feels entitled to?" He honestly felt it was a remote possibility at best that she would be satisfied with just one painting. Further, with Kit's wealth and age Thompson knew that if he were not careful, he could be at battle with Lucy Moran for many years to come. This thought alone, made him shiver.

At that moment, Thompson realized getting Kit's affairs in order was not only a priority for Kit, but for himself as well. Satisfied with all he accomplished for one day, Thompson Smith headed home to Sarah.

CHAPTER SIX

Friday, August 28th

The sun rose in a glorious peace at Northridge Friday morning and its warm light bathed the drawn window shades in Kit's bedroom with a glow that woke her ever so gently. She slept surprisingly well and gave credit to Our Lady for filling her with the grace and peace that always led to her most restful sleep.

Rising, Kit moved to the vanity table across the room where she reread John's criteria three-times and sat quietly, turning it over-and-over in her hands. She knew it was time to face the decision she hoped never to make, which was to exclude Lucy from her estate permanently. Considering Lucy's behavior on Wednesday evening, Kit felt she could no longer delay in this matter.

"Regrettably," Kit spoke her thoughts to John in a whisper, "if I'm to adhere to your directives, which as heir to your family's wealth I feel I must, I cannot include our beautiful granddaughter Ashley as a just heir to our estate either." While in today's world such a rigid interpretation might appear flawed, Kit Moran's conscience was concise. At that moment, she was struggling between John's wishes and Ashley's future, and had no idea how to reconcile the two.

Hearing Ashley's soft steps coming down the hall toward her bedroom Kit placed John's folded criteria between the lamp and a vase at the back of the vanity. Then she quickly began to brush out her hair with the silver-plate brush John gave her for their tenth anniversary.

"Nan?"

"Hi dear, come in," Kit said, as Ashley pushed lightly on the door. Am I disturbing you?" she asked.

"Not at all, Ashley."

"The house is so peaceful this morning, isn't it Nan? The air here is so beautiful in August."

"It's absolutely lovely," Kit replied. "After sixty-years at Olive Branch Ranch I can pinpoint precisely where we are in a season, just by its feel. There's definitely a hit of fall in the air this morning."

"I think you're right," said Ashley, as she crossed Kit's room and sat on the end of her bed. Catching her granddaughter's reflection in the mirror, Kit was astounded by her radiance.

"Ashley, I've never seen you look as beautiful as you do today! Your appearance right now, is so contrary to how you should look with everything you are going through. But instead you are absolutely radiant!"

Instantly Kit recognized that some sort of extraordinary grace or blessing had touched Ashley.

She knew by her own faith experiences that God delivers His grace at the moment His children have the greatest need, and sometimes in the most extraordinary ways. "The appearance of the golden cross on *Mountain of the Holy Cross* is one such sign," Kit thought, remembering Fr. Joe's full acceptance.

"I don't know how to say this Nan, but there's something I absolutely must tell you this morning."

"What is it, dear?"

"I had a dream about Jesus last night," Ashley said with a hint of hesitancy. "No, it would be more accurate to say that Jesus came to me in a dream."

"Really? How wonderful!" Kit answered with an affirmative tone, which she hoped would open the door for Ashley to describe the experience without fear. "Tell me all about it. But before you do, please let me tell you my dear, I already believe you."

"*You do?* But I haven't told you anything yet."

"I see the radiance of Our Living Lord, Jesus Christ, all over your face this morning so I already know that what you experienced while you were asleep last night was HE."

"All I remember before Jesus came to me was a feeling that the entire ranch was bathed in a glorious peace. This is the best way I can describe it. Then it seems to me a whole scene came to life. Rather than being here at Northridge, Jesus came to me in the grassy knoll at Starlight, which makes this vision all the more mysterious.

"He walked step-by-step from the river, one beautiful Foot before the Other, to meet me exactly where I stood. With each step Jesus took toward me, Nan, the moonlight increased in intensity until an exact moment when it crossed over from night to day."

"What happened next?"

"Well, Jesus called me by my full-name Ashley Therese Moran in the clearest and most enchanting voice I've ever heard in my life – so pure and so strong. His voice was extraordinarily rich. The only way I can really describe it is to say it was instrumental. The quality of His speaking voice was so far beyond the world's greatest soloists. I can't imagine what it's like to hear Jesus sing. Can you? All of this, and the tenderness and clarity of His words, were so exceptional. What He said to me will never leave me. Never."

Outwardly, Kit's eyes never left Ashley's face as she described the scene. Inwardly however she was sharing in the delight of the very moment that Ashley found her Savior and she felt incredible consolation stirring in her own soul as well. Ashley went on.

"Then Jesus said to me, 'Ashley, I want to baptize you.' He didn't wait for me to answer, or for me to move towards Him. He took the last steps toward me and held out His Wounded Hands to take my hands in His. His

Wounds, Nan, dumbfounded me and I'm sure He knew how badly I felt when I saw them. But without my saying a single word, He said to me, *'I died for you, so that you may have life in Me. Claim this life, which was previously denied you and follow Me.'*

"Then I followed Jesus to the river and He met me there with two big beautiful Angels. One Angel held a golden pitcher full of Shoshone River water and the other a soft white towel. Jesus blessed the water and asked me, 'Do I have your full consent to baptize you, Ashley?'

"'Yes, Lord,' was all I could manage to say. Then I *could actually feel Him* read my heart and I didn't need to say anything more. From that very moment, I belonged completely to Him."

"And did Jesus baptize you, Ashley?"

"Yes, immediately. He poured the water from the pitcher over me, and said to me, 'Ashley Therese Moran, I baptize you in the Name of the Father, the Son and the Holy Spirit.' Then the Angel with the pitcher disappeared. He instructed the Angel with the towel to wipe my face and hair and then the second Angel was gone as well."

"Was there anything else?"

"Yes, for you. Before Jesus left the scene as well, He turned to me and said, 'Please tell my faithful servant Kit Moran her prayers have been answered.'"

With this, Ashley looked at Kit sitting as still as an angel herself, her eyes closed and her hands clasped as if in prayer, while fresh tears streamed down her face.

"Oh Nan, I didn't mean to make you cry! What do you think Jesus meant?"

All that Kit could say in return was, "Oh my dear child, these are tears of great joy!"

"There is something else I need to tell you, Nan. This experience left me sleepless and in utter joy the entire night. I've had time to think over what I'm going to say next, so I hope you won't think I am being impetuous."

"Ashley, I'm so aware of your sincerity at *this point* in your life that I would never challenge it, no matter what you tell me."

"I want to be baptized Catholic. It seems to me that I've already given my consent and that Jesus has baptized me spiritually. But I know the Church must baptize me just as Jesus baptized those who followed Him physically. And Nan," Ashley added, "I must do this right away."

Ashley could think of nothing but the love Jesus had given her.

"This is such a great gift of consolation" Kit thought, "and one that I could never have brought about, no matter how much I love my granddaughter."

"If this is your will, my dear, then you should be baptized just as soon as we can arrange it. There'll be some instruction necessary..." her own thoughts left her speechless. Kit reached to pull up the window shades, which were now actually holding back the light of a bright new day and then turned back to Ashley to continue their conversation. She was however surprised to see Ashley had crossed the room and was standing with the phone in hand.

"Call Fr. Joe for me, will you Nan? Tell him I want to be baptized right away and that you will bring me over as soon as we can get ready." Kit did exactly as Ashley asked her to do without uttering a single word of apprehension.

The phone at the Rectory rang without answer. Realizing Fr. Joe was already saying morning Mass, Kit hung up.

"Ashley, it's seven-ten. Father's at Mass."

"Oh," was all Ashley could say as she gazed off in disappointment. After a moment, Kit suggested they go downstairs for breakfast.

"No, you get dressed, Nan," Ashley said, giving Kit no

opportunity to object, "and I'll head over to Amour. I have a special dress over there I want to wear for my baptism. Do you think that will be okay?" she said excitedly. Then she answered her own question, "Oh, of course it is.

"I'll fly right back to pick you up."

Kit was breathless though she had not uttered a word. She knew Ashley's excitement was the work of the Holy Spirit, and not to interrupt *His plans.* Therefore she trusted Fr. Joe would have the time to meet with them. In fact, she knew that he too, would find this day a day for rejoicing. For a moment, she lost track of Ashley in the house, but then finally heard her grab her car keys off the table in the front hall.

"I'll be back in twenty-minutes, Mrs. Kit Moran, and I expect you to be ready!" Kit heard the smile in Ashley's voice.

"Life," she thought, "is still alive and well in Ashley and if everything falls into place, she will welcome Jesus into that life this very morning." Kit trusted in Ashley's stability. It was truly a hallmark of her young life, and so she had no reservations about her swift entrance into the Catholic Church. She did not have the slightest doubt that the Lord was calling Ashley personally, that very day.

"I'll be ready," she called through the opened window in her bedroom. As Ashley opened the sunroof on her car, she called up to her grandmother, "Wear something blue, Nan. You've always told me it's Our Lady's favorite color."

Kit smiled at Ashley's remembering she frequently wears blue to honor the Mother of God. At that moment it appeared her granddaughter, absorbed more of her Catholic Faith than she realized. In obedience, Kit searched her closet and found the perfect light blue suit for the occasion.

As promised, Ashley pulled the car up to Kit's front door exactly twenty-minutes later. While the door to Northridge was wide open when Ashley dashed in, Kit was nowhere in sight. "Nan?"

"Excuse me, Thompson," Kit said as she dropped the phone from her ear.

"I'm out here on the porch, dear. I'm already to go, but I'm speaking with Thompson. We'll be through in a just a moment."

"Okay," Ashley said as she showed her glistening face from the hallway. "Really, Nan. Don't rush."

"Thompson, you will *not* believe what has happened. Actually, I can't tell you at this very moment. But it's a dream that's about to come true. And I mean this quite literally!"

"I just can't imagine what could possibly have you feeling so elated today knowing the stress and sorrow you carry," Thompson said in reply.

"Would it be too much to ask you to come by Northridge, this afternoon?" she asked.

"No, of course it's not too much to ask. In fact, I would like to see you in person today anyway, so I can explain Lucy's comments from our little meeting yesterday afternoon. Then you can fill me in on your news."

"I'm hoping to send Ashley off this afternoon. We'll be dining with the Crawfords at six this evening, and I'm sure I can persuade her to rest at Amour before our evening on Logan Mountain." Kit spoke softly to ensure that Ashley could not overhear.

"Can you come for tea about two o'clock?"

"I'll be there," replied Thompson.

"See you then."

Pausing a moment alone on the porch, Kit held John's

criteria in her hand and reread it with total amazement. Then she folded it four-times over and placed it in her bag. Next, she stood and straightened her rich sky-blue suit, which was far too elegant for any Friday morning in Cody, let alone for Kit's time of mourning. In this hour however, she had reason to rejoice that Ashley, the child she had loved and prayed for since birth, was about to be baptized in Jesus Christ.

As she headed toward the front door, Ashley emerged from the kitchen in a white chiffon dress that belonged to Corrine. Sleeveless, it belted softly at the waist, and skit flared to a tea-length hem. She looked absolutely, angelic.

"Do you think Mom would approve?"

"Not only would she approve, she would be honored that you've chosen to wear her favorite summer dress."

"I can't tell you how I feel inside, Nan."

"There's no need to. It's between you and Jesus. But I'll tell you that He's given away a bit of your secret by splashing His radiance across your face.

"We should hurry now, my dear. Not only am I a bit concerned that Fr. Joe will be busy, but we shouldn't keep the Lord waiting." With this, Kit wrapped her arm about Ashley's waist and led her out to the car.

As the women pulled up to St. Anthony's Rectory, they could see Fr. Joe's car was still in the parking lot. Ashley knew that before this morning she had never given much thought to being baptized. Today however, was different. She could think of nothing else.

The spiritual encounter she had with Jesus was electrifying and miraculous as it came on suddenly and left supernatural affects. Infused by the Holy Spirit with the knowledge that she must be baptized into the Body of Christ, Ashley knew not to delay. In fact, she was so profoundly changed by the experience that a priest committed to the work of the Holy Spirit, as Fr. Joe Evers was, would know her heightened desire to belong to Jesus was not humanly possible in her present sorrow.

"Ladies!" Fr. Joe said in exclamation when he saw the Morans coming up the slate stairs to the rectory. He was shocked to say the least by the way they were dressed.

"Fr. Joe, are you busy?" Kit asked.

"You know, I always have time for both of you, especially now. I was on my way over to the hospital but there are no critical patients this morning so I can go a little later. Please, come in."

"Father," again Kit led the way, "we'd like you to come over to the church and to the altar with us. We have a very special request of you today."

"What would that be?" Father asked with some concern, but greater curiosity.

Then Ashley stepped forward and looked directly into Fr. Joe's eyes.

"Father," Ashley said, "I want to be baptized."

"Oh, Praise Jesus!" Fr. Joe quietly rejoiced. "What a wonderful grace you have received from the Holy Spirit, to be moved to enter His Church in this time of sorrow."

"Yes, Father," said Ashley.

"I'll tell you ladies, your joy is palpable. Tell me what's happened to convince you of this decision," he said as they entered St. Anthony's together. Once before the altar, Ashley told Fr. Joe all about her experience with Jesus. Kit, who held John's criteria tightly in her hands, prayed her rosary before a statue of Our Lady at the side altar. It was here, before this same altar, that she had begged Our Lady for favors for her family countless times before.

When Ashley was finished explaining her reasons for seeking baptism, Fr. Joe was convinced of her authenticity. He was more than happy to baptize Ashley, not because of her extraordinary experience, but rather because he knew Ashley was sincere in her desire to follow Jesus.

When their conversation concluded, Fr. Joe excused himself to prepare the water, oil, candle, and stole needed for her reception of the Sacrament of Baptism. Then he called the women up to the main altar. Ashley and Kit went to the baptismal font hand-in-hand.

While waiting, Fr. Joe thought how good God was for showing such profound love and consolation to each of these women in their great hour of sorrow. Then he kissed the white sacramental stole he wears for baptisms and placed it around his neck. Next, he instructed Ashley to say, "I do," each time he asked her affirmation. Then as they blessed themselves, he began the Baptismal Rite.

"In the Name of the Father, and of the Son, and of the Holy Spirit. Amen."

"Ashley Therese Moran, you have come here to the Roman Catholic Church for baptism, by water, and the Holy Spirit, you are to receive the gift of new life from God, Who is love."

"Do you reject Satan?"

"I do."

"Do you reject sin, so as to live in the freedom of God's children?"

"I do."

"Do you reject the glamour of evil, and refuse to be mastered by sin?"

"I do."

"Do you reject Satan, father of sin and prince of darkness?"

"I do."

"Do you believe in God, the Father almighty, creator of heaven and earth?"

"I do."

"Do you believe in Jesus Christ, his only Son, our Lord, who was born of the Virgin Mary, was crucified, died, and was buried, rose from the dead, and is now seated at the right hand of the Father?"

"I do."

"Do you believe in the Holy Spirit, the Holy Catholic Church, the communion of saints, the forgiveness of sins, the resurrection of the body, and life everlasting?"

"I do."

"This is our faith. This is the faith of the Church. We are proud to profess it, in Christ Jesus our Lord. Amen."

"I will now baptize you, Ashley. Come right over here in front of the baptismal font. And Kit, please take this towel and dry Ashley's face and hair once she is wet, if you will."

Taking in the joy of the moment, Kit remained speechless as she reached for the white towel.

"Now lean over the font a bit Ashley, and I will make a sign of the cross with water over you and bring you into a new life with Jesus Christ.

"Ashley Therese Moran, I baptize you in the Name of the Father, and of the Son, and of the Holy Spirit."

Kit wiped Ashley's soaking face and hair with the towel, and then Father continued the Rite, anointing the crown of her head with holy oil.

"God the Father of our Lord Jesus Christ, has freed you from sin, given you a new birth by water and the Holy Spirit, and welcomed you into his holy people. He now anoints you with the chrism of salvation. As Christ was anointed Priest, Prophet, and King, so may you live always as a member of His body, sharing everlasting life."

Next, Fr. Joe placed a baptismal stole over Ashley's shoulders and said the following prayer:

"Ashley, you have become a new creation, and have clothed yourself in Christ. See in this white garment the outward sign of your Christian dignity. With your family and friends to help you by word and example, bring that dignity unstained into the everlasting life of heaven. Amen."

Then finally, Ashley received a lighted candle:

"Ashley, this light is entrusted to you to be kept burning brightly. You have been enlightened by Christ. You are to walk always as a child of the light. May you keep the flame of faith alive in your heart. When the Lord comes, may He go out to meet you with all the saints in the heavenly Kingdom. Receive this light of Christ."

Ashley accepted the light, which only added to the brilliance radiating from her face.

"You look so beautiful," whispered Kit, as she reached to take the candle from Ashley so Fr. Joe could continue with her actual baptism by reciting the *Prayer of Ears and Mouth*:

"Lord Jesus made the deaf hear and dumb speak. May He soon touch your ears to receive His Word and your mouth to proclaim His faith, to the praise and glory of God the Father. Amen.

"Ashley, the Christian community welcomes you with great joy. In its name, I claim you for Christ our Savior by the sign of His Cross.

"I'll now trace the Cross on your forehead," Father said

to Ashley. "And Kit, I invite you to do the same." Each traced a cross upon Ashley's forehead and her baptism was complete.

As yet, Fr. Joe had no knowledge of John Charles Moran's written criteria and therefore was completely unaware of the role he had just played in God's plan for restoring Ashley's life. Kit, who was brimming with happiness over God's grace, could not wait to share her news, this incredible turn of events with Thompson, and knew he would be pleased she was now free to leave her entire estate to the only one who qualified as heir – Ashley Therese Moran.

On their way home, Kit called Thompson to ask if he could make the meeting earlier. She thought how good it was to hear him say, "I'll be right there."

In the past, joyful occasions such as a baptism in the Moran family were great times of celebration at Northridge. Sadly, these were not days for outward joy and in fact, to a certain degree, Ashley's joy began to subside on her return trip to Northridge. She felt her early-morning joy in the Presence of Jesus begin to retreat, and the reality of her parents' deaths and approaching service, settle in her soul.

"Help me, Jesus," she said aloud as she exited the car and helped Kit into the house. Kit knew exactly why Ashley had spoken these words but she remained silent. What Ashley needed was beyond Kit's power to give. Still she thanked the Lord for all that had taken place.

"I'm going home, Nan," she said to Kit, with a spirit that was almost void of its previous joy.

"I'll pick you up for dinner at the Crawford's this evening at twenty-to-six," Kit said, as Ashley walked her to the door.

"I'll be ready."

When Kit entered Northridge, she found Elaine in a state of panic and she rushed to apologize for not letting her assistant know where and with whom she had gone.

"I'm so sorry, Elaine. I should have left a note. With my car still in the yard I can see why you were worried about me."

"At first thought I was worried about you, Kit, but when I realized Ashley and her car were gone as well, I presumed you were together.

"The reason I'm so upset at the moment is the fact that Lucy was here. She left about ten minutes before you arrived."

"Lucy was here at Northridge? Did she come into the house?"

"Yes. I'm so sorry. I unlocked the front door when I brought in this morning's groceries as I always do, then I went into your office to take down a couple of phone messages so I never saw her pull in. Lucy rang the bell but before I could answer the door, she was already in the house."

"Tell me everything," Kit said.

"Come and sit down and then I'll tell you exactly what happened." As Elaine helped her employer into her place at the head of the table, she pulled out the seat to Kit's left and sat down.

"Did she look all around? Did she take anything?" Kit asked, her own sense of panic rising considerably as she waited to here of Lucy's visit.

"She did none of those things, Kit, that's what was so strange. She never went beyond this chair next to me and I thought it odd that she didn't seem the least bit interested in the interior of Northridge.

"Did she go into my office?" Kit asked, afraid she left some significant papers lying about.

"No, she didn't. I watched her until she was seated."

"What did she do next?"

"Well, she had a portfolio from which she pulled a large camera. Once seated, she took several pictures of your painting including some close-ups of Thomas Moran's signature as well. Then she put the camera away and made a couple of illustrations of some kind.

"I carried fresh linens up to your room and Lucy seemed totally oblivious to my continued presence in the house. I continued to watch her from Ashley's room and she never looked up. When she left without calling out to me, I realized she had no idea I was watching her the whole time."

"I'm so glad you've told me all of this in detail, Elaine. Although Lucy's actions are really quite bizarre, this information will help Thompson and I discern her real intentions. Lucy is slick, my dear."

"Oh, here he is now," Elaine said when she saw Thompson approaching the door.

"Come in, Thompson!" Kit motioned.

"I'll leave you two, Kit. I know you have so much to talk about."

"And much to do," Kit added with a bit of a smile. "Thank you so much for everything, my dear."

Thompson took Elaine's place at the table and he began disclosing his own news. "Kit, I have something to tell you about Lucy's intentions."

"Yes, yes, Thompson. I've just discovered that she was here at the ranch twenty-minutes ago. Elaine saw her take pictures of *Mountain of the Holy Cross* and she made some sort of illustrations as well.

"Well, with that information and the news I have to share about my meeting with Lucy yesterday, I think we'll be able to crack her "mode of operation" sooner than later. Let me ask you first though, did she go upstairs at all?"

"Elaine said no, she spent her whole time here at my table."

"Good." Naturally, Thompson was relieved. Then he began at once to explain the dreadful information he felt compelled to tell her.

"Kit, Lucy paid me $1000 yesterday to come to Northridge and retrieve what she now believes to be a Thomas Moran, painting. She claims she hid the painting in your attic when she was a young child – around the time John was diagnosed with cancer, as she recalls."

"She was ten-years-old then," Kit replied.

"Yes, I think that's the age she mentioned."

"It's not quite clear to me at this time whether she knows about your complete collection, though I don't think she does. She knows the painting she hid was by Moran and we now know she is aware that *Mountain of the Holy Cross* is still here at Northridge. Finally, she also informed me of a third painting taken from Starlight Cottage by the young couple she left Cody with."

"Did she tell you this, too?"

"She did. That morning she knew only that Roy Winters carried a painting off the premises. Eventually she noticed the painting was of Venice but seems to be unaware there was a whole collection at Starlight, and this, in spite of her visit there yesterday."

"I think this is probably true, Thompson. If she'd known about the paintings all these years, I believe she would have pressured me to give her a few after Gary Gallow died. And about Lucy's desire to hire you, I have no words to express my disgust."

"I know. What makes matters worse is that while Lucy believes the painting is worth $10,000, she is willing to take it from your property without your consent."

"Does she really believe this is *her* painting?"

"Yes, she does. She told me that she confessed to John

the night he died and asked him if she could keep it. She took his moan that evening as a "yes' and has believed ever since that the painting is rightfully hers."

"Thompson, you have no idea how irate and how violated I feel over my daughter's actions. And to think she never made amends to me and far worse that she stooped to use her brother's funeral to take something that rightfully belongs to my estate, is positively revolting."

"Had you learned about Lucy's desire for the painting some time ago would you have arranged to give it to her in your will?"

"Not if our circumstances were as they are now. But what does this matter now?

"You may feel it matters a great deal when I tell you what the painting she is after is worth on the present market," Thompson said.

"And you know this?" Kit asked.

"Yes, I inquired through Annabelle Marsh while Lucy was still in my office. If in "mint condition" Annabelle told me, it is worth $662,500.

"For Lucy to take this painting off of your property without your knowledge, regardless of how she does it is a felony. The fact that I know beforehand and will be helping her to do so will raise some legal issues, should you ever decide to prosecute. However, I don't foresee this as an issue with any balanced jury, Kit."

"Using Sean and Corrine's deaths to retrieve the painting is no less than extortion as far as I am concerned," said Kit. "What if I allow it? What if for the sake of peace I give her the painting and then deal with my grief, as I should be doing, without this unnecessary drama? Is the price of one painting too much to get Lucy out of my life forever?"

"Is this what you really want to do?"

"It is. What else can I do in my situation? Besides, it's

been many years since she's been a daughter to me. I will only hurt myself if I lament over her flawed character. One day she'll have to answer to God on her own. That's all I can say. Give her the painting."

"So be it!" Thompson said in solemn reply.

"Then I should advise you this gift to Lucy will be final if you exclude it from your will. If however, you have reason to feel that for Ashley's sake or for your own, you want the painting back, it will become a matter for the courts. In addition to a felony, I agree with you that this is extortion but to just what degree I'll need to consult a specialist in that field. You may have to prove one day that you made your decision to cooperate under duress."

"I only hope that I do not live to see the day Lucy faces what she has done to me, to Sean, and ultimately to Ashley. I will never include this in my will. I'm leaving the avenue for her to steal it open, and I know I must deal with the consequences later on should I decide to prosecute. But Lucy will *never* inherit this painting or any other from me! With your help Thompson, I'll solidify this decision as soon as we hear the results of the Marshes' appraisal.

"What I haven't told you yet," Kit said to Thompson, her whole tone of hope renewed, "is that I now have fantastic news regarding the distribution of my wealth. Early this morning Ashley qualified as the rightful heir to our entire estate by meeting all of John's criteria."

"What do you mean?" Thompson asked urgently.

To his amazement Thompson, who watched Kit's anger flare just moments earlier, witnessed her entire demeanor change to one of deep inner peace. Certainly, he was puzzled. For a moment, she sat quietly then said, "I should have told you what happened this morning as soon as you arrived."

"Told me what? Did you decide to waive John's

criteria?" he asked gently.

"No, no, not in the least. That will not be necessary because God has truly provided.

"Ashley, who still knows nothing of John's criteria, awakened from an astonishing dream about Jesus Christ this morning and insisted she be baptized immediately. We just returned from St. Anthony's. Fr. Joe baptized Ashley into the Catholic Faith, at what now appears to be the very same time Lucy came to Northridge. Apparently, the Holy Spirit motivated Ashley to desire baptism through a vision of Jesus in order to secure her future.

"And to ease your pain, Kit. *This is absolutely incredible!*"

"It's beyond incredible, Thompson," Kit said firmly. "Ashley's baptism and subsequent qualifying as John's and my rightful heir is absolutely Providential!"

When she returned to Eagle's Inn Lucy took a seat at a table by the window in her room. There she uploaded the photos from her morning expedition home to Northridge onto her laptop. In reality, her interest in Thomas Moran's work piqued several months earlier when she received a copy of *The Encyclopedia of Painting* from an acquaintance running an estate sale. The encyclopedia was the catalysis that stirred Lucy's memory of *Mountain of the Holy Cross, Big Springs in the Yellowstone Park and The Splendor of Venice*. It was of course true that she was leading Thompson on by denying she knew the name of the painting she hid, as well as the one Roy Winters stole. Frankly, she felt Thompson knew too much, about what she knew already.

In recent months, Lucy began considering various pretenses under which she could return home to learn more about her mother's paintings, but all of the scenarios she embraced seemed contrived. Sean's sudden death however offered Lucy the perfect excuse to return to Cody.

Earlier that morning, when on a brief walk through Cody proper, Lucy saw Kit and a young woman she presumed to be Ashley entering St. Anthony's Church. At that moment, she recognized a perfect opportunity to steal away to Northridge and view *Mountain of the Holy Cross* with her own eyes.

Because *The Encyclopedia of Painting* indicated "no illustration available" next to each of Moran's works, until she sat in front of *Mountain of the Holy Cross* as she had that morning, she could not be certain her mother owned the original work. Now however, she was certain and overjoyed by the fact Thomas Moran's signature on the painting was a perfect match to a copy of his signature on one of his letters in *The Encyclopedia of Painting.*

Gazing off as she watched guests enter and exit through the main door of Eagles Inn below, all of the puzzle pieces began to come together. The Smiths at Starlight Cottage, the fact that her mother had never tired of *Mountain of the Holy Cross,* and that Roy Winters most likely pulled *The Splendor of Venice* from a whole stack of Moran paintings the morning she left Cody, were leading Lucy to believe the majority of Thomas J. Moran, Jr.'s paintings were at Starlight Cottage.

"The beauty and the integrity of *Mountain of the Holy Cross* are amazing," Lucy said to herself, as she reviewed the photographs on her computer. "I never knew Mother's painting is such a gem."

Lucy was now in need of her own appraiser to authenticate her findings. She had an excellent contact in New York and left word with his assistant that she would wait for his return call. As late afternoon moved on toward evening Lucy lit a lantern on the mantel then sat and stroked her ego over what she was able to accomplish that day. Her self-adulation soon ended however as her mind wondered off to Adam and what, if anything, to tell him about the paintings.

"If Adam knows the scope of my findings," Lucy thought, "he will invade my privacy and take charge of my affairs." Until she could make this decision, she felt the less contact with Adam the better. As she looked down at her cell phone on the table, she hoped Adam would not intrude on her time alone by calling.

Thompson stood up from Kit's stately table and pushed his chair in as he helped her from her seat.

"Shall we go up to the attic?" he asked as he took Kit's arm.

"Yes, let's go have a look."

Given the facts, Thompson did not expect to hear such strength in Kit's voice, but he was pleased with her perseverance. Neither spoke on their ascent to the second floor or on their way up to the attic. There Thompson followed Lucy's instructions and found the area she described between the studs and the chimney. Moving his hand down to where he estimated a ten-year-old could reach, he found the painting.

"Here it is!" he said, as he felt through the thick dust and cobwebs covering its frame. "Now, we'll see," Kit heard him say as she handed him an old towel and Thompson gently wiped the vibrant watercolor.

"It's beautiful!" he said to Kit, after his first look adding, "as though it was painted yesterday." Kit made a second swipe over the glass.

"Just to think Lucy disturbed her father's last moments on earth to ask for this painting distresses me so. I know she was just a young woman of eighteen when John died, but she knew better. She had a conscience back then." Kit spoke softly, as she remembered a much younger Lucy, to whom she contrasted the detestable behavior of her only daughter Wednesday evening. "She had a conscience then," she said again as she shook her head.

"I know she did, Kit. I know by Sean's character and by your own that you raised Lucy with values. I am sure there is no need to remind now you that for some reason Lucy now walks in the opposite direction. Maybe if you look at her in this light, it will be much easier to have pity on her."

"That's true," Kit said in agreement. "But right now, my pity will do little to help get my estate in order. I must be strong. Actually, at the moment Ashley was baptized this morning I decided not to take these problems out of the Lord's Hands. As always when in Kit's presence, Thompson was impressed.

"Now let's move on with tomorrow's appraisal, shall we?" Thompson asked. "I'll bring *Big Springs in the Yellowstone Park* to Sarah, so she can add it to the inventory for an accurate appraisal from the Marshes when she brings them out to Starlight. Then I'll ask her to return the painting to Brendan, who will place it in Lucy's car."

"How can I ever thank you, Thompson?"

"Get some rest," he answered with care. "I promise I'll bring all this to a positive conclusion for you, Kit. Please don't worry."

"It's getting late. I think I'll get a little rest before dinner," Kit said.

"May I tell Sarah about Ashley and her incredible experience this morning?" he asked.

"You may. Ashley said so. But I can tell you that until you both hear the whole experience from her directly, you'll not understand the magnificence of God's plan."

"I'll tell Sarah, but you know she'll want to hear all of the details. And of course, she will be thrilled to know all

John's criteria are now met in Ashley as well. I'll see you tomorrow, Kit," Thompson said with an air of dread, remembering Sean and Corrine's funeral was nearly at hand.

Early Friday evening Kit and Ashley headed over to Logan Mountain for dinner with the Crawfords.

"Everyone has been so wonderful to us," Kit told Fran and Ted as they dined out on the mansion's beautiful infinity terrace carved from the back of Logan Mountain. The evening and company had a very clamming effect on both women as they faced their dread over Saturday. Each accepted a glass of wine with dinner and experienced a much-needed reprieve from the emotional tension that continued to build with each passing day.

A bit relaxed for the first time in almost a week, they engaged in the thoughtful conversation of their hosts who were very sensitive and wanted only to offer peace and comfort in their time of need.

While Kit and Ashley dined with the Crawfords, Lucy began to craft a plan to confirm that Thomas Moran's entire collection was at Starlight Cottage. As she sat looking out her window at the inn she remembered first, seeing Kit's key in Thompson's hand Thursday morning, and secondly, how well she was able to use that information against him at their meeting Thursday afternoon. When she thought of these two separate events together, Lucy suddenly had a vivid and unexpected memory of the night before she left Cody.

She remembered placing her late father's copy of that same key on a deep ledge over a window inside Kit's garage that night, just in case her plans to go east failed. With nothing on her agenda for the evening, Lucy set out for Northridge to see if – against all odds – the key was still where she left it.

When she arrived at her childhood home, luck was on her side. There were no cars in the driveway and the garage door was wide open. Moments later Lucy found herself on an old stepladder where, from the middle rung, she was able to reach the ledge above the window. She could only hope the key was still there. Much to her dismay, there were layers of greasy dirt filled with insects and rodent's waste which she removed by her bare hand. In the end however, it was really a small price to pay. On her third try, Lucy found the key.

Leaving Kit's driveway, she realized had just taken a terrible risk, which made her even more delighted in her accomplishment. Although she wanted to stop at Starlight Cottage on her way back to Eagles Inn, it was nightfall and her first view would have to wait until the next day.

"Tomorrow will be a long day," she told herself as she opened the door to her room at the inn. "It's imperative that I get out to Starlight, and then of course there is the memorial service. I'll be dog-tired when I get back to Vermont tomorrow night, but I'm sure the painting Thompson promised to leave in my car will make this entire trip back to Cody worthwhile.

CHAPTER SEVEN

Saturday, August 29th

Saturday, a day full of sorrow for all of Cody, had finally arrived. Kit and Ashley spent the morning secluded at Northridge and as noon approached, neither woman could escape the fact that it was time to say a final farewell to Corrine and Sean.

There were many acts of love on behalf of the Morans that day and each took a different shape and form. Sarah offered a special gift of love to Kit, ensuring the Marshes got out to Starlight Cottage. As she rushed to meet Annabelle and Neil at her office early Saturday morning, she pointed out Eagles Inn where they planned to stay that evening. Then she led them out to Starlight Cottage by way of Highway 20.

As the trio traveled from the parking lot toward the cottage, silver beams of sunlight danced on the river before them. The morning sun poured down on Starlight and it was really a lovely day for taking on such an incredible assignment, the Marshes told Sarah. Together they found the setting at Starlight quite charming.

When they arrived at the door, Sarah took Kit's golden-key from her pocket and unlocked the door, as Annabelle finally revealed the depth of their assignment to Neil. Neil was amazed beyond words. Seeing his life in its final years, Neil Marsh considered it a great and unexpected privilege to be the first in his profession to view Thomas Moran's original paintings. Moran's work was a great point of discussion at many an appraisers' convention over the decades they were missing. Neil knew he would be the envy of his colleagues, if he were ever to disclose this appraisal.

As Sarah shined her flashlight over Moran's works in

the closet, the Marshes could scarcely believe their eyes. Finally, Sarah opened the portfolio she had carried along to Starlight and revealed *Big Springs in the Yellowstone Park*. Then she asked the Marshes for an immediate appraisal.

Upon seeing the painting firsthand, Neil and Annabelle both confirmed that Annabelle's projected estimate of $662,500 was accurate.

With this confirmation, Sarah handed Annabelle the key to Starlight then wished the Marshes much success with their assignment. As they set about their work with their usual diligence, Neil and Annabelle both had a deep sense of compassion for the Morans and all those gathered in Cody to mourn the loss of Sean and Corrine.

Lucy entered the dining room Eagles Inn for breakfast at nine. Margie Cooper ushered her to the table Lucy and Kit shared on Wednesday night and treated Lucy Moran with the same courtesy she extended to all of her guests – not that she felt she deserved it.

Lucy appeared completely detached from her brother's death as she ate a hearty meal of strawberry waffles, fruit cup, and date-nut bread without reserve. Her ability to detach from the present hour was uncanny. The truth however, was that she felt no real sorrow for Sean.

As she enjoyed her breakfast, Lucy checked in with her office manager in Vermont. Then she contacted a few real estate clients and reviewed materials from Sotheby's Auction House in anticipation of selling *Big Springs in the Yellowstone Park*. It was important to Lucy not to lose time or focus. Several minutes later she emerged carrying the two small gray suitcases she employed for her belongings in hand and her black-portfolio over her shoulder. She checked out of room 211 on her way past the front desk. At that point, Lucy had an entire hour to spend at Starlight if she hurried.

Driving toward Olive Branch Ranch, Lucy had a fleeting moment in which she realized she still had not met Ashley. "There will be no introduction," she thought. "A casual hello this afternoon or just a nod to Sean's daughter is all I can afford. In light of her father's death, the poor thing might actually think I would want something to do with her personally. Certainly, that's nothing I'm up for and of course Adam would simply have a fit if I became involved with her."

Lucy's roots of cold-heartedness were deep-seated. Her thoughts of Ashley, Kit's obvious favorite, filled her with jealousy. It was her immediate intention however to keep her jealousy of Ashley from brewing and spilling over today.

"I can see I absolutely must avoid any kind of a scene today, for my own sake," Lucy reminded herself. "Thompson will never come to my aid if I show any negativity toward Ashley or Mother."

With all these thoughts in mind, Lucy sped out Highway 20. Navigating at excessive speed, she nearly hit a van full of children when she took a hard left into the double parking lot. As she hit the lot with force, her car slid sideways in the dirt until it came to a full stop. When she finally regained her composure, Lucy was surprised to see a late model car parked a few feet away. Her excitement over having a key to the cottage however prevented her from reasoning there might be others on the premises once again.

For Lucy's sake common sense prevailed just in time. As she neared Starlight Cottage, she heard voices. When she heard the voice of an elderly man, she was convinced the Smiths were not there this time. Next, she heard the voice of a middle-aged woman and it became quite clear she would not be able to access the cottage.

Quickly Lucy decided on an alternate plan and veered off the beaten path. Now she approached the cottage from its shaded backside, ducking branches and pulling several spider webs from across her face and hair. Rounding the left side of the cottage, she came into a bit of sunlight. Then making her way to the single window facing Northridge, she looked inside. There she saw a middle-aged woman and an elderly man standing with their backs to her.

"Where's the key?" Lucy heard the old man say to the woman.

"Oh, I just don't know what I'll do if you don't relax, Dad. One day your anxiety is going to kill me."

"I'm sorry, dear. It's just that at my age, and after a lifetime of restoration, I want to leave you with an impeccable reputation. One slip-up can do you in this business, Annabelle," the old man said.

"I know it, Dad. You've always told me that. And I certainly don't mind a gentle reminder from time-to-time, especially when working on a special case. "Here's the key," Lucy heard the woman say and she watched in disbelief as Annabelle Marsh picked Kit's golden-key up off the table and showed it to the man she had called "Dad."

At first, Lucy could not imagine what business this odd couple was conducting at Mill House, but within seconds, she spotted two stacks of framed paintings leaning against the far wall just under the window where Sarah and Thompson tied their horses on Thursday. It was obvious from the profound beauty of the paintings, and the identical style she noted in *Mountain of the Holy Cross* her hunch was correct. There were many more of Thomas Moran's outstanding works at Starlight Cottage.

With her back still toward Lucy, Annabelle raised her head quite suddenly to look out the window ahead of her and then out the door to her right. Finally, she turned to her father and said, "Dad, I have a strange feeling we are being watched."

Neil Marsh never minimized his daughter's concerns the way she did his. In fact, he found Annabelle to be a keen judge of reality and not easily shaken.

"I'm going to check outside," she said to her elderly father as she went out the front door and turned right toward Northridge. Hearing Annabelle's warning, Lucy moved quickly back in the direction she had come. Rounding the corner at the back of the house, she was out of sight before Annabelle moved in front of the window where she had just been standing.

Lucy stood behind the biggest tree in a deeply shaded area and held her breath. Seeing nothing, but not yet convinced, Annabelle continued her way around the house until she finally entered the front door again.

"I didn't see anyone," she told her father. "But I just can't shake the feeling there is someone else here. The best way I can describe it to you, Dad, is a feeling of indescribable agitation."

"I think we'll be okay," Neil said with surprising calm. "Let's get back to work now or we'll never finish by the end of the day." Clearly, Neil Marsh was not about to let anything break his focus during this most distinguished assignment.

When safely out of view from Starlight Cottage, Lucy realized it was time to head into town for the memorial service. She would be home in Vermont that evening and would begin to consider what to do with the knowledge she gained that morning. With a better understanding of her mother's incredible wealth in mind, she considered for the very first time, that perhaps she was being shortsighted by not informing her husband, Adam Whaler. "After all," she thought, "Adam's family always says, 'to catch a big fish, two Whalers are better than one.'"

At precisely noon, A.J. Lawser pulled his black limousine up to Northridge to take the Morans into town. On their way, A.J. detailed the exact timing and movement of the funeral cortege. As they entered the funeral home, he respectfully ushered the two women into a private area for their last farewell to Corrine and Sean. No sooner had he closed the main door however than did Lucy enter the room through an employee entrance.

Kit was amazed at Lucy's gall. It never occurred to Lucy that she was unwelcomed. Her extraordinarily aggressive personality, never begged her to consider the feelings of others. Rather, the only insight Lucy Moran ever possessed was the one that helped her to navigate her own selfish plans.

With much grace, Ashley came forward. "Lucy, I'm Ashley, Sean's daughter," she said quietly. Ashley's beauty and her stoicism overwhelmed Lucy.

"A fragile girl this is not," Lucy thought. "I'll have to watch out for this one." Then she stepped forward to meet her niece for the first time.

"I'm sorry about your father and mother," Lucy said as she extended her hand.

"You are not!" Kit said, breaking the silent vigil she desired before Sean and Corrine.

"Mother, how can you say that? I've come to the funeral, haven't I?"

Thinking it would be better that Lucy had not come at all, Kit wished she could make her daughter vanish.

A.J., who overheard the women, realized Lucy was present without authorization and showed her out of Blackstone Funeral Home the same way she apparently came in. It was obvious to A.J. since their initial meeting, that Kit Moran made no effort to include Lucy in the family's memorial plans. Observing Kit's intentional omission, he was confident that ejecting Lucy was in accordance with his clients' wishes. With Lucy out of the way, at last Kit and Ashley have time to say goodbye to Sean and Corrine.

A few minutes later Lawser, dressed in a tuxedo and top hat, ushered Kit and Ashley down a manicured walkway and directed them to take their place behind the horse-drawn carriage now carrying the bodies of Sean and Corrine. There was no music for the procession and that was intentional on Kit's part. Silence alone would mark the way of five-hundred or so mourners on hand to bid her son and daughter-in-law farewell. To watch Corrine and Sean honored in this low-key yet reverent way brought the Morans great comfort, and the women in turn comforted those who witnessed their courage.

The striking white ribbons that adorned the town's black lampposts touched Ashley's heart, and Kit drank in Cody proper which glistened. While it was evident that the people of Cody cared deeply about Corrine and Sean, it was difficult for Kit dismiss Lucy from her mind.

"Burden upon burden," Kit said to herself in a moment of helplessness. "At least Ashley will have nothing to worry about as far as the ranch is concerned," she added as she thought back to the extraordinary events of the last few days.

Although only a couple of minutes had passed since the cortege left Blackstone, Kit's tears had already begun to fall to her toes for Sean and Corrine. As the cortege entered the high school grounds, the orchestra, band, and scores of mourners joined them as well. Kit tried desperately to maintain her composure as the crowd grew in around her. Suddenly she heard Lucy crying out, "M-o-t-h-e-r!"

Lucy pushed her way to the head of the line and caused

a great commotion as she did so. Finally, she succeeded in arriving at Kit's side and took her mother's left arm with her right. When Ashley realized Lucy had wormed her way to Kit's left side, she increased her support to Kit's right.

"Mother, let me sit with you in the gym, would you please?" Lucy pleaded. Lowering her head down to Kit's, she muffled her further plea. "I cannot bear to be seen as an outsider – not now when you need me." Kit was stunned into silence and Ashley who overheard these comments held fast to her grandmother. "She can do as she wants, as long as there is no scene," Kit thought.

Lucy's behavior infuriated Kit, but when the carriage ahead paused for a moment at Cody High's science building in honor of Sean, she experienced some relief. Thompson and Sarah used that moment to slip in line directly behind Kit and each put a hand upon her shoulder. Their presence offered immediate calm and the couple remained beside her the entire afternoon.

Upon entering the gymnasium, A.J. Lawser led the mourners past Sean and Corrine's caskets and across the room to the bleachers. A row of seating in front of the bleachers was designated for immediate family and friends. Moving quickly to the end of the row, Thompson counted out five seats for their group and was intentionally short one, forcing Lucy to the first row of bleachers. Initially she made a fuss, but Thompson's glare, shocked her into silence.

Ashley sat in awe of the great numbers of people in attendance, including many of her former classmates from Cody and present classmates from the University of Wyoming, some of whom had come great distances to share in her sorrow. She was particularly grateful to her three suite-mates, Megan, Shawna and Jen for wrapping up their summer studies abroad a week early, to be with her.

Her favorite psychology professor Mr. Martin and her advisor Ms. Crowell came from the University. All of her mother and father's colleagues, many of whom Ashley had as teachers in the Cody schools, were also present. In addition, of course, Olive Branch Ranch employees and associates including the Lewiston family: Jake, Rita, Patrick and Michael were among the mourners as well.

When everyone was finally in place and hushed into silence by Ted Crawford, the Grand Teton Orchestra began the memorial service with *Amazing Grace*. Then, alternating with the Cody High School Band, the musical ensembles played *On Eagles Wings, How Great Thou Art* and several other selections between readings from Sacred Scripture and the two minutes set aside for silent prayer. Finally, the couple's eulogy included various friends who all did an outstanding job in leaving the mourners with loving memories of both Sean and Corrine.

Kit thought of young Dylan Bates several times throughout the memorial service and readily included him and his family in her prayers. She thought the boy who caused the Morans' deaths would also be suffering greatly that day. As her sorrow grew for Dylan, and for Ashley, Sean, and Corrine, Kit felt insurmountable grief.

Ashley's experience at her parents' memorial service however was completely different. She, of course carried the greatest grief by the loss of both father and mother, so the Lord once again gave her special graces. During silent prayer, Jesus came to Ashley once again and a deep feeling of peace engulfed her. This time He entered her life through the depths of her conscious prayer.

"I Am the Bread of Life. I will give you strength," Ashley heard Jesus say within her heart. Suddenly she felt a flood of warmth in the depths of her being, and although she could not understand the meaning of the words Jesus

spoke, she was certain He etched them right into her soul.

Hearing these words within, Ashley opened her eyes to see the gymnasium filled with radiant light. The flowers she had instructed A.J. Lawser to lay upon each casket were more beautiful than if picked just minutes before.

From her experience of "meeting" Jesus at Starlight Cottage, Ashley was certain something supernatural was happening to her, yet again. This time Jesus did not provide her with an answer. For now, He would leave this precious child without a clear understanding of what He was doing in her soul.

As she ended her silent prayer Ashley heard a soloist, accompanied by the Grand Teton Orchestra, sing the *Ave Maria*, a tribute to the Mother of Jesus. Moments later Fr. Evers led the coalition of ecumenical ministers and rabbi in a final blessing over the congregation. Before she knew it, the Cody High School Band played the dismissal song *America the Beautiful* as A.J. Lawser led the mourners from gymnasium.

As Ashley took her place beside Kit in the cortege, she was well aware that Jesus had lifted her spirits once again. With certainty, she knew there was tremendous grief ahead, but she also knew that with the help of her Savior, she would not fall into despair – not today or any day in the future.

The memorial service, affected Kit too, but in different ways. The beauty of the ceremony and in the number of mourners who had come for Sean and Corrine touched Kit deeply. On a deeper level, she was able to find some relief in knowing that it would not be long until she would be with her Seanny again.

While Kit and Ashley had resumed their places in the cortege, Brendan Snyder noticed Lucy was deep in conversation with two women he did not recognize. To his relief, the women soon excused themselves to join the other mourners, which gave Brendan an opportunity to get control over Lucy.

"Come with me, Ms. Moran," young Snyder insisted, as he took Lucy's arm and led her firmly. "If you stay with me, I'll take you to your car after your brother's internment." Then placing Lucy's extra car keys in her hand to assure her he was in fact involved in her "transaction" he added, "I've left the package Thompson prepared for you on the backseat."

"Oh, Brendan, you are a friend for life! How can I ever thank you for supporting me in this walk over to Riverside Cemetery? I'm afraid without your help I might be overcome with grief today."

"Liar!" Brendan said to himself. "What a wonderful tribute this memorial service is to your brother and sister-in-law," he said as he stretched to control his anger.

"Yes, isn't it though," Lucy replied. She and Brendan finally turned the corner from Yellowstone Avenue into Riverside Cemetery, as the mourners gathered in around the caskets for benediction. "I don't see my car, Brendan," Lucy said with concern. Brendan pointed to her car at the second gate of the cemetery where he backed it in at the head of the line.

"Oh, thank you. You are a dear," Lucy said with an air of relief. "Let's stop right here if you don't mind," she added as she moved toward the shade of a large cottonwood tree some fifty-feet away from the burial site.

Although Brendan was surprised Lucy prevented them from moving to her brother's grave, he said nothing as the moment of silence at the graveside had begun. During the brief benediction, Lucy simply stared ahead at the mourners. The moment she saw the group relax at the internment's conclusion, she asked Brendan to take her to her car. Brendan shuttered in relief as he finally watched Lucy Moran drive away.

By late Saturday afternoon, Annabelle and Neil Marsh had completed the physical inventory of all the paintings at Starlight Cottage. Noting the three paintings not included in their physical inventory, *Mountain of the Holy Cross, Big Springs in the Yellowstone Park,* and *The Splendor of Venice*, they were able to account for all of Thomas J. Moran, Jr.'s named works, and then some.

"Perhaps we can come out to Northridge to see *Mountain of the Holy Cross* tomorrow, Dad. That is, if Mrs. Moran is up to having us come by."

"We can only hope, my dear," Neil replied.

After returning every painting and illustration to the closet in an orderly manner, Neil and Annabelle locked Starlight Cottage tight. On their return walk to their car, they agreed it would be a great honor to represent Kit on the open market, should she ever decide to sell Moran's work.

"There is time for Mrs. Moran to decide all this later, my dear. For now we have completed our professional assessment, the only job we have been offered thus far."

"How right you are, Dad," said Annabelle who was completely gratified with the assignment at hand.

Later that afternoon, Sarah called Kit to relay the Marshes' findings. "Annabelle and Neil Marsh have just reported to me that they can account for all of Moran's paintings including *Mountain of the Holy Cross*, in your possession; *Big Springs in Yellowstone Park*, which they appraised before Lucy took it home to Vermont; and *The Splendor of Venice*, which we now know was removed from Starlight by Roy Winters the morning Lucy left home."

"This is amazing, Sarah. Do you mean that with exception to *The Splendor of Venice*, I have had Moran's entire life's works here at the ranch all this time?"

"Indeed you have," Sarah said. "As we know, the

Marshes haven't seen *Mountain of the Holy Cross* yet, but even as the amateur in the group, I've assured them they'll find this painting in near-mint condition as well. I've suggested they might view *Mountain of the Holy Cross* early tomorrow afternoon, before they return home to Casper."

"How's one sound? Would you ask them?" Kit suggested.

"I'm sure that will be fine. They will stay here in town tonight in order to produce their report. I'll offer them the use of my office tomorrow morning. And Kit, there's something else I think might be of interest to you."

"What's that, my dear?"

"By coincidence, Annabelle Marsh has just checked into Room 211 at Eagles Inn."

"Is this significant?"

"211 is the same room Lucy checked out of this morning. Annabelle confirmed this with the front desk when she came across some "evidence" Lucy left behind in the desk drawer."

"What evidence?"

"Apparently, she left several pages of notes in the desk. It seems she made these notes while she was seeking an approximate value of *Big Springs in Yellowstone Park* while on the phone with an appraiser from Sotheby's in New York. Do you think Lucy has uncovered the span of your collection?"

"I hope not," Kit said, "but then again who knows what Lucy really knows."

"Well, I guess we'll know eventually," Sarah sighed. Then she continued, "There's something else I'd like to mention before we hang up."

"Go ahead, dear."

"Well, Thompson and I would like to ask if we may join you and Ashley at Mass tomorrow morning."

CHAPTER EIGHT

Sunday, August 30th

Before retiring on Saturday evening, Annabelle Marsh left the notes she found at Eagles Inn in the Smiths' mailbox. Early Sunday morning Thompson found Sarah reviewing Lucy's every mark on three double-sided pages as she sat over coffee in their mahogany breakfast nook, the centerpiece of their modern black and white kitchen.

"There you are," Thompson said to Sarah.

"Yes. Here I am," Sarah replied, as she smiled at her husband.

"What have you got there, Sarah?" he asked referring to the papers on the table.

"These are Lucy's notes from Eagles Inn," Sarah answered. Thompson reached for his wallet on the black granite counter-top where he placed it the previous evening.

"Here's her check, Sarah. It's obvious my handwriting specialist is not necessary this time. Have you made anything of her notes so far?"

"Well, apparently Lucy put together this list of *Hudson River* artists for some reason," Sarah said as she showed Thompson the list. "I'd guess that she was discussing this list with someone on the phone, wouldn't you?"

"Yes, because look, Thomas Moran, Jr.'s name is second to the last on the list."

"What do you think this means?" Sarah asked her husband.

"Well, I would say Lucy wanted to discuss the Moran paintings with an appraiser but at the same time wanted to make sure she showed no greater interest in Moran's work than in the works of the others listed."

"Apparently she contacted someone at Sotheby's New

York location," said Sarah.

"You're right. There is New York area code, 212."

"Look Thompson, she also scrawled Ashley's name on the second page along the rooftop of a house. Oh, look, this seems to be a sketch of Amour and the Centre at Olive Branch Ranch."

"It certainly does. What else is there?" Thompson asked as he began thumbing through the notes Sarah was done with. The final drawing he reviewed was a drawing of Northridge, over which Lucy had scrawled her own name.

"No matter how true our other suspicions about Lucy's motives for returning to Cody for Sean's funeral, Sarah, now we must be certain to include Northridge as well. It seems to me Lucy has the desire to claim Kit's home."

"We must be sure to let Kit know what we've discovered when we meet with her this afternoon," said Sarah.

"And I'll get busy tying up the Moran estate from my angle so there is no way possible for Lucy to become Kit's natural heir," Thompson added.

"Thompson, do you think Ashley knows anything about Thomas Moran's collection yet?"

"As far as I know, not yet."

"Do you think Kit will tell her soon?"

"I'm not sure what her exact plans are," said Thompson, "but I'll certainly advise her to do so any time now, whenever she feels it's best or necessary. Are we going to meet them for Mass this morning?" he asked.

"That's the plan. Then we'll all meet with Neil and Annabelle at Northridge.

When the Moran women rose at Northridge, Kit found Ashley to be in much better spirits than she expected the day after her parents' funeral. It was not that Ashley was lighthearted by any means, but there seemed to be something "extra" keeping her afloat.

"It's grace," Kit reminded herself, as she thought back to just some of many times God prevailed in her own troubles. "I can see He has blessed Ashley with an inordinate amount of grace and has also given her the hope she needs to carry on – at least for today."

On the way into town for Sunday Mass, Ashley hinted she had a second extraordinary experience with Jesus. This time however, she felt less comfortable sharing with Kit, the words she believed Jesus had spoken to her heart during the memorial service. While certain she had experienced the exceptional love of Jesus one more time, on one hand, the timing of such an experience, right in the middle of her parents' memorial service, left Ashley feeling somewhat bewildered, on the other.

With Ashley at the wheel, Kit's thoughts turned to Lucy's intrusion in the funeral possession, and she knew she must find a way to finalize the death of her relationship with Lucy. "It has to end today," Kit told herself. "Lucy has sealed her own fate with regard to any inheritance of her family's wealth." Accepting this truth into her heart, all Kit really needed to do now was make it legal. Then she could look forward to her coming years with Ashley.

When Father Joe Evers began the processional song for Holy Mass, the Moran-Smith foursome experienced a whirlwind of emotions. God had called all four to Himself that morning, even while they drifted in and out of their pressing thoughts and prayers. Thompson and Sarah were so happy to be back in Church and looked forward to receiving the Sacrament of Reconciliation at a meeting already scheduled with Fr. Joe for Monday evening. Clearly, they wanted to receive Holy Communion that morning, but recognized that doing so without God's forgiveness for their sins, was a true sacrilege – an insult to the Lord.

Ashley's mind moved back and forth, dancing between the joys Jesus had granted to her soul and her all-consuming sorrow in the loss of her parents, until Fr. Joe signaled for the congregation to rise for the reading of the Gospel. At last, she was able to settle her mind. Then to her great surprise, Ashley heard the exact words Jesus had spoken to her at the memorial service: *Jesus' Discourse*, John 6:34, *"I Am the Bread of Life..."* *

Her heart leapt at these words. Fr. Joe's homily explained the life that Jesus wants all to have in Him, and the fact that receiving the Holy Eucharist in the state of grace will feed the soul the Body of Jesus, which he said is necessary for a strong spiritual life. While she knew the words were the same as those she heard Saturday, Ashley was uncertain exactly how to discern this additional gift from the Holy Spirit – the fact that Sacred Scripture revealed this reading to her for the second day in a row.

"Nan, I'd like to catch Fr. Joe for a moment," she said at the conclusion of Mass. "Would you mind asking Thompson and Sarah to take you home?"

"Of course not, dear," Kit said. Secretly Kit was relieved she would have time to speak with the Smiths and the Marshes without Ashley being present.

"Then I'll go to Amour to see Cocoa," Ashley added. "I've decided to stay with you a more few days, if that's okay."

"Absolutely. I'll see you when you get home," Kit said as she left the church with the Smiths.

"May I tell you something, Father?" Ashley asked Fr. Joe, as she initiated what she thought would be a difficult conversation.

"Anything," Fr. Joe said kindly.

"I heard Jesus speak, *'I Am the Bread of Life,'* during my parents' memorial service yesterday."

"I know this phrase was in today's Gospel, if you recall," Father said.

"Yes, I do," said Ashley, "but I need some help with this if you don't mind, Father. Exactly what do these words mean?"

"Well, Jesus spoke these words to the crowd when they discovered Him in Capernaum," Fr. Joe answered. He was disclosing the fact that He was their Savior and through Him, by the Power of His Precious Body and Blood in the Eucharist, they would never hunger again.

"Father, I'd never heard these words in my life before yesterday, but I just heard them again today – the very next day," Ashley said with a touch of astonishment.

"Of course, that makes perfect sense to me," Father continued. "As you told me earlier this week you've learned nothing of the *New Testament* readings so far. Am I correct?"

"Yes, that's true. I heard these words for the very first time yesterday, when Jesus spoke them to me."

"During the silent prayer?"

"Yes. He spoke these as clear as day within me, during the moments of silent prayer. Then to these words, he added, 'I will give you strength.'"

"Well then, case closed," Fr. Joe, said as he clapped his hands together.

"What do you mean?" Ashley asked.

"What I mean, my dear, is I'm convinced that Jesus spoke to you once again."

"Thank you, Father," Ashley said with complete relief. She knew that if he doubted her in any way she might just break. Instead of diminishing her experience as a less spiritual priest might do Fr. Joe continued in a most positive way.

"Ashley, the Holy Spirit has already confirmed for me that you have received this second gift from Jesus."

"He has?"

"Yes. The Holy Spirit gives these confirmations quite often, actually, but most never bother to take note of His Works."

"How has the Holy Spirit confirmed this to you?" Ashley asked.

"Well, the cycle of readings we heard at Mass today were set years ago. I did not select *Jesus' Bread of Life Discourse* reading this morning, on a whim, but rather it is the Gospel at Sunday Mass today, all over the world. In discerning this movement of the Holy Spirit in your life, Ashley, it's important to examine the fact that you were completely unaware of this Gospel.

"To put it another way, the day Jesus whispered these words, which were previously unknown to you – *He knew* they would be read at Holy Mass the following day. It's only by God's Power that you could have received such a gift. And I say to you too, it's a true gift that only those who live by the Power of the Holy Spirit can confirm and truly appreciate."

"Can you confirm this for me, Father?"

"Without question. Those who allow the Holy Spirit the privilege of presiding over their lives learn that to receive words from Jesus one day, and to hear them again the next, especially in Holy Mass is truly a gift from God – a gift to believe in and through which to allow the soul to grow."

"Of course I've never known such a thing could happen," Ashley said.

"All the better reason to treat this as an extraordinary grace from God, Ashley."

"Fr. Joe, can you tell me why Jesus said these specific words to me?"

"I can. In the very same way the Lord brought you to the baptismal font just a few days ago, He is now bringing you to His altar."

"Yes, I have come to His altar, Father."

"You came to be baptized Ashley, and came again to Holy Mass today, but God is calling you to His altar quite literally to receive His Son – the Bread of Life. Your Heavenly Father wants you to live again. In addition, Jesus is assuring you, you'll be able to go on without your mom and dad if you allow *Him to* be your strength. Jesus wants you to receive Him in the Eucharist, to come to Him in Holy Communion often."

"Oh, now I see. When should I come to Holy Communion? Tomorrow?" Ashley asked in innocence.

"Well, you need to prepare, my dear. Unless the Lord leads you otherwise, we'll plan your First Holy Communion for some day in the next few weeks. Let me get back to you with a date."

"That sounds wonderful," Ashley answered with obvious rejuvenation.

"We'll meet again soon. Then we'll go over a few teachings for your First Holy Communion and discuss the details of your big day," Fr. Joe concluded.

"Until then, I'll look forward to receiving Jesus for the very first time," Ashley said. "And Father, I know Jesus will keep His promise to give me strength. I feel stronger already."

With this, Ashley wished Father Joe a good day and headed out to Amour to pack a few more things for her return to Northridge.

The Marshes car was already in the driveway when Thompson pulled into Northridge.

"I hope Elaine has made Neil and Annabelle comfortable," Kit said, with her usual concern for hospitality.

"Without a doubt she has," Sarah added, affirming her high regard for Elaine Cain.

There were the customary introductions once everyone had gathered in Kit's dining room. Then Elaine quietly took leave for the day, assuring Kit she would be in early Monday morning.

The news Kit was about to hear from the Marshes would astound her. Neil Marsh's handwritten report of ten doubled-sided pages, listed approximately twenty-five of Moran's works on either side of each page. As the group sat huddled in the dining room, the Marshes showed the trio they were able to account for all but one painting on Marcus Moran's original inventory.

While bypassing *Mountain of the Holy Cross,* the appraisers presented Starlight's inventory for thirty-minutes, calling each of Moran's works by name and giving an estimated value for each line item including $292,775 for *The Splendor of Venice* if found.

"Kit," Neil said solemnly as he tried to hide his elation, "Annabelle worked feverishly last night and this morning to assign the current market value to every work," he said as he passed the entire list to Kit. Together we have concluded that in the present market your collection, excluding *Mountain of the Holy Cross,* is worth a staggering $75,000,000," he said.

"This is absolutely incredible news, Kit," Thompson said. His excitement of course was two-fold. Just being part of Kit's private revelation of this lost piece of Americana was a poignant discovery in his present sorrow. Then, with Kit having received an actual dollar-value for this part of her estate from certified appraisers, he could now proceed with an initial transfer of her assets to Ashley for protection, if Kit was ever incapacitated. This transfer would allow Ashley the power to officiate over business at Olive Branch Ranch, and at the same time protect the Thomas J. Moran collection. At last, Thompson would be able to offer Kit the greatest consolation he possibly could during this devastating period in her life – a new will.

"Oh, my dears," Kit said to Annabelle and Neil, "How *am* I ever to thank you?"

With this Neil moved toward Kit, his contemporary and said, "No, Kit, we thank *you*. I do especially for the great privilege of reviewing Thomas J. Moran, Jr.'s work firsthand. This assignment has been the experience of my lifetime, at the very end of my long career.

"Now, let's look at *Mountain of the Holy Cross*, specifically," Neil said, as he pointed to the famous painting. "Like a fine wine, the best has been saved for last." Neil paused as he gazed thoughtfully on the gold cross in the mountain, and then turning to Annabelle at his left side excused himself from the others for a moment in order to speak with is daughter "privately."

"I'm certain the Whitney Museum's information stated that the cross on the mountain is snow white," Neil said softly, referring to the famous Whitney Museum in New York City, their frequent guide.

"Excuse me, Neil," Kit said, as she broke into their conversation. "The cross was white, that is, until this past Thursday."

"I'm sorry Kit, I don't understand."

"We don't either, Neil," Thompson joined in to relieve Kit. "That is, we don't understand how it happened, but we understand why." Thompson went on explain Thursday's events to the Marshes and they were amazed. It was their belief however, that in the negative era of spiritual events in the world, the value of the painting would not change in any way.

"The current market value for *Mountain of the Holy*

Cross is $4.9 million," Annabelle told Kit, "giving you a grand total of $79,900,000 for the entire collection."

After bidding the Marshes good-bye, Kit turned to Thompson and asked him to change her sole heir from Sean to Ashley, effective immediately. Then Thompson assured Kit that her signature on her new will would become binding as soon as her pen left the page. "I'll bring it out to you by then end of the day."

"Thanks so much," Kit said to Thompson. "I will also be informing Ashley of her cousin's collection of paintings today as well," Kit told her friends. "Because Lucy's intentions and her entire life really, seem to be shrouded in a lack of integrity, I simply must protect Ashley and myself from any future antics she may be planning."

"I really know so little about her," Kit said sadly. "Therefore, I simply must treat her as a threat to my estate."

"Kit, this is exactly what we were hoping you would do," Thompson said.

"A million thanks to you both," Kit said as she kissed each one.

"Sarah, you've given so much of yourself to us in this matter as well. I will never be able to repay you, my dear."

"Kit, the privilege of knowing you, is all the thanks I'll ever need."

When she arrived back at Northridge, Ashley found her grandmother reviewing some sort of report spread out over the dining room table.

"Nan, I'm surprised to see you working here alone," she said to Kit.

"Oh, the others just left."

"Others? I know Sarah and Thompson planned to stay

for a while. Did you have other guests, too?"

"No. Not exactly guests, Ashley. Please come and sit down with me. There is business I must share with you that absolutely cannot wait. Well, I should say for me it is business, but for you, dear, at long-last I want to reveal the mystery of Starlight Cottage."

"Starlight? You're finally going to tell me about Starlight? Oh, Nan, *tell me everything!*"

Kit noted an unexpected vibrancy in Ashley and once again, she knew God's grace was at hand.

"Come sit down here beside me," Kit suggested. Ashley sat at Kit's left, facing *Mountain of the Holy Cross*.

"What *is* this, Nan?" she asked when she saw the inventory spread out at an angle before her.

"This is a line-item inventory. It's actually an inventory of the complete works of landscape artist Thomas J. Moran, Jr., your distant cousin."

"I'm confused, Nan," Ashley said to Kit. "I thought you wanted to talk about Starlight."

"*This is* the mystery of Starlight Cottage, my dear child. Your grandfather and I inherited over five-hundred works of art: graphics, watercolors, oil paintings and many sketches too, beginning the day of our wedding reception in 1949. Thomas J. Moran, Jr. was a distant cousin of your Grandpa John and a famous American Landscape artist of the late 1800 to early 1900's."

"Is this some sort of assessment you're looking at Nan, to see what *this* painting is worth?" In her present state, Ashley found it necessary to scale down Kit's revelation. Without consciously doing so, she tuned out the inventory and asked Kit specifically about *Mountain of the Holy Cross*. As she looked at the painting before her, Ashley noticed for the first time that the cross was no longer white – but sparkling gold.

"Nan, *what* is going on with the cross on the mountain?" she asked.

"It's seems it's another miracle, Ashley. It just appeared on Thursday when Fr. Joe brought me the Eucharist. We can talk more about that experience a little later. Perhaps the Lord hid it from you until now for a reason. Let's put first things first, my dear. I want to answer your question about the value of this painting, and then move on with my story about Starlight Cottage. Stunned by the gold cross, Ashley had a difficult time keeping her eyes off the painting.

"First, I do have a realistic estimate of what *Mountain of the Holy Cross* is worth on today's market. It's worth $4.9 million dollars. Sarah introduced me to a father and daughter fine arts appraisal team, Neil and Annabelle Marsh, and they gave me this figure. The Marshes came to see *Mountain of the Holy Cross* today which concluded a complete evaluation Sarah supervised yesterday at Starlight Cottage."

Ashley was surprised that Kit conducted business on the day of her parents' memorial service. She deferred to Kit's judgment however, when she learned her grandmother was trying to protect the Moran estate from Lucy.

"Well, hopefully, there's nothing more to worry about, as far as Lucy is concerned," Kit told Ashley. "Lucy's gone."

"Gone?"

"Yes, she flew back to Vermont last night."

"Brendan Snyder assisted her to her car and then watched her leave for the airport."

"Brendan? Why would he be involved with Lucy's departure?"

"Well, he was helping Thompson and me, and you as well, though you didn't know it. Brendan was helping all of us to see that Lucy left town with what she came for."

"I'm sorry, Nan, but I just don't know what you are talking about."

"All that I can offer you now, dear, is the simplest of explanations. These pages in front of us are an inventory of over five-hundred works of Thomas J. Moran, Jr. With the exception to just two missing paintings: *The Splendor of Venice*, taken years ago by an acquaintance of Lucy, and *Big Springs in the Yellowstone Park*, which I gave to Lucy yesterday, every painting is here at Olive Branch Ranch."

It was obvious to Ashley, Kit did not plan to offer an explanation regarding her apparent generosity toward Lucy, and so she decided to forego any kind of inquiry.

"At Sarah's recommendation, I hired Annabelle Marsh and her father Neil who are renowned appraisers from Casper. The Marshes worked through last night and provided an assessment of every piece listed here before leaving town.

"Thompson took a copy of this inventory from Annabelle this afternoon and he's having Brendan digitize the list for a permanent record as we speak."

"Sadly," Ashley said, "I don't know anything at all about Thomas Moran's work. I remember that my dad hinted of our connection in the past, but as far as I can remember, he never really made much of it."

"Nor would Sean really, Ashley. I never said much of our connection to Thomas Moran, to Sean. I was afraid he would have questions I simply I did not want to answer. You see, I didn't take care of the collection as I should have and over the years this caused me incredible anxiety."

"Do you mean my dad didn't know about the collection?"

"Not about the entire collection per se, though if I had

had the chance to mention it, I'm sure he would have had some memories. I was planning to tell all of you on your 21st birthday, in October. Over the last year, I had been thinking that we could decide what to do with the paintings as a family.

"Now there's one final thing I must tell you. Despite not having been in a controlled environment, the paintings are in the best possible condition. In terms of the collection, Ashley, I've learned that every drawing or painting is in near-mint condition. In its entirety, the collection may bring $79, 900,000 at auction. You see my dear, the paintings are the secret of Starlight Cottage."

In spite of the women's extraordinary news and their labored grieving, peace surrounded Northridge well into that evening. Just before nine, Thompson and Brendan finally rang the front doorbell and stepped inside. After Brendan and Ashley were introduced, Thompson got right down to business. He asked Kit to sign, and Brendan to witness, all the documents he prepared with exception to her new will. Then he dismissed Brendan and Ashley so he could explain everything to Kit in greater detail.

"Put on the water for tea would you please, Ashley?" Kit's voice followed Ashley to the kitchen. "Perhaps while you're out there, Brendan would like something to eat."

"Please have a seat," Ashley suggested to Brendan, as she pulled a stool from under the counter. Would you like tea or something cold to drink?"

"I'd love something cold, if you don't mind."

Ashley appreciated Brendan's company and clearly, he welcomed hers. They had several mutual topics of conversation between them including the University of Wyoming where Brendan also did his undergraduate work, prior to receiving his law degree that spring.

As the two continued their easy conversation, Ashley gave nothing more than a fleeting thought to a call that interrupted Kit's meeting with Thompson.

"Hello," Kit said to the "Private Caller" listed.

Immediately Thompson read emotional distress on Kit's face, and heard Lucy's voice from where he was sitting. He could not believe Lucy called at the very moment Kit was casting her out of the Moran estate forever.

"Is there something you need, Lucy?" Kit was curt and obviously trying to get to the motive behind Lucy's call.

"Well, first I wanted to see how you are tonight, Mother. Sean and Corrine's funeral was beautiful, but it must have been such a strain on you."

"I'm managing," was all that Kit could say to this inquiry. She was careful not to disclose her true feelings.

"Mother, I've been thinking since yesterday."

"Yes? What about?"

"I would like to ask your forgiveness."

"Forgiveness? What do you mean?"

"Mother, I'd like to return to your good graces."

Thompson watched Kit's face redden with great concern. Although he could not hear Lucy's proposal, Thompson pushed the signature page of Kit's new will in front of her.

"Go on," Kit said to Lucy, as she reached for her pen and signed where Thompson indicated.

"I mean, if you can find it in your heart, I want to come back and spend some quality time with you. I am so, so, sorry for all of the hurt and pain I've caused you, Mother. I want to make it up to you."

"Lucy, I forgive you. However, as far as your coming back into my life in any way that will not be possible. Actually, I didn't want to interrupt you, but I must go now. Thompson Smith is helping me with some details that need my immediate attention."

Lucy, confounded by Thompson's presence at her mother's side especially at that hour, knew she must not comment or she might harm any chance she had left to reconcile with Kit. She held her tongue.

"All right, Mother. But please remember me. I'll talk to you soon."

When Kit hung up the phone, she told Thompson the details of the call.

"...Then she said, 'Please remember me.' How strange. Thompson, are you thinking what I'm thinking?"

"Precisely, Kit. That's why I signaled for your signature. I need to protect you from Lucy and I must make this point absolutely clear.

I know Sarah mentioned that Annabelle stayed in the same room Lucy did at Eagles Inn, and in the desk drawer, she found an illustration Lucy made and labeled. Lucy actually scrawled her name over a sketch of Northridge. There's no other way to explain this notation except by concluding Lucy wants your home. I'm sorry to break this news to you."

"I should have known," Kit said as she stood.

"Oh before you go, let me give you John's original criteria for our file."

"Absolutely," Thompson said, as he waited for Kit to retrieve the four-cornered paper she had been holding close to her heart the last few days.

"It looks as though they're through," Brendan said to Ashley.

"Oh, Ashley," Kit said, as she and Thompson made their way to the kitchen, "now I can rest in peace."

"Just as soon as Brendan signs as witness to your will." Brendan followed Thompson's directions. "There, now you are set. Yes, we've made all things legal tonight," Thompson, confirmed.

"Ashley, I've put Kit's mind at ease concerning any possibility that Lucy will be able to go after the Moran assets. Kit will explain everything to you," Thompson said adding, "but perhaps, that should all wait until the morning."

"I think you are quite right about that," Kit agreed.

"Brendan, thank you for all of your hard work and especially for seeing Lucy off."

"It all worked out well, Mrs. Moran. I just moved her in the direction we needed her to go. Really, she seemed quite willing to cooperate. I think her thoughts were on..." Suddenly, Brendan hesitated to mention, *Big Springs in the Yellowstone Park*, not wanting to hurt Ashley further by her aunt's outrageous lack of sympathy over her parents' deaths.

"We'll get all the copies of your signed documents everywhere they need to go, Kit. Now get some rest, my good woman," Thompson said lovingly.

As soon as the men departed, Kit gave Ashley a gentle kiss and headed off to her bedroom. Once both women were in bed, she called down toward Ashley's room. "Things have all worked out, Ashley. Remember my dear, *always let God unfold His Plan around you.*"

"I will. I promise. I love you, Nan. Sleep well."

"I love you too, my child. Good night and May God bless you, always."

Lucy made her second call to Sotheby's Auction House on Sunday afternoon and learned the projected value of *Big Springs of the Yellowstone Park* was $662,500. Now fully aware she received a painting valued far beyond her wildest expectations from Kit, her negative spirit churned over the sheer number of Thomas Moran paintings that remained at Starlight Cottage.

She was still waiting for Adam to arrive home. Her

husband had been at a real estate convention in New York over the weekend and would be home any minute. With *Big Springs of the Yellowstone Park* still tucked away in the trunk of her car, Lucy knew the hour for a decision had come. She had to decide whether to inform Adam of Kit's growing wealth or continue to keep these facts under wraps and protected from Adam's influence.

Ultimately, Lucy decided telling Adam everything was the lesser of two evils. Therefore, she began to strategize how to present Olive Branch Ranch and all of its magnificent assets in a way that would not consume her husband. In the past, their joint business ventures were usually all the better for Adam's input in the end. She knew this. She also knew that by including Adam in her affairs, she ran the risk that he would step out too far at some point and put their sensible calculations at tremendous risk. Even with these negative truths in mind, Lucy thought it best to go ahead and take Adam into her greater confidence. If he ever found out about Kit's wealth on his own, he would make things impossible for her.

"Lucy?" she heard Adam say, a few minutes after the garage door closed.

"I'm in here," she called in return from her black leather lounge chair. She had been sitting comfortably before the elegant glass fireplace since hanging up from her call to Kit.

Stopping only to say hello on his way to their wet-bar Adam said, "I'll be right in. The drive back from New York was brutal. I'm just going to make a Martini. How was your flight last night?" he asked, though he could not be bothered to wait for an answer.

"It was fine," Lucy said aloud to herself as usual.

Adam had been somewhat of a business companion

during their ten-year marriage, but the depth of their marital relationship never hit a level of true intimacy in any area of their lives. Frankly, Adam's mind and his perception were compulsive. Lucy was constantly starving for his attention as he attached himself to every possible media connection 24/7. Though she voiced her objections often, no amount of pleading ever changed the way Adam treated is wife. Lucy received second place in all things, something she eventually learned to live with. As an alternative to emotional starvation, she promoted her self-interests aggressively.

As she thought about how to deliver her news to Adam, Lucy tried to imagine how overbearing he would be once he knew the true extent of her family's wealth. While she waited for him to join her in their family room, she said a quick farewell to her old way of self-protection. Quite consciously, she moved into a side of their relationship that felt uncertain but which she felt was quite necessary, if she was to accomplish her goal of becoming an heir to her mother's wealth.

"How was the funeral, Lucy? Are you glad you went?"

"I am, but not for the reasons you think."

"Your brother and sister-in-law's deaths must have been an incredible blow to your mother and your nephew."

"You mean my niece, Ashley," Lucy corrected Adam.

"Oh, that's right. I think you did mention you have a niece."

Skating on his own film of uncertainty, Adam was not sure how far to push Lucy in discussing her weekend. Clearly his mention of her family in the past had caused utter fury, and he was simply too tired to get involved in a conversation that could cause an explosion on a Sunday night. To his surprise, however Lucy began speaking about the Morans, and this time without apparent reserve.

"Ashley is my brother Sean and his wife Corrine's only child. She is about twenty-years-old and as I understand, due to enter her final year in college."

"She must be devastated by the loss of her parents," said Adam.

"I am sure she is but she has incredible strength too, at least from what I could see."

"Do you mean that you didn't spend time with her or your mother?"

"I spent no time with Ashley at all. There was not much point in it really. And while I did have dinner with my mother, our strained conversation continued on to the bitter end.

"While in flight last night I reflected on my future as far as the ranch is concerned. It dawned on me, like a new reality rising, that Ashley and I are Mother's only living relatives. In addition to this, when I was out at the ranch on one of the three very brief stops I made there, I discovered my mother owns a complete collection of landscapes painted by Thomas J. Moran, Jr., who lived from 1837 until 1926. Are you familiar with Moran, Adam?"

"I am. Did you know about this collection before?" he asked as he settled into a deep oversized couch facing their home's floor-to-ceiling windows, which in the daytime framed a perfect view of Lake Champlain.

"Once I let a friend of mine take a painting from an old cottage on the ranch, but I had no idea there was an entire collection of Moran's works inside. That is until yesterday, when I saw two appraisers reviewing countless paintings with my own eyes."

"Let me see, Lucy. If I know you, you have been sitting here trying to devise a plan to ensure your mother will consider you in her will."

"Exactly!"

"I've never known you to be so blunt, at least with me, regarding Olive Branch Ranch," said Adam.

The fact that Adam mentioned her mother's ranch by name was not lost on Lucy. She was now certain Adam knew more about her family in Cody than she previously realized. Perhaps she had allowed a small fact here or a memory there to escape over the years. Or more likely, as Lucy thought longer, Adam may have checked on her past before they married. When they met, she vowed never to use the name of the Moran ranch with Adam, and she was absolutely certain she never had.

"Knowing Adam it is more likely he delved into my past, than my letting the facts slip," she thought. "But either way, what does it matter now? I simply must find a way into Mother's good graces once again and become a viable presence in her future estate plans."

"Adam, I have something I want to show you."

"What is it?" he asked with great curiosity. He was now onboard with whatever plan Lucy decided to use to become part of Kit Moran's estate once again.

"Well, although Moran is a common name, in this case the artist is a relative of mine."

"This does not surprise me, given the paintings have been with your family."

"All but two paintings are with my family now. One, as I have explained has been lost to an old friend, and the second one Mother gave to me yesterday."

"She gave you a painting? Why in the world would she do that if they are of value and you have had so little contact with her?"

"Oh and they *are* of value. I mistakenly believed the painting I have with me was worth ten-thousand dollars."

"Mistakenly? Ten-thousand dollars is a fair amount of money for a painting, don't you think?"

"I did think so, until my Sotheby's contact called this

afternoon. He informed me that if the painting I have, *Big Springs in the Yellowstone Park* is authentic, and in near-mint condition, its present value is $662,500."

"What?" gasped Adam. "And what would possess your mother to give it to *you?*"

"Well, she didn't exactly give it to me. She heard about a conversation I had with my father on his deathbed, asking for the painting. She gained this knowledge after-the-fact however, as I had already paid a visit to her lawyer and paid him $1000.00 to deliver the painting to me.

"Her lawyer did this, Lucy?"

"Yes, of course."

"Are you crazy? Your first inclination was to make an incredible error? Do you really think this guy did not inform your mother?"

"Well, I've known him since he was a boy, Adam. Please don't be hard on me," she pleaded. She tried to avoid Adam's answer.

"Adam, I need your help. Two minds are better than one. Let me show you the painting. It's in my car."

True to form, Adam was relentless. "Lucy, you've made a foolish mistake in asking this lawyer to bring you the painting. This may be construed by the authorities as a form of extortion, if he did so reluctantly. I can see you need my help going forward and I simply cannot afford to have my wife incriminated in something illegal. It just would not sit well with my New York clients."

"I accept your criticism," Lucy said. She was more than happy to put an end to this grief.

"Let me go get the painting from the car, so you can see its beauty firsthand." Although deep down Lucy was hugely skeptical over Adam's intention of helping, as she desired, once he saw the beauty of Moran's work firsthand, Adam was willing to become an equal partner with Lucy. As a binding force, they talked well into the night.

"Adam?" Lucy said when they finally headed upstairs.

"What is it?" he asked.

"There is one more thing I need to mention. I called my mother this evening and tried to get back in her good graces – but she would have no part of it.

CHAPTER NINE

Monday, August 31st

"Elaine!... Elaine!... Elaine!"
"What is it, Ashley?" Elaine called out in alarm.
"It's Nan. I can't wake her! *I can't wake her!"*
Ashley ran from Kit's bedroom while Elaine grabbed her cell phone from her purse and sprinted up the stairs.
"Where is she?" she asked mindlessly, for surely she knew Kit was still in bed.

Ashley could not speak but followed Elaine into the master bedroom where Kit's head lay upon her pink satin pillow.

Elaine laid her head upon Kit's chest and listened to the silence.

"The Lord has taken her, Ashley," she said with conviction.

Elaine's hope in Eternal Life filled the air as she reached for Kit Moran's cool and lifeless hand. Ashley succumbed to Elaine's peace, the greatest gift Elaine was able to offer Ashley since her entire ordeal began eight days earlier.

"Our Lord has called your dear grandmother Home. Let me call Sarah, Ashley, Kit's passing will need a medical pronouncement. Then I'll call A.J Lawser as well."

"And Fr. Joe, too please, Elaine," Ashley said, choking back her tears. "I'd like to have him pray with Nan and with us before we decide what to do next." Already, young Ashley was speaking with the voice of one experienced with death.

Elaine made the two calls while Ashley sat with Kit. Sarah arrived just minutes later with Thompson and Fr. Joe followed. The dreadful news surprised all but

Sarah, who had recently been seriously concerned about Kit's level of stress.

Ashley grew numb to the voices around her and even to the prayers Fr. Joe recited over her beloved Nan. Her elders recognized her immediate need for greater comfort, as there had been no reprieve from her established grief, and clearly, she would have no rest for quite some time going forward.

Within the hour, Kit left her beloved Northridge, her home for over sixty-years. Those remaining stood in the driveway briefly where from their shock they heard Thompson say, "I will call Lucy." Moreover, all present agreed, though reluctantly.

This decided, Ashley turned to Fr. Joe and said, "I'd like to have Nan's funeral Mass tomorrow, if possible. If Lucy can make it back to Wyoming in time, then she can make it. I feel I should be the one to make the arrangements for Nan unless someone here objects." The group gave their support to Ashley with no further discussion.

"In consideration of everything that's happened, and the fact that all of Nan's friends and associates were in contact with her last week, I see no reason to have a "parade" of folks come by again. Nan would never want this, especially because she would not want to trouble the good souls for additional generosity, and neither do I.

"I'd like the service to be very small, the five of us and of course Fran and Ted Crawford, Christina and Drew."

"I know Peter Travers and Jake Lewiston will want to be there as well," Thompson interjected.

"Lee Farley and a few of the other long-time employees, too," said Ashley, "but that should be everyone."

"I'll call them all this morning," said Sarah, "and if anyone other than these inquires we can simply mention that Kit's arrangements are private."

Fr. Joe added from the spiritual side that Kit had such a wonderful relationship with Jesus that she would be most pleased with a simple presentation of her body to the Church for a final blessing.

"It's settled then," said Ashley with a profound sense of confidence. Though overcome with grief once again, she wondered where the young self-centered college student, her former-self of just two weeks ago, had gone.

"Oh, and Fr. Joe, if you'd have time to discuss a few things with me this afternoon I would appreciate it."

"Of course, Ashley. Come by around two if you feel up to it," said Father, hoping he could help her with whatever was presently on her mind.

When all had been decided and Elaine and Ashley were alone at Northridge, Elaine offered to stay with Ashley until the end of the week. In turn, Ashley accepted her kindness.

"Lucy, there's a call for you," Adam shouted out to the kitchen from his home office. "The guy said his name is Thompson Smith. Some client of yours?"

"Not exactly," Lucy whispered as she snapped the phone from Adam then employed a coy tone of voice.

"Thompson?" Lucy said as she began a brief release of all that was on her mind. "You do know by now that I have Sotheby's proposed value of my painting. I also want to inform you I am also aware you and Sarah were covering up the rest of Mother's collection at Starlight. I saw your appraisers out there Saturday morning."

"Lucy, wait," Thompson said, hoping that she would give him a full pause in which to interject the real reason for his call. "Lucy, I'm not calling about the Moran collection in anyway today, although at some point it is likely we will need a discussion on that matter. I am calling you to tell you that your mother has passed away."

"Really? Mother has passed away? I just spoke with her last night," she admitted in a rather startling tone.

"I know you did. I was there. I heard Kit tell you I was there. Remember?"

"Then you know that I tried to make amends," Lucy said, her voice pleading for Thompson's reassurance.

"I know Kit graciously forgave you but unfortunately you waited too long to make amends. Now your chance is gone. I informed Ashley I would call you this morning to tell you about Kit's funeral Mass which will be celebrated tomorrow. That's all."

"Is that set in stone?"

"Yes."

"By whom may I ask?"

"It has been decided by Ashley and supported by a close group of your mother's friends. The funeral is tomorrow. Come if you like – or not. Quite frankly, it means nothing to us if you do. You should know however, there is no one who will be any less than gracious towards you. The decision is all yours."

"And Adam's," Lucy replied.

"Adam?" Thompson asked.

"Yes, Adam Whaler, my husband of ten-years. I'll be there if Adam will fly out with me tonight."

"Spare me the details," Thompson thought.

As far as Thompson was concerned the conversation had been far too long already, and he hastened it further to a close. "So be it, Lucy. Either way."

After her call from Thompson ended, Lucy stayed in front of the large glass windows. When she turned from the beautiful morning view of Lake Champlain, Adam was resting comfortably in his easy chair behind her.

"Who is Thompson?" he demanded to know.

"Thompson Smith is my mother's attorney. He called

to tell me that Mother has passed away."

"What? Really? When did this happen?"

"Apparently she did not wake up this morning."

"I'm sorry, Lucy."

"The funeral is tomorrow morning," she added.

To her surprise Adam followed with, "We should be there." When she mentioned Adam as a travelling companion to Thompson, she never really thought Adam would agree.

"I really don't see the point in returning for Mother's funeral. We said our good-byes, and that's that. In fact, I just spoke with her last evening before you got home. I tried to apologize for the past and really got nowhere."

"That's exactly the point, Lucy. Because you were at odds, unless you return home, you will never get a handle on what your niece and your mother's friends are instigating with regard to her wealth. Is there a will, for instance? Or is there some other binding agreement made recently? Or perhaps it has been years since your mother put anything on paper.

"As I see it, you really have two choices, the first, to sit here and wait for some sort of notice that may never come, or the second, to be present at your mother's funeral and remain in town for a few days afterward to glean whatever you can through the few contacts you have.

"Personally, Lucy, as your new business manager, I must insist we head out to Cody tonight. I'll check the flights immediately."

Adam's insistence on this fast-moving plan stunned Lucy. She trusted him and then she didn't. She wanted him onboard with her plans to obtain as many of her mother's assets as possible, but she was well aware she simply could not disengage him whenever she wanted to.

Lucy knew well that to try to direct Adam in any business endeavor would only make him all the more aggressive. "No," she thought to herself, "if I want things to remain relatively peaceful, I must let Adam in and further, allow his control."

A half-hour later, Adam told Lucy, he had booked the flights and did so with far greater enthusiasm than she expected. They would be attending her mother's funeral after-all, a fact that was just beginning to haunt Lucy's inner emotions.

"Come in," Fr. Joe said as he opened the rectory door to Ashley. "What do you have here," he asked when he saw some sort of list in her hand.

"I've brought Nan's funeral on a single sheet. Actually, Father, I am bringing *her* requests to you, which clearly match what was decided this morning. Elaine remembered Nan told her where to find this list if anything happened to her.

"You see Father, I think Nan has sent me to you with her needs all settled so you can help me with mine."

Fr. Joe reviewed the list of requests, which quite simply included three readings and five hymns.

"Just the usual," Father thought as he marveled at Kit's humility.

"This is easy enough," he said to Ashley.

"Now, what can I do to help you in this additional cross Our Lord has placed so heavily upon your shoulders?" Fr. Joe asked gently.

"Well, I'll get directly to the point, Father. I'd like to make my First Holy Communion at my grandmother's funeral. I'm asking because of the revelation we discussed yesterday, Jesus' words to me, *'I Am the Bread of Life.'* This next step for me would have made my grandmother so happy. If possible, I'd like my First Holy Communion to be my final gift to Nan."

"Well, let's just see," Fr. Joe said as he digested

Ashley's request and led her into his library. There he quickly referenced *The Rite of First Holy Communion* and *Canon Law* for an answer to Ashley's request. Finding nothing of help in either resource, Fr. Joe decided to call his bishop.

"I'll call Bishop Needham at the Archdiocese in Cheyenne, and I'll explain everything to him. Deciding these sorts of matters is one of the roles of a bishop. What I do know, my dear, is that whether or not His Excellency grants you this request, you must receive the Sacrament of Reconciliation before you receive the Eucharist for the first time. Do you think you will be able to handle this today?"

"If you teach me, Father, I will do this. Will you make the call right away?"

"Absolutely."

While Fr. Joe made the call, Ashley went out for a breath of fresh air. She strolled across the lawn and said a prayer before an exterior statue of Our Lady, which St. Anthony's parishioners frequent with their personal needs. There she could only imagine how many times Kit had stopped there and prayed to her Heavenly Mother for Ashley as well.

"It's Fr. Joe Evers, your Excellency," Father heard Bishop Needham's assistant say. "He said it's urgent."

"Joe? You there? You have an urgent matter? What do you need?"

"Yes, Your Excellency. I'm hoping you could make an immediate decision on an issue of extenuating circumstances. First, I'll give you a bit of the background."

"Go ahead, Joe."

"Well, this has to do with the Moran family of Cody."

"Stop right there, son. Do you mean Kit Moran's

family? Her dreadful tragedy is still haunting me. Such a fine woman, Kit Moran. God seems to ask so much of his best people."

"Do you know Kit personally, your Excellency?" Fr. Joe asked with sensitivity, understanding he would be the first to deliver the message that Kit, too, had passed away.

"I knew Kit well many years ago. I became acquainted with her just after I became bishop. She was instrumental in coordinating the Archdiocese Outreach Program for Wyoming's poor through my office."

"Joe, how is she holding up in all this? Is Kit the reason you are calling?"

"Your Excellency, Kit Moran passed away unexpectedly this morning."

"Oh, gracious. Oh, I'm so sorry to hear that. God bless her lovely soul."

"Actually, Your Excellency, I'm calling you for an interpretation of the *Rite of First Holy Communion* on behalf of my newest convert and parishioner, Kit Moran's only grandchild Ashley Moran. Ashley is the daughter of Sean and Corrine Moran."

"Good Heaven's, son, tell me about this situation and your request."

Fr. Joe explained the details of Ashley's spiritual journey over the last eight-days to Bishop Needham. In doing so, he brought forth Ashley's authentic claim that she saw Jesus in a dream, which motivated her to receive the Sacrament of Baptism without prompting. Then Fr. Joe explained how Jesus put His words inviting Ashley to receive Him through His Body and Blood upon heart during her parents' memorial service.

"Enough said, my dear man," was the good bishop's response. "I have the power to issue a dispensation under *Canon Law* for an extraordinary decision such as this. I grant Miss Moran her First Holy Communion at her beloved grandmother's funeral tomorrow. She must however receive absolution for past sins by your administration of the Sacrament of Reconciliation beforehand."

"She's already aware of this obligation, Your Excellency, and has agreed to it. Ashley is a beautiful young woman with incredible inner strength, just like her grandmother."

"Fine, Joe. Please express my deepest sympathies and promise of my prayers to Miss Moran. Tell her that it's my ardent hope that she will progress toward her Confirmation in Catholicism within the next year. The Gifts of the Holy Spirit will bring her the strength and consolation she needs to rebuild her life. May God bless her."

"I'll tell her, Your Excellency. Please allow me to thank you on her behalf."

"All set," Fr. Joe called out to Ashley who was seeking Our Lady's aid in granting her request. Clearly now she had a new understanding of her grandmother's devotion to Mary.

As she entered the rectory again, Fr. Joe assured Ashley of Bishop Needham's prayers and informed her she received his blessing on her First Holy Communion as well. To this news, Fr. Joe added, "And further my dear, he asked that you continue growing in the Church's blessings. Because he knows the Gifts of the Holy Spirit will strengthen you, he would like you to do this by planning to receive your Confirmation as soon as possible."

"I will," was Ashley's simple response. "And, thank you, Fr. Joe."

"Now Ashley, I want to give you a brief overview of the Rite of Reconciliation – Confession – as it's often called."

"Oh, yes, I've heard Nan and some of my friends speak of it." As Ashley thought of Kit again, she held her bottom lip hard to keep her emotions from rushing forth. Successful in holding back her tears, she thought to ask the question most adults ask when making their First Confession.

"I've always wanted to know, Father, why do Catholics have to tell their sins to a priest?"

"I think this is the number one question from those inquiring, Ashley. I'll explain. You see, when the Sacrament of Reconciliation begins with the opening blessing, Jesus Christ becomes present, by the Power of the Holy Spirit. For that period, the priest is the concrete and infallible sign that Jesus is there and that He has heard the penitent's sins. Then by the Power of the Holy Spirit, Jesus gives His absolution, and the Spirit of God gives direction for the penitent on how to pray and how to avoid the individual's most difficult temptations in the future through His priest."

"Is every sin always forgiven?" Ashley asked.

"The answer is "yes," always, but there is one qualifier as well. The penitent must be *sincerely sorry* for his or her sin. This is *all* that Jesus asks in order to forgive every sin no matter how grievous."

"Oh, I'm *so sorry* for all of my sins, Father. Now that Jesus has entered into my life I cannot bear the thought of my sins having caused His afflictions."

"With your degree of sincerity, my dear, I can absolutely assure you that your *every sin* will be forgiven by Jesus through me and by the power He has given me to absolve them.

Then Fr. Joe took a Bible off a nearby shelf and said, "Ashley, I want you to go over to the church and sit before Jesus in the Tabernacle. While there, please read

Exodus: 20, where I have placed the marker. Spend a few minutes in prayer over the *Ten Commandments*. Then try to see where your greatest weaknesses, past and present, fall. Then I'll join you. How does this sound to you?"

"I think it will be fine, Father," Ashley said, without her usual confidence.

"I'll carry you through it, Ashley, and then I'll widen my shoulders and do the best I can to serve you well tomorrow and in the future, too."

While Ashley prayed in front of the magnificent white marble altar and baptismal font at which she had become a Catholic, she could feel God's grace keeping her calm.

Opening the Bible to where Fr. Joe placed the marker Ashley read:

The Ten Commandments
Exodus 20: 1-17

I. I am the Lord your God. You shall not have other gods before me.
II. You shall not take the Name of the Lord, your God, in vain.
III. Remember to keep holy the Sabbath.
IV. Honor your father and mother.
V. You shall not kill.
VI. You shall not commit adultery.
VII. You shall not steal.
VIII. You shall not bear false witness against your neighbor.
IX. You shall not covet your neighbor's house…nor anything that belongs to him.
X. You shall not covet your neighbor's wife.

True to his word, Fr. Joe entered the church just a few minutes later. When he arrived at the altar, he kissed a small purple stole, the outward sign of his authority to absolve sins, and placed it around his neck. In all of his priesthood, never was he called to greater compassion for anyone than Ashley Moran at this very moment.

"Are you ready, my dear," Fr. Joe asked softly.

"Yes, I am," Ashley said with confidence.

Then Father began. "In the Name of the Father, and of the Son, and of the Holy Spirit. Amen."

"Ashley, this is your First Confession," Father announced officially. "I'm going to read you a list of sins that relate to *The Ten Commandments*. What I am hoping to help you uncover are patterns in your behavior that keep you from a loving relationship with Jesus for example: any disregard for authority, the *Fourth Commandment*; any thoughts or acts against sexual purity, the *Sixth Commandment*; or gossip, a sin against the *Eighth Commandment*. Do you understand the process?"

"Yes, Father," Ashley replied.

"We'll work our way through the list in no time.

"Jesus will wash every sin away through your sincerity, my dear. My job is to will help you understand the sins for which you are totally responsible, and those for which you are less culpable because you have had no prior religious training. I want you to have every confidence in the fact that with sincere sorrow on your part, Jesus will take away your *every sin* today. This is His promise to those who follow Him.

"When we have finished discussing your failings," Fr. Joe continued, "I'll ask you for the one sin for which you are most sorry. Then I'll ask you to pray this brief prayer for forgiveness." Fr. Joe handed Ashley the traditional Catholic, *Act of Contrition*. I will then give you absolution in the Name of Jesus Christ and your sins, even those you may no longer remember, will be forgiven.

"Finally, before you leave church, I want you to do penance for your sins by saying the Hail Mary, three-times," Father said, as he pointed to the Hail Mary on the reverse side of the card.

"Fr. Joe is so gentle," Ashley thought to herself. For a moment before Father began to read the general list of sins, Ashley realized how well he had cared for her over the last week. Although they had known each other just one week, plus one day, to Ashley it already seemed a lifetime.

Through Fr. Joe's presence at Confession, Jesus came to Ashley for the third time since her parents left her. This time He came to her through the Sacrament of Reconciliation – His sacred gift to the soul.

"Have I really been forgiven?" she asked when her First Confession was complete.

"Absolutely," Fr. Joe replied.

Ashley pondered this thought, which led her back to her conversation with Kit. She remembered how Kit had forgiven Dylan Bates with such ease.

"Jesus forgave me as easily as Nan forgave Dylan Bates," she said to Fr. Joe.

"Kit learned to do this because of all the times Jesus forgave her transgressions over her lifetime. Once a soul recognizes the true forgiveness of Jesus Christ, and feels this wonderful freedom from sin within, it is much easier to reconcile with others."

"I feel this freedom, Father."

"Of course you do," Fr. Joe added.

"I must go and forgive Dylan in person and let him know that Nan forgives him as well," Ashley said, as her time with Fr. Joe concluded.

On what her friends would call an impulse, but what she now knew was a movement of the Holy Spirit, Ashley drove to Sunset Boulevard on the edge of Cody proper to where she learned the Bates family lived.

Dylan was at home and sitting on a swing on the front porch when Ashley pulled up to the simple white turn-of-the-century home. He recognized Ashley immediately because he had seen her picture in the paper at her parents' funeral over the weekend.

Ashley thought Dylan looked gaunt. It was quite apparent he was suffering the pains of his mistake physically, as well as emotionally. Although she had never seen the young man before, she recognized his agony. He was living in a devastation he could not resolve.

A puzzled Dylan Bates stood as Ashley approached the bottom step of the porch. "Dylan, may I come up?" she asked.

"Of course, Miss Moran," he said softly. Ashley breathed a sigh of relief over the ease with which the young man's words flowed. She was happy he knew who she was.

"I'll only stay a moment," she said as Dylan offered her a seat across from him.

"Dylan, I've come to ask you to accept my forgiveness for the unfortunate accident that took the lives of my parents."

Dylan was speechless so Ashley repeated her statement again.

"I've come to ask you to accept my forgiveness for accidently ending my parents' lives."

"You want *me* to accept *your forgiveness?* How can you do this – offer me forgiveness? I've killed your mother, your father – two of my favorite teachers. I'll never forgive myself."

"You will. You'll see," Ashley said. "And by accepting my forgiveness as I ask you to, you'll forgive yourself much sooner. Sooner rather than later is what I am asking of you on both accounts. Dylan, this is the only thing I'll ever ask of you."

"How can you do this?" Dylan asked. "How are you able to do this? And what about your grandmother, how does she feel about me?"

"She feels the same. My grandmother forgives you,

Dylan. She told me she forgave you and prayed for you, from the very first hour she heard the news."

"How will I ever face her, Miss Moran? I've hurt her so much. These last few days people in Cody have said so many wonderful things about her."

"Actually, I've come to share her forgiveness with you, as well as my own. My grandmother will never be able to do this for you directly, although she will continue to pray for you and watch over you, too, as you go on with your life."

"Watch over me? What do you mean?"

"Dylan, my grandmother passed away this morning out at our ranch." Ashley stood, hoping a change in posture would help her to keep her composure.

"I thank you so much for allowing me to come and give you her forgiveness. And I thank my grandmother for teaching me to offer you my forgiveness as well. Please accept these gifts from us and go on with your life. Do something wonderful for humanity and know that my dad, mom and grandmother are all praying for your great success."

A shocked Dylan Bates watched Ashley drive away. The impression she left upon him was that of an angel from Heaven who moved him from total despair into new hope. His gratitude toward Ashley was beyond measure.

As Ashley approached the end of Sunset Boulevard, Thompson called. "Hi Ashley. I just heard back from Lucy. She and her husband Adam will arrive in Cody tonight."

"Lucy has a husband?" Ashley asked.

"I just found out myself. It's apparent to me Kit didn't know either."

"Does this mean I now have an uncle to deal with as well as Lucy?"

"Ashley, let me assure you, I'll deal with Lucy and Adam, unless you decide otherwise. For now, I want you to put their arrival aside completely and depend on those supporting you. We won't let you down on any account and that includes dealing with Lucy and her husband, as well."

CHAPTER TEN

Tuesday, September 1st

Sarah called Northridge around eight on Tuesday morning. "Hi, Ashley. How are you holding up?" she asked.

"Pretty well, I'd say," Ashley answered.

"I wanted to check in on you, dear, and also to tell you that Thompson and I will be receiving Holy Communion with you today. We met with Fr. Joe last night and we both received the Sacrament of Reconciliation for the first time in many years. I'm speaking for Thompson too, when I say to you this morning, God is bringing some good about in our lives with the trials we are going through with you now. We are so pleased to receive Communion with you on the day of your First Holy Communion."

Even through her sorrow, Ashley was touched by the Smiths' new commitment to their Faith and especially by their desire to stand in unity with her as she made her First Holy Communion. "Thank you, Sarah," was all she could manage to say.

"You're welcome, love," Sarah said tenderly. "We'll see you at St. Anthony's at eleven.

While Ashley sat at the dining room table digesting Sarah's call, Elaine presented her with a small white box.

"It's a First Communion gift for you, Ashley, but it's not from me. It's from Kit."

Astonished, Ashley asked, "How could this be?"

"Many years ago, when you were seven to be exact, Kit came to me bearing a heavy degree of sorrow."

"She did?"

"Yes. From time-to-time when she found something

truly upsetting, she would entrust me with her feelings. You see, although I was her employee, our relationship was truly one of deep friendship. After my own mother passed away, Kit was a gentle soul for me as well.

"One day, right around the time many of the little girls and boys in your school were making their First Holy Communion, your grandmother came to me. She was heartsick over the fact that you would not be among the angelic faces clothed and veiled in white, meeting their Savior for the first time in the Eucharist. We talked for quite a while and although Kit knew that you would not be among so many of your friends, she prayed that would change someday."

"To assuage her sadness over the whole situation your grandmother put a little plan of action together. She called me into her office several weeks later and drew this little box, from a secret compartment under her desk. She was just dying to show me what she had done for you."

"Go ahead and open it," Elaine insisted. "It's your First Holy Communion gift from Kit."

Ashley pulled the white ribbon from the box. Inside she found a small leather jewelry box. Lifting the cover, she removed a snug protector from inside, and there in the crevices of royal-blue velvet lining Ashley found her first Rosary.

"These are special, Ashley. Kit drove down to Cheyenne to Bartholomew's Jewelers and had this Rosary designed, especially for you."

Ashley pulled the beautiful gold beads slowly from the box one decade at a time.

"I've never seen anything so beautiful," she said. "Each bead is a tiny rose. Look at this little glass medallion, Elaine, there's a diamond inside."

"Yes, there is. Kit gathered several things from her jewelry box to have these beautiful beads made for you.

Every gold rose came from her engagement ring and wedding band, from your Grandpa John's wedding band and the matching Crosses and Miraculous Medals they wore throughout their married lives.

The diamond in the center is from Kit's engagement ring."

"Oh, Nan," Ashley said softly through fresh tears, "I love you!" Elaine's eyes too, filled with tears.

Before the hour passed a small group of Kit's closest friends, assembled to meet her cherry wood casket at the front door of St. Anthony's Church. Just as Fr. Joe gathered the last of the attendees into the main vestibule, Lucy and Adam arrived.

"Mother, mother," Lucy cried as she left Adam's side and pushed her way through the other mourners.

"Mother if only things had been different!"

Ashley, already well trained in human behavior, recognized the manipulative tone in her wayward aunt's voice. She resented Lucy for blaming Kit for the failure of their relationship. Although she knew little about her aunt Lucy, she knew she had seen quite enough.

And as far as Adam was concerned, Ashley disliked the man immediately. He was slick in personality and in dress. He appeared accomplished, but vain and aloof. Adam reminded Ashley of the only man to con her grandmother. Several years earlier, an outsider sold Kit tainted vitamins and all of her newly broken stallions became sick. Forced to her withdraw from the Annual Show of Excellence, she lost her a substantial portion of her annual revenue. Eventually, the man was arrested and imprisoned. These memories served Ashley well, as she gathered her first impressions of Adam Whaler.

Hoping Lucy's would show restraint, Fr. Joe suggested that A.J. Lawser lead Lucy and Adam into the church.

A.J. sat the couple on the side of church opposite Ashley. Once settled Lucy realized all eyes were upon her and she knew not to cause another scene.

The altar was beautifully dressed that morning with white roses in honor of Kit and for Ashley's First Holy Communion. This was Fr. Joe's way of proclaiming the Church's hope in Kit's entrance into Heaven and in celebration of this joyous, though appropriately understated day in Ashley's growth in the Catholic Church as well.

Kit's funeral was an intimate gathering. The incenses offered over her body and burning candles of natural bees' wax filled the air with reverence. After the opening prayers, Fr. Joe moved along gracefully through the readings Kit had selected, *1Kings 8: 22-23, Psalm 37: 23-24, and John 7: 37-38,* * each at the appropriate time as he continued to pray Holy Mass.

A young female parishioner with a glorious voice sang the *Ave Maria* during the Offertory of the Mass. At Communion, Fr. Joe called Ashley to the altar and pronounced these words to her for the first time, *"This is the Body of Christ,"* as he held up the Bread of Life briefly before her adoring eyes.

---

1 Kings 8: 22-23   "Solomon stood before the altar of the Lord in the presence of the whole community of Israel, and stretching forth his hands toward heaven, he said, "Lord, God of Israel, there is no God like you in heaven above or on earth below; you keep your covenant of kindness with your servants who are faithful to you with their whole heart.
Psalm 37: 23-24   "Those whose steps are guided by the Lord, whose way God approves, May stumble, but they will never fall, for the Lord holds their hand.
John 7: 37-38   "On the last and greatest day of the feast, Jesus stood up and exclaimed, "Let anyone who thirsts come to me and drink. Whoever believes in me, as scripture says: 'Rivers of living water will flow from within him." New American Standard Bible, 1995.

Ashley bowed, said "Amen," then took the *Body of Christ* into her hands, and consumed precious Jesus. Next, Father offered her the *Precious Blood of Christ.*

"This is the Blood of Christ," Fr. Joe said as he held up the *Blood of Jesus* before Ashley who bowed again, said "Amen," then took and drank from the chalice. Fr. Joe guided Ashley back to her seat where overcome with emotion from all-sides she bowed her head and cried. Several moments later, Father concluded Kit's funeral rite and small congregation gathered in the vestibule for *The Song of Farewell*.

On the way out of the church, Sarah and Thompson overheard Lucy comment to Adam, "Of all the days for Ashley to pick for her First Holy Communion!" Sarah, incensed by this comment, grabbed Thompson's arm so as not to cause a scene with her own anger. In silence, they followed Kit's coffin through St. Anthony's front doors. Then leaning into her husband's shoulder Sarah said in a hushed tone, "Of course Lucy wouldn't understand. Ashley is experiencing an intimacy with Jesus that most of us will never experience, certainly not Lucy! Let's remember this moment Thompson, and maybe we'll be able to anticipate Lucy's next moves." Thompson agreed.

Ashley left St. Anthony's in silence and entered A.J.'s waiting limousine with Christina and Drew. In Jesus, she remained strong, never losing her composure again. She remained at peace as she watched A.J. Lawser turn Kit's hearse through the gates of Riverside Cemetery, throughout the graveside rite, and as she left Kit behind with Sean and Corrine.

"Thompson," Ashley called out softly to him as he and Sarah left Kit's grave, "Sarah mentioned you want to see me at your office, is that right?"

"Yes, I'd like to see you this afternoon if at all possible. Can you come to my office about five," he asked as he drew Ashley in between Sarah and himself and grasped her hand. Looking deep into her eyes he said, "It's very important."

"I'll be there," she said as she climbed back into A.J.'s limousine.

When the last of the mourners had finally returned to their cars Adam stepped back to give Lucy a moment alone with Kit. "I'm sorry, Mother," Adam heard his wife mutter. "Truly I am, *but you...*, Oh, never mind, you would never understand." With this soured attempt as a last-farewell, Lucy rejoined Adam and together they returned to Eagles Inn where they stopped at the bar for a glass of wine before heading back to their room.

"Our accommodations are adequate," Lucy said as Adam put their key pass in the door, "but room 211, where I stayed last week was really lovely."

Settling into a chair overlooking Inn Road below, she fired-up her computer. Then Adam announced he was going to ride out to Olive Branch Ranch.

"You are?" Lucy asked.

"Yes, I am," he said with a certain authority over his wife. "Don't forget our new arrangement in this cause," he reminded Lucy. "I'm the manager of this trip to Cody and I'll also manage any financial interests we find worth pursuing here. Certainly you know better than to ask me to hang around a hotel room all afternoon when I could be making money, Lucy."

"Yes, I do. Go ahead then. See what you can see. Just don't talk to anyone and you should be okay. While you're gone, I'll see if I can track down a recent inventory of Thomas J. Moran, Jr.'s works somehow." Purposely Lucy did not bring the *Encyclopedia of Painting* with her, as she had been viewing it at her office where it was out of Adam's sight.

Just hours after laying her mother to rest, Lucy's entire

focus in life was Kit's estate and the Thomas J. Moran, Jr. collection. While she thought having Adam involved would end the burden of hiding Kit's wealth from him, she was not beyond calculating *his* worth to her plans, or even the possibility of dismissing him if he did not prove to be an asset to her. Time would tell.

Adam, on the other hand was reaching far beyond the scope of any plan Lucy was contriving. Unbeknownst to his wife he was not concerned in the least over what Lucy may or may not inherit. The plan he was brewing on his own, consisted of contacting the heir or heiress of the majority of Kit's estate, and then proposing an offer he or she could not resist. He hoped to entice this individual into selling off parts of Olive Branch Ranch so he could develop several planned communities. Regardless of Lucy's interest in the existing buildings and paintings, Adam had other plans.

When he left Lucy, Adam headed off to the airport to meet Chezworth Ford, a commercial real estate mogul he convinced to fly out of New York that morning to give his initial opinion on Adam's plan. Adam's present goal was to board the helicopter Chezworth Ford hired and survey Olive Branch Ranch from the air.

By the time Adam left Eagles Inn, he was exasperated with Lucy. He could not understand why she was making the Moran collection and Olive Branch Ranch the cornerstone of her potential assets. Of course, Adam had no idea of what made Lucy tick. As a husband, he was void of every quality that might lead him to understand Lucy's interest in her family's ranch. Behind the scenes, the Lucy and Adam Whaler lived lives of fierce competition with one another. Adam, who had a definite plan for making money and no attachment to Olive Branch Ranch, would likely attempt to bowled Lucy over.

Unaware of Adam's plans for development, Lucy's goal for that day was to put an end to her conjecturing over Kit's material assets and begin to investigate what was going on at Thompson's office. "Quite a load but not beyond my abilities," she thought with spiteful self-confidence.

At three o'clock, Lucy emerged from her room to call on Thompson Smith. After Adam left, she was successful in securing an online version of Thomas Moran's missing inventory from the Whitney Museum of American Art. The information she gained about the proposed value of the Moran paintings increased her knowledge tremendously and she now felt confident in handling Thompson on every level.

As she headed over to Thompson's office Lucy began to consider Kit's estate at-large and she mulled over the fact that she, as Kit's only living child, was entitled to at least a portion of her mother's assets.

Certainly, there'll be a formal "reading of the will," she told herself aloud. "But, first-things-first," she added as her inner excitement rose. "I have to learn whatever information I can about Mother's assets, including her business holdings. If I'm not prepared, I will never gain anything."

When Thompson heard the front door of his office close, his gut instinct told him it was Lucy.

"I'll get this," he whispered to Brendan as he passed by his young assistant's office.

"Lucy, please come in," said Smith as he tempered his voice and managed a look of compassion.

"What can I do for you this afternoon?" Thompson asked.

"I'll get right to the point, Thompson. I've come to inquire about the reading of Mother's will." Lucy made absolutely no attempt to hide her motives and Thompson was not at all surprised.

"I'm assuming you are the executor of Mother's estate now that Sean is deceased as well."

"You are correct, Lucy. Kit made me executor of her estate the day after Sean passed away."

"Then I'm correct in asking you personally when do you plan to read Mother's will?"

"You are. And because I believe it's best in this case to have everything out in the open I've already petitioned the court for approval on all of Kit's documents. Assuming there are no liens of which I'm unaware I'm planning to read the will within several days."

"Will you be staying in town?" he asked Lucy.

"Yes, until the reading, presuming it will be sometime before the end of the week."

"Most likely it will be."

"We'll stay in town until then. As usual you can reach me on my cell phone."

"Very well," Thompson said as he showed Lucy out the front door.

"Has Ashley no idea?" Thompson asked himself, as he prepared the conference room for his young client's arrival. "She accepted the fact that I needed to meet with her this afternoon. She must have at least some unspoken suspicions that this meeting concerns Kit's will," he thought. "Or does she?"

"What did you need to see me about, Thompson?" a pale Ashley asked as she settled into a chair at his conference table. Thompson felt Ashley's naïveté was detectable and knowing he was about to change her life forever, he was concerned. He certainly hoped she would be successful in learning to deal with her completely new world.

"Does it have to do with my future? Some grant or trust Nan has left for my education? I know she wants me to find my way in the world even if this takes me away from Olive Branch Ranch."

"Obviously, Ashley has not thought things through. Who does she see as owner of Olive Branch Ranch if not herself?" Thompson thought.

"Ashley," he spoke firmly, "I have a copy of the documents Kit signed Sunday evening while you and Brendan were in the kitchen at Northridge. I need to give you a copy and to explain a few things about them. Moreover, because Lucy is in town I need to do this right away. She was in my office just an hour ago to inquire about the reading of Kit's will."

"So you're worried about Lucy? Is that what this is about?" Ashley asked Thompson.

"Yes, in one sense I am worried about Lucy."

"Is Sarah, too?"

"Yes and we both want to help you with any defense you might need as far as Lucy is concerned."

"A defense? What do you mean? Somehow I'm missing your point."

Thompson drew a strong breath as he stood from her side where he had been leaning against the conference room table. Then he took the seat directly across the table.

"I'm sorry, dear, but I must be frank with you," Thompson said, as he pulled Kit's silver-beaded key-case from the center drawer of his conference table. "Ashley, this key belongs entirely to you."

"Nan's key?"

"*Your* key now."

"The key to Starlight Cottage?" she asked with lingering doubt.

"Yes, Starlight Cottage and its entire inventory of Thomas J. Moran, Jr. paintings. Everything is yours."

Through her conversation with Kit, Ashley had concluded only that the collection was worth a tremendous amount of money. Nothing more.

"Isn't Lucy heir to Nan's estate?" she asked in complete innocence.

"Your grandmother has left everything to you," Thompson said again. He was now fully aware Ashley had no idea what he was about to say. "Kit signed a new Last Will & Testament on Sunday night when Brendan and I were at the ranch. Her new will leaves the entire ranch and all of its properties, personal and business to the heir or heir(s) who fit a set of criteria John Charles Moran wrote long ago, actually fourteen-years, before your birth. In fact, it was through a concerted effort between Kit and my office just last week that everything is now in order. Ashley, your grandmother has left her entire fortune to you."

Ashley looked dazed. Clearly, she was wrestling with complete disbelief and this, yet another new reality, all at the same time.

"I'll explain everything to you step-by-step. Would you like a glass of water before I go on?" Thompson asked.

"Yes, please," she answered. Her voice was fatigued. "If you don't mind that is," she added, never failing to be true to her courteous nature.

When Thompson returned, Ashley cleared her thoughts and asked Thompson to explain things again.

"All right. I will give you your Grandpa John's criteria for the inheritance of the Moran estate to start, and then you'll see that without the slightest question *you* have met all of John Charles Moran's criteria.

"The final item, to be a practicing member of the Catholic Faith, has been a "true miracle" indeed, if I may borrow these words directly from Fr. Joe. Without this miracle, of Jesus' appearance in *your* life, Ashley, you would not qualify as owner of Olive Branch Ranch. You are now the only one who qualifies. There will be no other who qualifies, not now, or ever.

"Furthermore I could testify under oath if need be, that just ten-days ago Kit conversed with me about being unable to sign the Moran Estate over to you without your meeting John's criteria. It was not that she did not love you enough but that she felt bound to your Grandfather's final word on their assets. After all, their wealth was originated by the sweat and tears of your Grandpa John's parents."

"But what about Lucy? Doesn't she meet the criteria?"

"She does not. This was both a relief and a sorrow to your grandmother. When it was time however for Kit to sign her final will Ashley, she was greatly relieved that Lucy was disqualified by John's criteria."

"So, what are you trying to tell me, Thompson?"

"Ashley, all of Olive Branch Ranch, its homes and buildings, assets, land, livestock absolutely everything, including the Thomas Moran, Jr., collection belongs to you. It's yours, and yours alone and no one can ever take any part of it away from you. There are no loopholes in your grandmother's will and there will be no valid contest against your inheritance. Kit's signature on Sunday night made *your* inheritance of her entire estate – ironclad.

"If Kit had left things undone, which happens more often than not in these situations, I'm sure Lucy would contest her mother's will. If John's criteria were not found, Lucy would contest Kit's will. However, I am telling you Ashley, no one on earth will ever be able to contest your grandmother's will and win.

"And what makes your situation even better is there are no unpaid bills, no liens against the property, no disgruntled employees."

"That doesn't surprise me, Thompson, because I've

always been aware of Nan's evenhandedness in all the ranch's most complex affairs. What I couldn't comprehend in my youth, my parents helped me to understand later on. Nan's all-around integrity was genuine and impeccable."

"How do you feel about inheriting the entire Moran fortune, Ashley?"

"Of course you know I'm in a state of shock. That's just the reality of my life right now. Actually, I'm quite numb and not sure what's happening in any aspect of my life. It must be my grief."

"That's absolutely the case, my dear, and unfortunately will remain so for quite some time."

"And to be honest," Ashley added, "I still don't understand what you mean by Grandpa John's criteria."

"Let me show you," Thompson said gently as he pulled John Charles Moran's handwritten criteria from Kit's file.

"Your Grandpa John Moran was hopeful there would be one or more descendants who would meet three specific criteria for inheriting his family's wealth. He hoped his heir(s) would have: a deep love for the Moran family heritage, a great love for America, and would be a practicing Catholic(s).

"You see Ashley," Thompson went on, as he unfolded the four corners of the criteria and exposed the "6 x 9" document. "Kit told me recently that as a young man John Moran never imagined there would be no remaining Catholics in the Moran family. In his last years however, he apparently saw a shift in the dynamics of faith in America and added the need for the recipient(s) to be practicing Catholic(s) just in case the Catholic Faith weakened some in his own line."

"But Thompson," Ashley said in amazement, "that almost happened."

"Yes, without the miracle of your baptism, surely it would have happened. In addition, I don't think Kit knew exactly what she would have done with the ranch in that case. She did tell me, that in good conscience and out of respect for John's wishes, she was considering other options such as leaving the ranch to charity.

"This was such a great burden for her my dear, a silent burden, which God chose to remove from her by granting you an extraordinary recognition of His love just last week."

"Now everything is becoming clear to me. You asked me how I feel about the news of my great inheritance. It's too soon to say." Ashley paused thoughtfully. "I'm proud, but lost. I'm overwhelmed, full of grief and frightened, all at the same time. It will," she continued, "certainly be life-altering for me. Somehow, in all these negative emotions, I also feel a sense of hope. There's new life abounding, I just know it, even though I'm hibernating in a dark, dark winter in my life. I must learn to believe in a new spring," she told Thompson.

"Then I'd say to you, Ashley, that you'll find hope in a new spring through your new-found friendship with Jesus Christ."

"If I didn't have this new gift of faith maybe I'd freeze solid right here in this chair."

"Well my meeting with you today is as much about transitioning the daily operations of the ranch to you as revealing Kit's wishes. I should point out to you now that whenever a corporate owner ceases to have power by death or illness or for any other reason, the corporation will inevitably undergo a period of stress. I want to help you with this transition, Ashley. There are checks waiting for your signature already. I'm here for you as legal advisor, and of course, Sarah and I will be with you as friends and confidants anytime you need us going forward.

"Ashley, I'd like to have a formal reading of Kit's will tomorrow at ten. And of course Lucy will be here."

"I have confidence in everything you've told me, Thompson. I promise I won't worry."

"Good," said Thompson. Ashley brushed back her hair from her face and as she left his conference room Thompson saw a new and unexpected ray of survival.

Next, Thompson sent a text to Lucy confirming he would read Kit's will on Wednesday morning.

When Adam returned to Eagles Inn that afternoon, it was difficult to keep his enthusiasm under wraps. In all that he learned of Lucy's family and its wealth through Richie Mitrell, never did he imagine the size and the shape of Olive Branch Ranch to be so incredibly beautiful or so well suited for development.

Chezworth Ford carried an aerial software package on board the chopper when they began their excursion over Cody. Later he would be able to offer a detailed topography report to help Adam decide on his development plans. What they saw with their own eyes was beyond words. According to the surveying instruments they employed, the boundaries of the Moran ranch were far-reaching. Olive Branch Ranch actually crossed the Shoshone River at the northern quadrant, and Ford's preliminary design for three planned-communities seemed feasible.

"If you consider connecting two bridges over the river," Chezworth explained to Adam, "there is room for three communities in triangular form."

"Clearly," Adam thought, 'the beauty of the rural part of the ranch far surpasses any of the buildings and artwork Lucy is consumed with."

At the conclusion of his three-hour tour, Adam Whaler was certain of only two things. He must have that land for development at all cost, and in the present hour he must refrain from giving Lucy even the slightest indication his sole interest in the Moran ranch was only in its future development.

When Adam returned to Eagles Inn and Lucy informed him, that Thompson would read Kit's will the next morning he insisted he attend. "I can't let you sit through it alone, Lucy. You know I'm here to support you and in this case I think it's true that two heads are better than one."

Later at dinner, Lucy asked Adam one simple question about his afternoon, "How did you find the ranch?"

"A bit worn," was all Adam offered before he deliberately turned their conversation toward their businesses waiting at home.

While Adam seemed not to want to discuss the ranch any further, Lucy knew exactly why. Before they returned to the dining room that evening, a loyalist in her Vermont office sent Lucy a text to inform her of Adam's meeting with Chezworth Ford. This employee knew Lucy disliked Ford and wanted to protect her employer's business interests. When she read the text, Lucy decided not to discuss any aspect of the ranch with Adam until she could figure out exactly how to handle him. Her one and only inquiry was a simple ploy. His curt answer in response convinced Lucy that right from the beginning of their trip, Adam was never on her side.

CHAPTER ELEVEN

Wednesday, September 2nd

Wednesday morning, Lucy and Adam sat in silence and browsed through the *Wall Street Journal* over breakfast. A few minutes before ten, they left the inn and headed over to Thompson's office.

Meeting the couple at the door Thompson ushered Lucy and Adam into his conference room.

"I'll have you wait here for just a few minutes, folks. I hope to have the proceedings underway promptly at ten."

As Thompson passed Brendan's office, Brendan waved to his boss in silence, then pointed out the window to Ashley, who had just stepped out of her car. Thompson signaled for Brendan to remain silent. Then he entered his office, closed the door, crossed behind his desk, and signaled Ashley to come in through his private exterior door.

"Hi," Thompson said quietly as he held the door for her. "Lucy and Adam are waiting in the conference room. I've decided to read Kit's will in my office, so I want you to stay here in this chair," he said, as he guided her to the furthest of four red leather chairs facing his desk. I'll go ask Brendan to come in in case we need his assistance. He can sit in the chair next to you. Then, I'll seat Lucy and Adam in the last two seats next to Brendan.

"It's a bit of a power-move actually," he continued. "Lucy will never expect you and Brendan to be waiting when she enters the room which should catch her and Adam off-guard. This should put them on the defensive – exactly where we need them."

Finally, it was time. Thompson placed his right forefinger over his lips to let Ashley know she should be silent as he opened the door, then he stepped out just far enough to signal for Brendan to join them. As soon as Brendan took his seat next to Ashley, Thompson stepped into the conference room and asked Lucy and Adam to follow him.

"Hello, Ashley," Lucy said awkwardly, when she saw her niece already seated. "This is my husband Adam Whaler," she said clumsily, knowing Ashley had seen Adam at Kit's funeral.

"Hello, Lucy, Adam," Ashley said calmly.

Leaving no time for Lucy to realize Brendan was no longer her ally, Thompson began the proceedings.

"Ashley, Lucy, I've called you here today for the formal reading of Kit Kiley Moran's final Will & Testament because you are Kit's only two living relatives. I would like you both to know that this Will & Testament reflects all of the Olive Branch Ranch's stock, holdings, assets, properties, horses and livestock, homes, buildings and out buildings, and all of Kit's personal effects, which includes everything on the property. In addition, I want to make it clear to you both, that Kit was the sole heir of the same, with the passing of her husband John Charles Moran in 1968.

"I should also tell you both that while there could be an assumption on each of your parts that there will be some loose ends with regard to all of Kit's properties because of her untimely death, there is, I say without a doubt, not a single thread left dangling from the Moran estate. In other words, Kit's will is 'iron-clad."

"Well, *that's* good to know," said Lucy abruptly.

"Clearly," Thompson thought, "Lucy expects nothing." Still Thompson remained undisturbed, as he continued the procedure. Clearing his throat, he eased into the crux and the finality of the matter-at-hand.

"Lucy, Ashley," they both looked on, as did Brendan, who was now making mental notes on Thompson's brilliant performance, "let me begin by telling you that your mother Lucy, and your grandmother Ashley, left nothing to chance. She contacted me several weeks ago, before Sean and Corrine passed away, and asked me to begin work on her estate. Brendan and I reviewed my files on Kit's estate, as well Harry Loft's files with a "fine-tooth" comb.

"Whenever there was a question or a clarification needed on a title or a personal note, I contacted Kit. When I saw her last week, I asked her for a full-page of her current handwriting, in case there was ever a need to verify its authenticity. And so with this entry from her gardening journal dated August 1st this year, I have proof of her most recent handwriting, right here." Thompson gently pushed the single page before him to the top of his desk for all three to see.

"In reviewing the Moran Estate, actually on the very day you arrived in Cody and met Kit for dinner, Lucy, Brendan discovered a note from your father, which was dated the morning of his death, Easter Sunday, 1968. This note directed us to one of John's books in Kit's library, *The Old Man of the Mountains,* in which we found an envelope John had left, listing his criteria for distribution of the Moran estate to his and Kit's heir(s). Cody District Court has accepted the certification of authenticity issued by a handwriting analyst who has deemed John's handwriting authentic.

"Kit reviewed John's criteria for the first time last week. Until then, she was completely unaware that it existed. However, the night before she passed away she signed-off on her new will, which clearly states that John's original criteria were her wish as well.

"What do you mean by criteria?" Lucy shot.

"What I mean, Lucy, is that your father, John Charles Moran, set down specific personal characteristics for the person or persons to whom the Moran estate would pass. At the time of his passing he of course had no idea who would out live Kit but his wishes, which Kit abided by in her final hours, are the criteria that must be used now for the distribution of your family's wealth."

"Well, *what are the criteria*, Thompson?" Lucy's impatient voice raised several decibels.

"Surely, *I* must qualify for something. Especially since, you've mentioned that my mother abided by my father's wishes in her final hours.

"*You know* how much I love Daddy" Thompson, "and that I called Mother Sunday night and begged her forgiveness," Lucy said, her voice rising once again.

"As I mentioned to you already Lucy, I was present during your phone call and I heard Kit say that she forgave you for all that you've done. However, I also heard her say that she was not interested in having you enter her life again. Her exact words were, 'but as far as your coming back into my life in any way – that won't be possible.'" Lucy grew flushed over Thompson's accuracy.

"I'll show you Kit's signature on the final document which I date-stamped. This electronic stamp provided the time as well. If you check your long-distance telephone bill, Lucy, you'll see that at the precise moment of your call, your Mother turned over her entire estate, but not to you – to Ashley."

Lucy was horrified. She stood and looked at Brendan with vengeance, then at Thompson with vile contempt. Finally, her piercing eyes sent daggers to Ashley, and she screamed at her beautiful niece, *"You little witch!"*

"Lucy, don't do this!" Thompson warned.

"Do what? ..... Oh, I get it! Don't turn on little prissy, here?"

"Lucy, please," Adam said, "you will only make matters worse."

"Stay out of this Adam. It's none of your business. I dissolve our partnership and for that matter our marriage as well. Don't think I don't know about your little expedition yesterday with Chezworth Ford. I am sharper than you think, believe me. And as far as Richie Mitrell, your private investigator is concerned, I know all about him and his reports about my background and family. You never did marry me for love Adam, or you never would have had me investigated."

In her rage against Adam, Lucy turned to Thompson and Ashley and revealed Adam's plans.

"Here's a little piece of information that I'm sure neither of you have discovered," she said sarcastically, "Adam, here, is planning to buy you out Ashley, and develop Olive Branch Ranch into three planned-communities."

Lucy's truthful accusations shocked Adam. Sadly, he knew that she meant what she said, and that he had actually brought this new era of misery down upon himself.

Without the least concern for anyone else in the room, Lucy took a deep breath and then continued. "I demand a copy of my father's criteria, my mother's handwriting, and the signature page of her will."

"You cannot demand it, Lucy, but you may obtain it by subpoena. Have your lawyer contact me. However, be forewarned, the County Seat has already examined every document. Your mother's handwriting and her final signature are just back from District Court this morning.

"Kit's will is final, Lucy. You must face the fact that you have not measured up to a single line item of John Moran's criteria, and that Ashley has. Your father asked that his heirs honor the Moran family name, have a love for America, and be practicing Catholics. What I'm going to say to you now is quite foreign to your manipulative ways, but I'm going to say it anyway – and I know I speak for Kit – *SO YOU LISTEN UP LUCY!*

"Not only have you *not* lived up to any measure of the criteria stated, you have been known to be in opposition to all three. You have had decades to reform your life to the integrity set forth by both John and Kit Moran.

"Instead of qualifying as heir to the Moran fortune, *and I do mean fortune*, you have dishonored your family numerous times – and this, as recently as twice in the last week by showing up here in Cody to honor three people you apparently despise. Secondly, you have never shown an ounce of gratitude for your father's service to *your* Country, Sean told me this himself. In fact, we all know you've been guilty of burning flags and demonstrating against the United States and your family's patriotic values. And finally Lucy, you removed yourself from your Catholic Faith, abandoning the gift of faith that was given to you by God and fostered by your parents."

"It's interesting Thompson, that *you* make all of these judgments against *me*."

"Oh, no, Lucy. Let me be clear. My allegations against you are not personal. Your business was your business, until Kit made it mine. I now represent your mother's interests through a promise I made to her. Take it or leave it Lucy, this is an open and shut case."

Thompson's unquestionable authority dumbfounded Lucy. Storming from the room, she "warned" everyone, including Adam, "See you all in court!"

Shaken, Lucy left Thompson's office alone and headed back to Eagles Inn where she learned room 211 was now vacant. Remembering the calming effect of that room from her stay the previous week she checked in at the reservation desk, then moved her belongings across the hall. There she hoped to regain a sense of calm, as well as attend to some personal business before heading home for Vermont the following day.

A red-faced Adam Whaler left Thompson's office immediately after Lucy and strolled down Sheridan Avenue to Buffalo Bill Saloon, where he remained for several hours.

After a short debriefing, and Thompson's advice to take things easy and not to worry, Ashley thanked Thompson and Brendan for their unwavering dedication then drove out to Amour, to draw some peace from its familiarity. At Amour, that afternoon, she made her first decision as owner of Olive Branch Ranch. Ashley decided to leave Amour for good and make Northridge her new home.

While sitting briefly at the kitchen table at Amour, her head resting down on her folded arms, she said the following to Sean and Corrine. "Mom and Dad, I'm leaving home permanently today. I won't be coming back to live here again. I hope you don't mind. Of course, you know I own the ranch now and our workers and their families are depending upon me for their livelihoods. So, I will take the reins of Olive Branch Ranch today and I'll do my very best. Please pray for me. I love you both."

With these thoughts spoken, Ashley brushed away her tears, and then she walked through the door of Amour for the last time. Her new responsibilities were very different from the gentle introduction to the world she had planned – her college degree, then enrollment in a master degree program while still living with Sean and Corrine.

Courageous Ashley Moran would not step away from her new role as rancher, which, with only her intuition as guide, seemed to be the cornerstone of her future – not the one she planned, *but the one planned for her by Almighty-God.*

When Adam returned to Eagles Inn and Lucy's things were no longer in their room, he inquired at the front desk about her departure. To his relief he learned that his wife had engaged room 211 for another night. Knowing that Lucy did not intend to return to Vermont, at least until the following day, Adam decided to fly back home immediately. After all, this was not the first time Lucy threatened him with divorce, and it would probably not be the last. "A night apart," he thought, "might just do us both some good."

Departing for the airport, Adam slipped a note under Lucy's door.

"Dear Lucy, I forgive you. If you want to come home to me,
I'll be there for you as always, with Martini in hand.
Love, Adam

Clearly, Lucy needed time. The fact that Adam thought only about his need to forgive her, and not her need to forgive him for scheming over her family's ranch behind her back, was very revealing to Lucy. This was the real Adam Whaler, not the man she pretended him to be. This was the man she married. Today, and for the very first time however Lucy realized Adam was a despicable human being.

Quietly she turned the word "despicable" over and over in her mind. "Adam is despicable," she thought as her spirit shook violently within her. Her true uneasiness was not due to her admission that she had married a despicable man, but rather that the word despicable was resonating in the darkness of her own soul. If she admitted Adam was despicable, and she knew they were so much alike, then Lucy had to be honest with herself – she was despicable too.

As she sat by the window all that afternoon, Lucy did everything possible to justify her behavior toward Kit, Sean, Corrine and Ashley. The more she tried however the more her reasons rang hollow.

When evening approached, Lucy lit the fireplace in her

room, and ordered dinner. There she spent several hours before the fire evaluating her marriage and then her own life. The more she thought about Adam the more she realized he had few redeeming qualities and worse, the very things she disliked so much in Adam, she recognized in herself. In the space of one evening, Lucy Moran's decades-long façade crumbled to her feet and she saw the person *she* had become. She hated what she saw.

"How did I come to this?" she asked herself. She tried to push away the memories of all the ill will she had spread in her lifetime, but was unable to do so. Hurtful things she had done both recently and years ago came flooding back. When she could no longer stand the emotional upheaval she was experiencing, she crawled into the four-poster bed.

After twenty-minutes or so of non-stop tossing and turning a strong cold breeze, strong enough to wake a sleeping soul, rushed over Lucy and she reached for the quilt at the end of her bed.

"Allow me," she heard from the darkness as the heavy quilt glided over her and rested just under her chin. Lucy was terrified.

"Whose there?" she asked, as she reached for the phone on her nightstand to call the police.

"Lucy, Lucy, where have you been?" the deep warm voice asked.

"Daddy? Daddy, is that you?"

"It is, little one."

"What are you doing here? I mean, how did you get in here? Oh, you know what I mean," Lucy said as she flew out from under the covers and stepped toward John Moran who was lighting the lantern on the mantel.

"How I got here is not as important as why I'm here, Lucy."

"It's so wonderful to see you, Daddy. So incredible,

really. Tell me why you've come."

"I've come to console your grieving mother."

In these remarks, Lucy felt utter shame as she had not felt since childhood.

"You see Lucy, your mother cannot be consoled over your behavior, and now that I have the wonderful good fortune to finally be in her presence again, I simply cannot stand by and watch her suffer."

"Daddy, please don't tell me all the things I've done wrong in my life, I simply cannot bear it." Lucy seemed to know what was coming.

"Lucy, there's no need for me to tell you, as my Lord above has allowed me only to stir your spirit. He'll guide you if you are willing. My job in this is simply to wake your soul for your own sake and for your mother's sake as well.

"I'm going to leave you now."

"No, don't go," Lucy pleaded, "I love you, Daddy. I miss you."

"I must. However, what I have to say to you before I go is important. Be very careful to live a life of integrity from this day forward. Everything you do is of the utmost importance in this regard. You have received a second chance in life. You have a long way to go and so little time in which to do so. I will always love you, Lucy. Turn back from your sins, I beg of you. You have done enough damage to yourself and have contributed more than your share of grief to the world."

When Lucy looked up to John in order to reply, he was gone. Weary she tumbled back into bed, where she laid awake all night and watched scene after scene of her life and all of her sinful actions flash like a movie before her eyes. Though she begged for relief, none came. Lucy Moran was left alone to face the remnants of her own despicable life.

CHAPTER TWELVE

Thursday, September 3rd

At daybreak, Lucy purchased a tall cup of coffee from a main street bakery and walked slowly through Cody proper. Suddenly nothing in her life was the same as it had been just the day before. She was softened by the gentle touch of her father's presence and powerfully aware that she did not miss Adam. Purposely she ignored the half-dozen calls he made from their home in Vermont. After John Moran's visit, the condition of her marriage was secondary; her only real concern that morning was saving her own soul.

This new memory of John forced Lucy to face the "unforgiveable" things she had done in her life. For the first time she truly recognized the unnecessary suffering she caused Kit and Sean. What was causing Lucy the most pain in the present moment however, was her father's revelation that Kit was still suffering over her lost daughter, when she deserved the peace and glory of a true saint.

Walking down Sheridan Avenue, Lucy's interior life stirred even more and she found this most unsettling. She had no idea what was going on inside of her, but she knew something was. In reality, God's grace was now at work in her and her present state of turmoil, although she did not know it, was a Divine Intervention.

In His benevolence, God prevented Lucy from seeing the error of her ways head-on. For most living in serious sin, facing their wrongdoings is unbearable. God knows this. In Lucy's case, He allowed the stirring that started the previous evening with John's visit, to fan out gently in every way possible. Moreover, by the grace earned or her through Kit's countless prayers, Lucy would soon be able to face her sins.

As she walked through Cody that morning, her memories of her hometown turned from bitter to sweet. She felt her hardened soul softening within. Melting, was the best word Lucy could find to describe her experience as the first hours of the new day moved on. "It feels as if my hard inner core is just melting away," she said to herself as she reflected on her innermost feelings.

Nearing the end of Sheridan Avenue Lucy came to St. Anthony's Parish. Suddenly she had perfect recall of the days she received the Sacraments of First Confession, First Holy Communion, and Confirmation. She had not remembered any of these events when she stepped into her former parish for her mother's funeral on Tuesday. Instead, Lucy focused then only on the material things she thought needed attention such as the interior paint, outdated artwork, crosses and chalices, and all these things simply annoyed her.

Because her perception about everything in her life was superficial, Lucy was not capable of seeing St. Anthony's interior, its warmth and the comfort it offered so many parishioners who felt wed to the parish as Kit had. How could Lucy see anything beyond the mere esthetics, when her entire view of life was shallow?

None of St. Anthony's flaws crossed Lucy's mind this morning as she looked at the parish grounds. Rather she could see her younger self, dressed in white for her First Holy Communion, smiling and standing between Kit and John and holding each of their hands.

"Where have I been?" she asked herself. "Why have I allowed myself to become a person, whom the girl I now see standing across the street would never recognize? Just when Mother needed me the most, I abandoned her."

Lucy stepped from the curb and crossed the street. She then walked toward the front of St. Anthony's. Quietly and reverently, she climbed the six marble steps up to the double doors and entered the vestibule. Each of her senses woke suddenly. The fresh smell of incents and extinguished candles filled the air. She breathed in the lovely aromas as her eyes took in the beauty of the sun streaming through the stain-glass windows. The original woodwork now appeared warm and rich to Lucy. The fact that so few renovations were done in all the years she had been gone was no longer her revulsion, but her delight.

With each passing moment, a new memory returned. The most cherished of them all was the day her brother Sean, dressed in his little white suit, made *his* First Holy Communion. Suddenly grief was Lucy's constant companion. She stepped quietly into a seat where she laid her head on the bench before her and broke down. She cried for Sean. She cried for Kit. Most of all she cried over her own sins and all of the arrogant moves she made in her adulthood, just so she would never have to admit that she was wrong about anything.

Entering the church from the main entrance as well, Fr. Joe immediately noticed a woman in a back pew in complete distress. Before he realized he was speaking to Lucy, he asked the distraught woman, "Is there anything I can do to help you?"

Brushing the tears from her face Lucy sat up and said to Fr. Joe, "Would you hear my confession, Father?"

"Of course I will, Lucy," was Fr. Joe's gentle reply.

Offering Lucy the reconciliation room at the back of the church, they both entered. Father helped her into a comfortable chair and then placed on himself the same purple stole he used when Ashley received her First Confession on Monday.

Lucy admitted to Fr. Joe that it had been well over forty-years since her last confession. In turn, Father did not bat an eye. Rather, he used the brief time they were together to assure Lucy of her Savior's mercy, love and forgiveness. Then he advised her that from this point on it would be wise to allow the Church and Her teachings to help her build a new way of life. Lucy readily agreed wholeheartedly.

After she received absolution, she asked Fr. Joe if he had another moment or two. She wanted to explain how it was that she came to St. Anthony's that morning.

"You see, Father, my father John Charles Moran appeared to me last night."

"Do you mean in a dream?" Fr. Joe asked.

"Not in a dream, Father, in an apparition."

"How interesting," Fr. Joe said. Lucy wrongly interpreted Father's comment as a note of disbelief. Father clarified.

"Lucy, I must be honest with you. Had you not been Kit's daughter and you mentioned this to me today, it would take me some convincing. But I believe you without question."

"Really, Father? Do you believe me because I am Kit's daughter and she was a holy woman?"

"No. I know you are Kit's missing child and I am quite aware of her holiness, but these are not the reasons I believe you. I believe you because since Sean and Corrine died, your family has had one miracle after another."

"Is this true?"

"It certainly is. However, I not at liberty to tell you more."

"You could get more information from your niece, Ashley, if she is willing to tell you.

"I'm sure she would never tell me anything. She has been so cool to me since I came to town."

"Lucy let me be blunt with you. All of Cody has been cool to you because you have been so hateful to everyone. Ashley Moran, whom I have just gotten to know recently,

238

is a fine young woman. Her life was suddenly ravaged by death, and she has every reason to be bitter, but she is not. You know, Lucy, Ashley paid a visit to Dylan Bates. He's the young man responsible for Sean and Corrine's deaths. She went to him and asked him to accept her forgiveness."

"That's incredible," Lucy said.

"What's really incredible, Lucy, is that today you finally understand just how wonderful your young niece really is."

Lucy thanked Fr. Joe for his assistance then returned to her room at Eagles Inn where she recorded her experiences of the previous twelve-hours in her personal journal.

About that same time Thursday morning, Ashley made her second decision in her new role as owner of Olive Branch Ranch. She decided to have breakfast in Kit's chair at the head of the table at Northridge. On one level, she knew it was her duty to fill the empty chair, but her decision to do this now was for self-protection. She simply could not stand the pain she would experience if she left Kit's place empty indefinitely. Further, she worried that if she postponed this or any other similar decision, it would only delay the inevitable and might actually hold her back in accepting her new role as owner of the ranch.

Taking Kit's seat for the first time, Ashley noticed a pile of correspondence Elaine left on the table. On top of the letters and bills was a note from Lee Farley, the ranch's general manager:

Ashley:

I know this has been an incredibly difficult time for you, but I must remind you the Annual Show of Excellence this year, is this coming Monday, September 7th.

I need your signature on the attached form, authorizing the ranch's participation. The only thing you need to do beyond this is meet with Jake Lewiston and sign for the emergency medical kit.

Please give me a ring on my cell phone when you've taken care of these two items, or if you have any reservations about our participation this year.
Thanks. Lee Farley

Suddenly it hit. She would be the one to authorize this year's participation in the Annual Show of Excellence, the ranch's greatest source of revenue. She knew Kit would want the broken stallions put up for sale, and while Ashley knew little about corporate finances, she was confident the liability in participating was small in relationship to the ranch's incredible wealth. Therefore, for the sake of morale, for Kit, and the precise rhythm of the life cycle of the stallions on the ranch, Ashley signed the form.

Then following Lee's instructions, she called Jake Livingston and asked him to come out to the ranch as soon as possible. Jake told Ashley he and his son Patrick were on their way over to the Centre and would stop by Northridge when they were through. He explained they would like to return Kit's statue of Our Lady, which Kit loaned Rita Livingston when Patrick was in the Sudan.

"I'll bring the statue to the door, Dad," Patrick informed Jake when they arrived. "I think it was Mrs. Moran's prayers that got me home safely this time, so I want to express my condolences on her passing to Ashley in person."

"Okay, son," said Jake, "you go ahead."

"Hello, Ashley. I hope I'm not intruding," Patrick said, when she answered the door.

"I've come to return Our Lady," he said as he lifted Kit's statue of Mary slightly.

"Oh, *you* had her," Ashley said as she smiled at Patrick. "I asked Nan who she gave the statue to this time just the other day. As usual she would not tell me."

"It was my mother," he told Ashley. "I spent the summer in the Sudan working to train paramedics. Apparently coming out of Mass one morning, my mom expressed some concern about my safety. Before the end of the day, Mrs. Moran dropped Our Lady off to comfort my mother. She insisted you should have Mary back now to comfort you.

"Ashley, I'm so sorry." Patrick said.

Ashley gently placed her finger over her mouth to signal that she could not continue that particular vein of conversation. She could feel Patrick's sincerity and much to her surprise she was no longer put-off by him, as she had once been.

"What's so different about him?" she asked herself. Then suddenly she realized there was nothing different about Patrick, there was something different about her perception of him.

"I got your note. Thank you," Ashley said awkwardly.

"You're welcome. May I put Our Lady down somewhere?" Patrick asked as the statue began to grow heavy.

"Of course," she answered. "Why don't you leave her on the dining room table for now. Your dad is waiting."

"Is there another place you would rather I leave her?"

"Actually, she belongs on a pedestal out back on our lower lawn."

"My dad won't mind," he answered.

"Hey Dad, I'll just be a minute," Patrick called out.

"Son, Lee just called me and has a question about injecting one of the medications. If it is not an imposition on Ashley, I can pick you up in about fifteen-minutes. Tell her I'll catch her at the Centre Monday morning for her signature on everything."

Having heard Jake's instructions Ashley called out, "That's great, Jake. I'll see you Monday." Then turning to Patrick she said, "There's just time enough for coffee, if you'd like to join me out on the porch."

Patrick headed out and placed Kit's statue of Mary in its proper resting place, while Ashley filled two coffee mugs. She thought right away that there was something very comforting about Patrick's spirit and his demeanor. The more they talked the more comfortable she felt with him. His brief visit certainly provided a momentary rest bit from her sorrow and the tremendous responsibilities of the ranch looming over her.

Acknowledging her life had changed completely in an instant, Ashley mentioned that she would not be returning to the University for her final year.

"I'd be happy to listen, if you need someone to talk to," he told her as he took in her news. In truth, the way things had turned out of late, she welcomed the idea of his friendship. Because she was so familiar with his father, mother and brother Michael, she did not feel threatened in the least by Patrick's generous offer at this most vulnerable time in her life. Already she was missing her college friends and conversing with people her own age.

"Would you come by again Saturday?" she asked.

"Absolutely," said Patrick with quiet affirmation.

"Would one, work for you?"

"One it is," said Patrick, as Jake pulled up to the door.

CHAPTER THIRTEEN

Friday, September 4th

Ashley left Northridge for Amour at dawn on Friday morning. There she saddled Cocoa and headed down to the Centre where she spoke with Lee Farley and informed him she was taking a brief ride to Heart Mountain in nearby Powell.

"I'll be back before things start getting really busy here," she assured Lee as she tightened Cocoa's reigns and headed off the ranch by crossing the Shoshone River.

Heart Mountain was an unlikely destination for a young woman in Ashley's present circumstances. When she woke that morning she felt the need "to touch" her deepest roots, to feed her growing conviction that she was to live out her own life on Olive Branch Ranch as the fourth-generation of Morans to do so. She felt moved to touch the spirit of her Grandfather John Charles Moran who had once confronted this same decision, to live his life where he was born as well.

Heart Mountain in Powell, Wyoming, was the site of the Heart Mountain Retention Center where Japanese Americans were detained during World War II and where John Moran served his last year in the U. S. Army.

This morning Ashley felt the need to be away from the ranch, to be away from the grief that possessed her at every turn. As she rode to Heart Mountain, she hoped she would "find" her Grandpa John as well as a sense of peace. Instead, as she approached the mountain, Ashley felt the spirit of the children, some orphaned, and who were stripped of their basic childhood freedoms at the Japanese American refugee camp.

"It's the children I feel," Ashley said aloud into the emptiness as she rode where 465 tarpaper barracks once stood. "I feel the children who were here." It was not the depth of their suffering that Ashley experienced. Rather, she found her spirit ignited once again with her own passion, her own aspirations of contributing to America's most precious resources – its children. She was not disheartened, as she knew others might be if "forced" into a family business. Rather, as she rode Cocoa over the land, Ashley experienced an interior sense of well-being and knew that if she turned things over to God, He would include her dream of working with children in the life *He* seemed to be arranging for her at the ranch.

Before her day was to begin in earnest, Ashley enjoyed every last second of her time alone at the base of Heart Mountain. She soaked in a final look at its beauty, the mountain's curvy grasslands which draw a visitor's eyes from bottom right to upper left and then across the narrow flat-top summit which distinguishes Heart Mountain from all others in the Cody area.

As she turned Cocoa back toward the ranch, Ashley opened her heart to the possibilities owning the ranch might offer her. In the spirit of John Moran that morning, she decided she would live her life on Olive Branch Ranch and her decision was final, just as her grandfather's had been.

When she crossed her property line, Ashley noticed the ranch had come alive with the day's activities in her absence.

"Ashley, would you like to spend this morning reviewing the first of the stallions going up for sale?" Lee asked.

"That would be great, Lee," she said as she dismounted Cocoa and joined him and several ranch hands for the review.

As the men placed the first 10 of the 43 stallions for sale in the main ring, Ashley enjoyed seeing the products of Kit's last year of intensive labor.

That morning's goal was to replicate the way the horses would exhibit on the show grounds so the animals would be less likely to balk. As the third batch entered the ring, Elaine called Ashley on her cell phone.

"Ashley, Lucy just called and asked for your number. I told her I'd get in touch with you instead."

"Did she say what she wanted?"

"She did not."

"Well, I'll have to deal with her sometime," Ashley said reluctantly. "Did she leave her number?"

"She did." Elaine gave Ashley Lucy's number. Then Ashley returned the call.

"Lucy, this is Ashley. Elaine said you called."

"I did," Lucy said without of drama.

"Ashley, I am hoping you would be willing to have a late lunch with me today. I am planning to head back to Vermont this evening and would like to have an opportunity to get better acquainted with you before I leave."

Not knowing how to answer, Ashley simply bent to her own peaceable inclination and accepted the invitation.

"What time is best for you?" Lucy asked in a clear unadulterated tone.

"I think two would work out well. Are you still at the inn?"

"Yes."

"I'll meet you there," Ashley said, not yet wanting to invite Lucy to Northridge.

"That will be fine." Lucy was grateful and she knew she was altogether undeserving.

When Ashley ended the call, Lucy was fully aware that God's grace was moving her, and this type of experience was entirely new to her. While spiritually awakened in her humanity she was however, utterly shaken by the changes she felt her in her spirit. The only fact of which she was certain was that she planned never to turn back from the grace that was seizing her.

In terms of her humanity, Lucy had no idea how to proceed. God was renewing her life in ways He would leave her to discover as she moved along. She had been totally "blind" most of her life, but now she could see – though only partially.

In the infancy of her new life in Jesus Christ, Lucy had decisions to make. The first of which she knew must be to make amends to Ashley. This of course she felt would be much easier than deciding what to do with her marriage.

Amid all these thoughts, Lucy found solid ground in only one area of her life, her real estate business. She made good use of the time she had left that morning, by checking in with her office back home and considering temporary housing in Vermont. Returning to Adam was now out of the question, unless he too made some necessary changes, and she knew not to rely on that. For the first time in her adult life, Lucy could now see that God had been after her to make change for years.

On her way to Eagles Inn just before two, Ashley prayed to remain open to what her aunt had to say. If she knew about Lucy before her parents' deaths she might feel years of contempt, but this was not the case. Her dealings with her aunt were limited and while she was not pleased with what she saw thus far, Ashley felt she would do an injustice to her father and grandmother's memories if she did not meet with Lucy at least once.

Earlier, when deciding what to wear, Ashley chose a black suit from the three suits she owned. Upon entering the dining room at Eagles Inn, Lucy was impressed with Ashley's poise and her professional manner.

Lucy rose from her seat the moment she saw Ashley coming and greeted her with a warm smile and handshake.

Immediately, she expressed her gratitude to her niece for meeting with her. Her gentle behavior was very different from the hostility she imposed upon her mother at their reunion. Humbled by her experiences over the last twenty-four hours, Lucy was a changed human being.

"I thought it would be imprudent not to come," Ashley responded in confidence.

"I've asked you here because I'm seeking your forgiveness for how I've behaved while in Cody," Lucy began.

Immediately Ashley remembered her own dealings with Dylan Bates and she prayed to be open to what Lucy had to say.

"You are a young woman, Ashley, and it's obvious you have already chosen to live a life of integrity. My mother and father gave me the gift of their integrity and I destroyed it. I've done many, many things in my life to offend other people." Then for the first time in her adult life, Lucy further admitted, "And far worse than this, I have done many things to offend God. I know this now."

Ashley was flabbergasted by Lucy's frank revelations and more so by the spontaneity with which her aunt asked forgiveness. While she was willing to forgive Lucy for the insults she endured at her expense recently, the depth of Lucy's contrition overwhelmed her.

Remaining open but believing Lucy's conversion "must stand the test of time," as she heard Kit say many times with regard to her workers, Ashley softened some toward Lucy, but remained reserved as well.

"Really, Lucy," she responded, "I don't think I'm the one to address your life's failings. Perhaps you could speak with Fr. Joe Evers. He's wonderful."

Realizing she had frightened Ashley, Lucy answered gently. "I've seen Fr. Joe, Ashley. He heard my confession yesterday and did quite a lot to set me straight.

But actually it was my fathe..." Lucy stopped suddenly when she realized she was about to tell Ashley that her father, Ashley's grandfather, appeared to her and that *he* was responsible for her change of heart.

While she held her tongue on this note, she recalled Fr. Joe's suggestion that she ask Ashley about the "Moran miracles." When her calmer senses prevailed, she asked a question Ashley never saw coming.

"Ashley, do you believe in miracles?"

Ashley answered the question with a question. She moved cautiously, offering only limited trust.

"Why, do you ask?"

Surprised but not under-minded, Lucy decided to be frank. "I've asked you this question because Fr. Joe suggested I do so. However, I can see now I've been unreasonably blunt. Therefore, if you please, I'd like to clarify why I've asked you. Ashley was relieved.

"I believe in miracles," Lucy began, "but only recently has this been so. When I informed Fr. Joe of a particular event that happened in my room at Eagles Inn, he said he believed me because you and my mother had received some extraordinary graces since your father and mother passed away."

"This is true," Ashley finally admitted. "If you want me to discuss my experiences with you, Lucy, I'm afraid you'll have to reveal your experience first. Then, if I feel it's the right thing to do, I'll share mine."

Ashley felt at peace with this decision. She sat quietly as Lucy told her of John Charles Moran's visit to her room at Eagles Inn. She never imagined that through Lucy her grandfather could be so close to her in the present hour.

"Wasn't I just out at Heart Mountain this morning with Grandpa John in the forefront of my mind?" Ashley asked herself. "This is the first time that his presence has ever been part of my life," she thought. The fact that her aunt's experience involved her Grandpa John was enough for Ashley to conclude the Holy Spirit was confirming Lucy's experience was real. In her brief time in formation, Ashley had learned this much about the mysteries of the spiritual life.

As yet, she felt no desire to reveal anything about her trip to Heart Mountain to Lucy. She was willing however to share her sudden Baptism and the reason she received her First Holy Communion at Kit's funeral.

Not only was Lucy astounded by the news of Ashley's apparition of Jesus and how her baptism came about but also she was greatly ashamed when she learned the real reason for the unusual timing of Ashley's First Holy Communion. At that moment, Lucy had no idea how to respond with regard to her own hateful attitude toward her niece. She felt however that she could not leave Cody without attempting to do so.

"Ashley, I'm so sorry to admit to you that I made some absolutely hateful comments about the timing of your First Holy Communion. And of course I compounded all this by my despicable outburst in Thompson's office," Lucy added.

"Lucy, you didn't know," Ashley said as she attempted to excuse her aunt's behavior.

"And it's because I've thought of nothing but my own wants, that I didn't know. This is true about so many things in my past and present life.

"I forgive you, Lucy. You'll straighten things out with God's help," Ashley said kindly.

"With God's help," Lucy agreed.

There were no promises made to keep in touch as the women departed. Lucy thought it was too soon and Ashley agreed. Quite simply they were grateful to one another for the single visit, each believing their lunch was worthwhile.

"Good luck with everything at home," Ashley said.

"You too," said Lucy to her young niece. Surely, Lucy saw the irony in the present moment. By her mistakes in life, Lucy's true home was in Vermont not in Wyoming. Olive Branch Ranch now belonged solely to the one who deserved it, the youngest living Moran.

When Ashley returned to Northridge, she called Lee Farley to see how things were going at the Centre. Lee assured her things went as well in the afternoon as when she was there that morning. She was pleased.

As she hung up the phone, the bell at the front door rang. She passed through the kitchen and glanced out the window to the driveway. Alone at home she hoped she would recognize the car but it was unfamiliar to her.

A tall man, perhaps sixty-years old Ashley thought, offered a nervous greeting when she opened the front door. The stranger, with short curly white hair, was well groomed and impeccably dressed. He wore a navy blue suit, which made Ashley think he was representing one of several insurance companies Thompson mentioned would be in touch with her.

"Are you the present owner of Olive Branch Ranch?" the man asked.

"I am."

"Does the Moran family still live here?"

"I am Ashley Moran, Sean Moran's daughter but my father passed away several days ago."

"Oh, I'm sorry to hear that. Is Lucy Moran still living?" the man dared to ask. Ashley stepped back.

"I'm sorry to bother you, Ms. Moran. I'll get right to the point," he said. "I'm from New York. I was once a guest here at Olive Branch Ranch and an acquaintance of your Aunt Lucy. My name is Roy Winters."

250

Ashley's mind reeled. "Where have I heard this name before?" she asked herself. "Nan mentioned him to me," she thought. "This is the man who took Lucy to Woodstock."

Suddenly Roy Winters read distrust on Ashley's face and sought to reassure her.

"I've come to Olive Branch Ranch today to right a terrible wrong I have committed against your family. If Lucy is not here, I have something to return to your grandmother." Ashley remained silent, though she no longer felt afraid.

"Several months ago I lost my wife Samantha to cancer. Before she died, we had time to discuss her final wishes with regard to our making amends for some of our youthful indiscretions.

"A few years after our visit here to Olive Branch Ranch, we settled down in upstate New York. There Samantha and I both experienced a conversion from our heathenism to Jesus Christ.

"I'm here today to admit I took a painting from a little building here on Olive Branch Ranch. I'm certain I have a Thomas J. Moran, Jr. painting in my car and I want to return it to you. It's your grandmother who deserves my wholehearted apology," Roy said.

"I know my grandmother would be so happy that you and your wife found Jesus Christ, but she too passed away just Monday."

In his present state of vulnerability, Ashley's losses overwhelmed Roy Winters. He listened intently as she went on, "My grandmother mentioned you and Samantha to me for the first time a few days before she died and she held no animosity regarding the painting. She was always ready and willing to forgive anyone in need of forgiveness. I'll gladly accept the painting back. Then on behalf of my grandmother I ask you to please forgive yourself."

Roy Winters marveled at Ashley's wisdom, which far surpassed his own.

"I'll find a special place for *The Splendor of Venice*, Mr. Winters," she called out as he returned to his car after leaving the painting with her. Then she watched as the tear-filled man simply drove away.

CHAPTER FOURTEEN

Saturday, September 5th

All throughout the morning, Ashley wondered if she would really enjoy seeing Patrick again. She hoped she had not made a mistake by asking him to come by at one, but at the same time, she had no desire at all to cancel the visit.

Earlier that morning she dressed in soft olive corduroys and a lightweight ivory cotton sweater, the same attire she wore for a day of shopping with Corrine the previous spring. She loved what she was wearing because of Corrine, and clearly made no particular effort to impress Patrick.

As the morning passed, she dealt with some feelings of grief and wondered if she was not putting too much pressure on herself by entertaining a friend. She was uncertain she could maintain her composure on one hand but welcomed Patrick's company even if nothing more than a brief distraction from her grief, on the other.

When she stepped into Kit's office to review several financial statements on her desk, Ashley stopped to take a closer look at *The Splendor of Venice* on the chair by the window where she placed it Friday evening. Its beauty impressed her as the mid-morning sunlight streamed through the riverside window. As she began to appreciate the painting, she pondered what she would do with the collection. Then she thought the paintings might be a good topic of conversation when Patrick arrived.

"Ordinarily I wouldn't be so trusting with someone I don't know well," she thought. "Although I don't know Patrick well personally, I know Nan trusted his father with her livelihood."

In this fact, Ashley released all apprehension and

decided she would show Patrick *Mountain of the Holy Cross* and *The Splendor of Venice* at Northridge. Then, if he were willing, she would offer to take him out to Starlight Cottage to see her favorite place and its astounding contents as well.

Patrick could not wait to see Ashley again. Secretly he had carried a distant crush on her several years, which he never gave serious thought to pursuing, because their families were business associates.

Patrick Lewiston was a compassionate young man who combined sociology and pre-med into a bachelor degree from University of Colorado. When he graduated, he decided to give a year of his time to the American Red Cross who offered him the opportunity to design a program for training paramedics in the Republic of the Sudan. Within a week, he would be returning to the Sudan for his final mission and was presently considering what his next career step would be.

"Hi Patrick," Ashley said as she opened her front door. "I'm so glad you could make it."

"Thanks so much for inviting me," he said awkwardly in return. Ashley's natural beauty completely distracted him.

To avoid those first few difficult moments experienced in every new relationship, Ashley decided to "roll out" her idea of how they might spend the afternoon without delay.

"If you'd be interested I have something special about our ranch to share with you," she began. "I know you and your family have been well-acquainted with my family for many years, but I'm certain what I'm about to tell you is beyond anything my grandmother ever shared, even with her closest friends." In this, Ashley drew back naturally and looked for a little reassurance that Patrick could keep a secret.

"Actually, I could use a friend in this matter," she went

on. "In my opinion what I want to show you is beyond the scope of what someone in normal circumstances would include in regular conversation. But of course there is nothing normal about my life right now."

"If you're wondering, you can trust me, Ashley, I promise you I will not betray your confidence not matter what you share with me." Patrick gave her a warm smile.

"Thank you," she said quietly. "I do appreciate your promise and I do trust you."

First Ashley introduced Patrick to *Mountain of the Holy Cross* over the fireplace. "I've seen this mountain in person on a hiking trip with the University of Colorado," he told her. "The mountain itself is absolutely beautiful!

"A bunch of us took a trip in the late spring one year and the cross of snow remained. Why is the cross gold in this picture?" he asked.

"That's a long story which is better saved for another day," Ashley said with a bit of humor. Secretly she was delighted that he could see the gold as well.

"Come up here," she said as she led Patrick up to the foyer, then into her office. "This was Nan's office," she said sadly, "but now it's mine. Come take a look at this other Moran painting, *The Splendor of Venice*."

"This one is beautiful as well," Patrick said as he took in the masterpiece. "Is this by the same artist?"

"Yes, a cousin of mine who lived in the 18th and early 19th centuries. Would you like to see the rest of the collection?"

"Of course. Where is it?" Patrick asked.

"It's in a little cottage on the edge of our property. We call the cottage Starlight Cottage," Ashley said.

"It's really a nice walk. Actually, I knew nothing about this collection until last week. I've always known there was something special in the cottage, but my grandmother sealed it years ago. You can imagine how surprised I was to find that not only are there five-hundred more of Thomas Moran's works stored at Starlight Cottage, but they are apparently all in excellent condition as well. This will be my first trip out to see them firsthand.

"I'd love to see the paintings," Patrick said as Ashley led him out onto the back porch across, the lower lawn and onto the path to Starlight.

Along the way, the young couple found conversation easy and recognized so many things they had in common. They discussed their individual careers being in a state of flux and their altruistic attitudes toward life.

When they arrived at Starlight, Ashley opened the front door and they entered. It was at that time that she first mentioned she would soon be making a decision on how to auction off the collection and establish some sort of service program for children in need on the ranch.

"I've been thinking about working with disadvantaged children for years," she explained to Patrick. "Everything has changed for me in the last two weeks. Through it all though, I've managed to do a little soul searching on this matter. I think I'll try to incorporate my background in education, into a viable program here at Olive Branch Ranch.

"You see, my grandmother has left the entire ranch to me and I've already decided to live out my life here as the fourth-generation of my family to do so. Yesterday morning I took a long ride off the ranch to think about my grandfather and the fact that he came to this same conclusion in his own life. I am sure his prayers have been helping me find peace in this decision.

"I know it's the right decision. If I plan my career to incorporate teaching and social service by selling this wonderful collection, it will be possible to build a school or shelter for disadvantaged children here before too long.

"Oh, I'm sorry I have gone on and on," she told Patrick

as she put away the last of the few paintings she took out to show him.

"Don't be," he said in return, "I love to hear you talk." Ashley blushed.

"I have one more tour in the Sudan beginning this weekend then I'll be leaving the American Red Cross to look for permanent work," Patrick began to share some of his goals in return. For me it's not so important where I work but that my work is fulfilling. This time I plan to stay in the United States. While there is so much work to be done in other lands there are so many people in need right here in our own Country."

"Will you stay with the Red Cross?" Ashley asked.

"No, I'll be moving on. I've explored all options with the Red Cross and there are no possibilities, except in their local training program. I just don't see myself in one of these positions permanently.

"What you've done so far is admirable," Ashley said sincerely.

"Believe me, I've received far more through these service trips than I've given. That's the way it always seems to be in service fields."

Patrick would love to have talked about their school days in Cody and in having Ashley's parents as teachers in high school, but he sensed it was too soon for her to hear his fond memories of Sean and Corrine.

As they entered the clearing at Northridge, their conversation turned to seeing each other again. "You could come back to Northridge tomorrow," Ashley said as she sought his company and the security of her home in her continuing grief.

"I could come by about the same time tomorrow if that works for you," Patrick said without hesitation. "My family is celebrating my grandmother's 90th birthday at her nursing facility in Rowley where we'll have Sunday Mass and breakfast. We should be back in town sometime around noon."

"Why don't we meet at Starlight? I love it there. It's my favorite place on the ranch. From there we could take a trail that leads into town or we could sit by the river," Ashley suggested.

"That sounds great," Patrick said as they rounded the corner at Northridge and he walked her to the front door.

"Let's meet there," she added thinking it might be nice to bring a lunch for them to share. She knew she needed something to occupy the long morning at home alone after she attended Sunday Mass. She dreaded Sunday's hard reality of the sudden loss of Sean, Corrine *and* Kit.

"You can park in the small lot out on Highway 20," she told Patrick.

"Oh, I've seen it," he said.

"The pathway leads directly to Starlight."

"Great. I'll see you there at one," he said, as he thanked Ashley for the wonderful afternoon.

"See you then," Ashley said in return as she waved goodbye.

On his way back to town Patrick could think of nothing but Ashley, her beauty, her personality, the lovely way she spoke. More than once over the years, he dreamt of Ashley Moran.

However, what Patrick Lewiston wanted most in life was to serve God and his feet were planted firmly in this directive. Whenever he pushed away his attraction for Ashley, he wrestled a bit inside but then let it go. During that early phase of his life, he took good care of his soul and God gave him other interests to protect him in times of temptation. While in college, he dated two women but not seriously. Several times during those years, he thought he wanted Ashley in his life, but he ultimately decided to allow God to work out *His plan* for his life including whomever He wished to be his wife.

In truth, Sunday afternoon could not come fast enough for Patrick.

CHAPTER FIFTEEN

Sunday, September 6th

Ashley made her way to St. Anthony's early Sunday morning. Sitting alone at Mass she felt the anguish of her losses and nothing more. The Lord, Whom had been so close to her these last few days, seemed now to have simply walked away.

God was now asking her to place her blind trust in Him. In the simplicity of her new faith, however, the best she could do was "muddle through." At the end of Mass, she asked for God's blessing then made the painful ride home all alone.

On her way back to Northridge Ashley swung down to the Centre where Dan Matthews was overseeing the Sunday shift. An extremely capable middle-aged ranch-hand who filled in for Jake Farley on weekends, reported all was well.

"There are a few things in your "in" box," Dan reminded her. "Don't worry, Ashley," he assured her, "before long running Olive Branch Ranch will be second nature for you."

Ashley loved Dan's humility and his confirmation of the deference she also felt from Jake.

"We've got your back," Dan said, as she took a stack of files from her office.

"You have no idea what that means to me. Thank you for your support, Dan," Ashley said. Then leaving the Centre to his care for the rest of the day, she headed home.

"Not a bad start to a day in which I feel so miserable," she thought as she opened the front door to her new and but empty home.

She heard it was good to keep busy in uncontrollable grief. "There will be days that you just can't manage, my dear," an old neighbor told her at Sean and Corrine's memorial service. "Give in for an hour or so but no longer if you want to recover quickly in the long-run."

"That must be true," Ashley thought. "That's what so many people along the way have recommended I do." Today however, she would see Patrick again, so whatever misery she was dealing with in the present hour would, she hoped would soon have an end.

"Actually," she thought as she closed the stack of invoices left for her review, "if I can just get myself together for a moment, I might be able to make a decent lunch for this afternoon."

Ashley's grief began to lift like a rising shade. A new ray of sunshine filled her every few minutes. Before long, she entered this new purpose. She put a batch of Kit's famous lemon squares in the oven then collected a basket and linens from a closet in the kitchen. Next, she began filling the basket with fresh sandwiches, fruit and iced tea. As she watched the clock continue to move ever so slowly, she decided to walk to her flower garden at Amour to harvest what she could for a bouquet.

The sun at Amour warmed her heart and her entire being and at last, the dreadful darkness lifted. Ashley returned to Northridge to finish her lunch, and then left for Starlight to meet Patrick whose image now filled her mind with quiet anticipation.

She knew she was a half-hour early when she left Northridge, but thought the extra time would allow her to set up lunch then collect her thoughts for a few moments at the river's edge. When she came through the clearing, however Patrick was already waiting.

"Hi," Ashley said to the handsome young man standing in the hollow exactly where she met Jesus in her dream. Patrick did not answer. Rather, he moved to where she placed her basket and took both of her hands in his.

Drawing her close to him, he whispered, "Hi, Ashley." Then he kissed her for the very first time – the kiss he had dreamt about for as long as he could remember.

Ashley kissed Patrick back then put her arms high around his neck as he drew her closer. Finally, she placed her head on his chest and whimpered. Then she cried.

"Please," Patrick said, "let me help you. Let me take care of you in your grief. Of all that I've seen in the Sudan, even in the little children, nothing compares to the pain I feel for you in what you are going through."

"Ashley, I love you," Patrick said with his arms still around her. He was genuine. He had no qualms or concerns that she might not feel the same way. If she did not return his feelings, he would deal with it. Then she spoke the words he wanted so much to hear, "I love you, too. I don't know how it happened," she said as she looked up at him. "All I can tell you is that today I love you too and I never want you to leave me."

Patrick pulled Ashley toward him in a very protective way. He knew she was vulnerable and would remain so for some time but he assured her he would never take advantage of her weakened state. He knew at that moment that he would love her and cherish her all the days of her life if she allowed him to.

Raising her face to his with his right hand, he continued to hold her close with his left. He brushed her drooping hair up off her forehead, he ran his fingers below both eyes and collected her tears. Then he kissed her lips softly once again.

"Ashley, I've been waiting all of my life for this moment."

"Thank you," she answered sweetly. "Thank you for waiting for me. I have this strong feeling that I should catch you up on all the details of my life on one hand, but on the other hand, I feel like I've known you forever."

"I feel exactly the same way," he told her, "it must be the bonds of new love that make us feel this way. Please tell to me anything and everything you want. I could listen to you talk all day."

Together they spread out the blanket Ashley carried under her arm and the contents of the picnic basket. As they broke open the basket before them, they broke open the story of their individual lives as well. Along with some of the most painful details of the last two weeks of her life, Ashley was also happy to share the joyful miracle of her recent steps into the Catholic Church.

"Sharing these blessed happenings with Patrick," Ashley thought, "will bring light into the darkness I carry." Clearly, she was worried that her present state of grief might overwhelm him, but he thought nothing was further from the truth. Just to be with her was his delight.

Not only did he assure her he was able to stand at her side no matter how rough the going got, he gave her every indication he would believe even the most treasured of her supernatural experiences.

"Ashley," Patrick said, "I've been brought up on these beliefs. I believe in the Gospels of Jesus Christ and in the Power of His Holy Spirit to manifest God's works spiritually and even physically in His world if necessary. What I am trying to say is I believe you, absolutely, I believe you."

At that very moment, she found so many things in Patrick that she could not deny were necessary to further her journey in faith. She wasn't afraid that she was falling in love too soon or at a time of extreme vulnerability as her mother might have counseled her, if she had been there.

Instead, not only did she find love in Patrick but she found someone to lead her on in her new Catholic life as well.

Late that afternoon as they walked back at Northridge,

Ashley told Patrick about the gold cross in the painting.

"Another man might have been filled with skepticism," she said to Patrick, "but you're a true gift from God."

"And you are to me as well," he answered. They both smiled.

Before he left for the evening, they spent some time discussing how they would remain in touch over the next few weeks.

"I'll be around until Friday, Ashley."

"The Annual Show of Excellence is tomorrow," she told him. "I'll be there all day with Jake and our team."

"Maybe I could meet you there if I wouldn't be intruding."

"That will be great," Ashley said. She was happy to have his personal support her first time through the sale.

"I leave on assignment this weekend for six weeks. I'll miss you."

"I'll miss you, too. While you're gone I'll be giving some serious thought as to how I'm going to bring new life to Olive Branch Ranch."

"You'll figure all of this out, Ashley, and I'll help you reach this goal, if you want me to. I'll do anything for you.

"I'll call you before I turn in this evening, if you don't mind," he told her. "Are you sure you are okay here alone?" he asked still with an outsider's look at the size of her home and ranch.

"Absolutely," she said. "I'm quite comfortable here and feel well-protected, too. You go along now and don't worry about me. We'll speak later. I'll be looking forward to it."

It was difficult for the two new lovers to part that evening. Ashley knew however, there were several other items of business that needed her attention before Monday's Annual Show of Excellence. She was grateful her outlook was now so much brighter and more conducive to handling the ranch's business than it had been that morning. Suddenly, and because of Patrick, everything seemed just a little easier.

Placing the kettle on the stove for tea, she felt a new beginning within. While the kettle boiled, she went to her office to listen to three phone messages she missed that afternoon.

"Ashley, this is Thompson," she heard first. "Sarah and I want to let you know we're thinking about you. Call us soon."

Next Fr. Joe said, "Ashley, this is Fr. Joe. I hoped to see you after Mass today but when I looked for you, you were gone. Please let me know if there is anything you need."

Then finally, the last was from Lucy. "Ashley, this is Lucy. I'd love to come and rent a house in town next spring. Thank you for being so kind to me. I'll be in touch again sometime."

With this call Ashley wondered not so much about whether or not she would be comfortable with Lucy's presence in Cody next year, but what next year and a new spring would bring into her own life."

As she returned to the kitchen to stop the boiling kettle Ashley noticed Patrick's jacket hanging in hallway. I'll have to tell him he left it when he calls," she thought.

Just then, the doorbell rang and she assumed Patrick was returning to claim his jacket. She was wrong.

As she opened the door, she saw a young woman, thin, frail and beaten about the face and neck. She was obviously pregnant and getting wet, as she stood all alone in a new falling rain.

"Ms. Moran?" she said with a desperate note in her voice.

"Yes, I'm Ashley Moran."

"I'm Rosie Hart. I'm a patient of Dr. Sarah's. She has been helping me with my pregnancy because my boyfriend is abusive," said Rosie as she started to cry.

"Come in. Come in, Rosie."

"I'll call Dr. Sarah." Ashley was worried. Clearly, Rosie's bruises were new.

"No, please don't. I'm so ashamed."

"Come sit down and tell me what happened." Ashley said as she made the young woman a cup of tea. Rosie shook so badly she needed Ashley's help in holding the cup. She was however able to collect herself enough to tell Ashley about her situation.

"Dr. Sarah asked Chief Travers for a negotiator to work with my boyfriend Randy because he has a terrible temper. When I mentioned someone wanted to help him he became extremely angry and hit me.

"It looks like he hit you more than once," Ashley said. Rosie did not deny it.

"It's not the first time. The only reason I went back to him was that my family said I couldn't return home if I ever got pregnant. I want to keep my baby, Ms. Moran. *Please help me keep my baby,*" Rosie said as she sobbed uncontrollably.

"I know this is an awful time to show up on you. It's all over town what's happened to your parents and grandmother. As selfish as this might sound I knew you'd have extra space. It's not for me but for my baby I'm ask'n. Could you please let me stay with you for a while?

"Of course you can on one condition, that you let me call Dr. Sarah. She's a close friend, Rosie, and you have nothing to fear."

Rosie agreed and Ashley made the call.

Sarah arrived at Northridge within minutes and examined poor Rosie in the living room while Ashley went upstairs to prepare her old room for the expectant mother and child.

Just as she turned on the light on the nightstand Patrick called and mentioned he left his jacket. "But I'm really calling to tell you that I love you and miss you already."

"I love you too," she said sweetly.

"Ashley," Patrick said. "There's one more thing I want to say."

"What is it?" she asked, as she unfolded the fresh top sheet she had in hand on Rosie's bed.

"On my way home I thought over and over again about your need for new life at Olive Branch Ranch. Are you open to a suggestion?"

"Yes, anything."

"*Always let God unfold His Plan around you.* At least that's what I do. Maybe this will work for you."

As Ashley bent to unfold the sheet for Rosie, she realized Patrick had just spoken Kit's very last words of wisdom: "Remember my dear, *always let God unfold His Plan around you,*" Kit had said. Ashley felt these words ring deeply in her heart.

Then topping off Rosie's pillow with a small white teddy bear Kit saved from Ashley's childhood, she said to Patrick through tears of joy, "Oh, Patrick, He just did! He just did!"

Made in United States
North Haven, CT
10 May 2025